One Step Beyond

Rediscovering the
Adventure Attitude

Alan Hobson

One Step Beyond

Rediscovering the Adventure Attitude

Based on the ideas of John Amatt

One Step ▲ Beyond Publishing
Canmore, Alberta Canada

Dedication

To my parents, Isabel and Peter Hobson, who have supported me through it all; through the happiness and the pain, through the victories and the disappointments, and who have loved me completely through it all – unendingly and unconditionally. Two finer parents a son could never hope for or ever dream of having. They are, quite simply, the best friends a man could ever have.

Third Printing, 1997

Canadian Cataloguing in Publication Data
Hobson, Alan, 1958–
One Step Beyond
ISBN 0-919381-06-5
1. Adventure and adventurers – Canada. 2. Achievement motivation.
I. Amatt, John, 1945–   II. Title.
G522.H62 1992   904   C92-091160-9

Edited by Maggie Pacquet
Design: Robert MacDonald, MediaClones Inc.
Toronto, Banff and Vancouver, Canada
Photographs: *Sharon Wood and son Robin* by Ingo Kalk, *Laurie Dexter* by Christopher Holloway and *Alan Hobson* by Dorothy Tenute.

One Step▲ Beyond Publishing
Suite 200, 838-10th St., Canmore, Alberta, Canada T1W 2A7

Printed in Canada

Contents

Acknowledgments

We don't do it alone. We do very little of significance by ourselves. If this is a good book, it's because of dozens of people who helped me along the way, or who actually showed me the way.

They are numerous. My friend, Dorthy Tenute, who was so critical in the early research stages; Barbara Clark, Theresa McCurry and Valerie Wilson, who also shared in research and review duties. I could not have hoped for more supportive and efficient assistance.

Lois Hunter of the One Step Beyond Adventure Group in Canmore, Alberta, provided the project with administrative backup and me with moral support. She spent many hours on the phone with the people featured in these pages, as well as with dozens of others whom we consulted on a huge range of adventure and achievement issues.

Peggy Amatt kept me fed and housed. She signed the cheques.

Dale Ens of Calgary deserves special mention. He volunteered dozens of hours in doing a preliminary but thorough read-through of the manuscript. Without his constant demand for clarity, this book would never have achieved the quality I feel it has. Although he was conscripted, he did a remarkable job. More than that, however, he became a true friend; one who believed in the product and who believed in me even when my belief in myself sometimes wavered. Friends of this quality are rare, and I consider myself blessed to know him and his wife Cathy.

My brother Eric was essential in providing me with business advice when it was most needed. And publisher Stephen Hutchings of Altitude Publishing in Banff, Alberta, kept me on time and on track. Designer Robert

MacDonald was an inspiration with his gifted eye and imagination; and Maggie Paquet of North Vancouver, British Columbia, gave the book the final touch with a careful and balanced edit.

Of course, this book would never be here without the support of Marlin Travel. It is not often I meet colleagues with the business foresight and intestinal fortitude of Rod Marlin, Gary Elliott and Ron Millette, but somehow they appeared, as if by providence, to save the project from extinction. Larry Regen, Marlin's Alberta sales manager, was especially important in getting the book into their hands.

Then there are those people whose influence has substantially changed my life. They showed me the way. I have the highest respect, admiration and appreciation for:

– Ken Allen, my gymnastics coach at the University of Wisconsin at Oshkosh, who, through his high standards of excellence taught me all the essential elements of achievement: discipline, mental and physical toughness, commitment to a goal, teamwork and courage. He wasn't just one of the finest gymnastics coaches in the world and the alternate US Olympic coach, he was an educator who, through gymnastics, taught me about life. His affect was life-changing.

– Pat Morrow, world-class outdoor photographer and filmmaker, author, adventurer and the first person to climb the tallest summits on the seven continents. I marvel at his dogged determination and quiet humility. He is the man I admire most in the world because he has created a life for himself unparalleled in common dreams.

– Barry Blanchard of Canmore, Alberta, leading Canadian alpinist. He has incredible sensitivity and eloquence coupled with extreme mental and physical toughness. He taught me that, "The essence of achievement is courage,

courage, courage."
– Laurie Skreslet. Simply one of my greatest heroes and a fellow warrior. He has a kind heart.
– Sharon Wood. If we all had her quiet strength and composure, we could move any mountain.
– Laurie Dexter. On July 1, 1990, as I cycled beside him while he ran 52 miles in eight hours, he took me to the high point of my writing experience to date.
– Mike Beedell, because he has never lost touch with the boy inside him. We could learn much from Mike. One day, the Lord willing, he may grow old, but he will never be old.
– John Hughes. He redefines solitary excellence in a way few can comprehend.
– Jamie Clarke of Calgary, friend, broadcaster, former junior national cross-country ski champion and fellow adventurer. He showed me the power of *carpe diem* – "seize the day." If we all could live as freely and fully as Jamie, we would pass into the next adventure with smiles on our faces. He is one of my best friends.

And finally, John Amatt, friend, colleague, mentor, a guy for whom the word "quit" does not exist when it comes to the stuff of dreams and the one man who more than any other made this book a reality. Aside from shepherding the project to completion, coordinating all the many and varied pieces, he has become a role model for me, a man I look to for direction in times of crisis. He is a very private man, but he took huge financial and personal risks with this book. If it is a success, then to him will go the spoils. I cannot thank him enough because he has always done more than enough. He lives and breathes the adage that "Good enough isn't good enough when better is expected." He took me many steps beyond with this project and I will forever be indebted to him for his patience, tolerance and perseverance.

8

Foreword

Marlin Travel is pleased to be part of this book. We are supporting it because we believe in the philosophies developed in it. Many of these philosophies have been integral to Marlin's growth over the last few years.

If you are an achiever aspiring to succeed, we encourage you to think deeply about the ideas presented in the pages that follow. They can help you make dramatic changes in your professional and personal life – for the better.

This is not really a book about adventure. It's a groundbreaking look at life. May your personal exploration bring you closer to your goals, to your family and to your dreams.

Rod Marlin   Gary Elliott
Chairman   President

Author's Preface
An Adventure in Achievement

This is a book about excellence – and how to produce it by examining our attitudes. When John Amatt first asked me if I would write this book, I had no way of knowing then that we were about to embark on a four-year odyssey that would push us further creatively, financially and interpersonally than we had ever been pushed before. To succeed in seeing this book to reality, we would survive an adventure as psychologically harrowing, although not as physically threatening, as the stories of the five individuals profiled in it.

To succeed, we would personally have to apply every element of the Adventure Attitude ourselves. In short, in order to write a book about achievement, we would learn even more about achievement first-hand. And we would have to practise what we preached.

Our journey began innocently enough. I called John Amatt, whom I had never met, but knew by reputation. I'd just finished work on the official book of the 1988 Olympic Torch Relay, *Share the Flame*, and once again found myself facing what self-employed people face dozens of times a year: I had to find work. As John and I were both professional public speakers and adventurers, he agreed to a meeting.

Within a month of that meeting, John presented me with a two-page outline for a book. It was an anthology of adventure stories; everything from the discovery of the Arctic's most northerly shipwreck to an epic ski journey to the South Pole designed to re-create the journey of Robert F. Scott, "Scott of the Antarctic." In all, there were to be 15 stories, complete with maps, photographs and diagrams.

The purpose of the book was to use adventure as a metaphor for life. John's hope was that those who read the book would be able to use some of the lessons it would outline to face the challenges of the twenty-first century.

His short outline lit my creative fires like nothing I have seen in my ten years as a professional communicator. This was the perfect book for me. It combined my two greatest interests: people and adventure.

I accepted John's offer in a shot and immediately began work on a full-blown book proposal. A few months later, it was in the hands of 14 publishers who had a track record of publishing books of this kind. Had I known then the heartache and soul-searching that that step would create for myself and John over the coming years, I might never have taken it.

Within weeks, a major national publisher called expressing serious interest in the idea. It seemed like Christmas had come early. I was over the moon.

Then, early the following year, I approached a major national corporation to be a potential sponsor. They were also interested in the idea. Even government assistance to help write the book looked feasible. Everything was falling into place.

The publisher was pleased because it would have automatic pre-sales of the book to the sponsor. The sponsor was pleased because it had a potential marketing tool. John and I could see our dream becoming reality.

Somebody wise once said that "Life is what happens to you while you're waiting for it to begin." Well, just when John and I thought our baby was about to enter the world, the world turned upside down.

The corporation pulled out, citing poor financial performance in their industry. The publisher consequently lost its pre-sales and the government declined to fund the project. Within a year of starting the effort, both the sponsor and publisher had come and gone, outside funding had been refused, John was out a lot of money and I was left with the sinking feeling that I'd just wasted a year of my life on something that might never see the light of day.

But I had underestimated John Amatt. This was his dream, and when John Amatt has a dream, he doesn't let it die. With the tenacity of a pitbull terrier, he bit into the problem and flatly refused to let go. "Finish three chapters," he said. "We can't sell this concept until people can actually hold a product in their hands. You write. Let me worry about financing."

The whole thrust of the book changed. Anthologies, we learned, are very hard to market. Thus the book became a series of personality profiles of specific adventurers. By the end of that year, things were looking up. John and I submitted the three chapters to our original publisher. They said they wanted to talk turkey in the new year.

So, the new year came in with John and I feeling optimistic again. At a meeting in early January, John made the publisher an offer it could hardly refuse. He agreed to sell 5,000 copies of the book himself. That's how much he believed in the project.

I remember coming out of that meeting feeling so proud of John and privileged to work with him. He had by that point in his life accomplished some amazing things, and I got a first-hand opportunity to see how attitude can actually produce excellence. I'd seen it in my career as a national-level gymnast, but this was my first look at the application of the "Adventure Attitude" in business. We came out of that meeting soaring.

But our flight was short. We were still financially strapped. In the midst of a recession, John's finances were

12

pushed to the limit. I couldn't help but be frustrated with all the effort it took to promote what I knew was national greatness: the people profiled in the book. I wondered if John and I weren't really coming face-to-face with what some have called the Canadian inferiority complex; that, as a nation, we really don't like to promote our achievements, even among ourselves.

Then came the crunch. After a meeting with his board of directors, John told me his financial partners were losing faith in the project. He sounded exhausted, as if he'd been beaten with a stick.

Later that evening, I was on the phone interviewing an Arctic adventurer for the book. Towards the end of the conversation he said something that instantly stuck in my brain: "If I were to leave a message with people, it would be that if you want to do something, go out there and do it. Set your mind on it and don't let anybody tell you you can't do it, because you can."

Buoyed by this statement, John and I persevered. During a subsequent meeting with the publisher, there was good news and bad news. The good news was that they agreed to publish. The bad news was that substantial changes would have to be made to my work before it would be ready for publication.

After having worked for ten years to get my work to the point where it was accepted by a major national publisher, I was faced with the most difficult professional decision of my life: do I swallow my pride, make the changes requested and see my work in print? Or do I hold to its existing structure and risk that my work will gather dust, unpublished, unread and unseen?

There are these pivotal moments in life for all of us. Sometimes we're not immediately aware of them. But at other times, they hit us straight in the face. Whatever the circumstance, we are forced to look within ourselves for the answer. No one can give it to us.

Oddly enough, my decision didn't boil down to publishing or not publishing. It boiled down to a deeper issue, one that all creative people face many times in the course of their careers: "Do you really believe in the quality of your work?" Because writing is an intimately personal part of you, the more difficult question I was facing was: "Do I really believe in myself?"

The answer came to me one morning while I was looking in the mirror. "If you change your work," I asked myself, "could you look yourself in the eye and still be happy with yourself?" The answer was no. John backed me in that decision and we began to look for a publishing alternative.

We've never looked back since. Marlin Travel, Canada's largest travel agency, agreed to support the book financially and, thanks to the fantastic coordinating efforts of Altitude Publishing in Banff, Alberta, we self-published this book. If you enjoy it, I'm flattered. I gave it everything I had. However you feel about it, I can still look myself in the mirror and like who I see.

Tribute to Bill March
The Iron Leader with the Warm Heart

You may never have heard of Bill March. If that's so, it's a shame. He was a leading figure in British and Canadian mountaineering for some 30 years, had an incredible 70 first ascents to his credit and was a prolific writer on adventure activities with over 100 articles in print.

In 1982, he was the leader of the first Canadian expedition to Mount Everest, an assault which saw four people die, six climbers choose to leave and six people stand on top of the world – two of whom were the first Canadians ever to do so.

But that's not what made him so special. Bill March had charisma and a personal force that made him an instant leader. He was tough, but kind; strong, but sensitive. In short, he was a paradox – an iron leader with a warm heart.

As an associate professor of physical education at the University of Calgary, Bill March touched the lives of hundreds of students of all ages. Although I was never enrolled in his classes, like so many people with whom he came in contact, I became one of his pupils. He showed me the power of believing in a dream, the guts it takes to lead, and gave me inspiration in being one of his followers. I have literally followed his footsteps up mountains and felt his power.

I remember clearly my last extended visit with "Big Bill." It was a few years ago in June. He'd just come out of the hospital after back surgery. His wife Karen had just returned from another chemotherapy treatment and his mother-in-law had recently had a stroke. I remember him lying in obvious discomfort on the living room floor, his head propped up against the foot of the sofa at an odd angle, munching away on Karen's oatmeal and raisin muffins. John Amatt and I were there to interview him for this book. He was, as usual, waxing philosophical, in spite of his physical and emotional pain. It was vintage Bill March – tough as nails.

While we were chatting, he suddenly became intense. His jaw set, his lips went straight and his eyes began to burn through us. It was not a look of anger, but one of intent.

"It's an interesting age in which we live," he said quietly. "It's interesting because we're really short of leaders. We're really short of people who will make decisions and accept the consequences."

If there is one person who epitomizes the attitudes, ideals and values presented in this book, it is Bill March. That is why John Amatt and I have decided to make this book a tribute to him.

I could write an entire book on Bill March and, in fact, we seriously discussed it. He had a depth of character and knowledge of life which was as broad as the mountains he climbed. Consider, if you will, this brief sampling of his words: "To me success is being happy with oneself and knowing oneself; knowing it and accepting it – warts and all."

"You can do it. If you believe in yourself and you work and commit yourself, and make the sacrifices and grow; and if you get out there and drink from the cup of life, you can do it. I think we all can. I really believe that."

"The essence of achievement is to not accept failure."

"I deeply believe that you should love and care about people. When you first think about it, it sounds idealistic, but you only go through this journey once and if you can go through and leave it as a good journey rather than a bad one, that's what's important."

"The biggest gift is good friends, whether they be your wife or your children or the friends you've got. To make meaning of life is to have those people you can sit down with and talk – really communicate with and share."

"It's a terrible thing, but we're born into this world alone and we die alone. There's no way around that. That's the way life is. But on the way through this journey, there are people – our family and our friends. Our relationships with them and how we relate to them are going to be the highlights of our lives. If you think about mountaineering, apart from solo climbing, mountaineering is probably the most intense personal relationship you'll ever have."

"I've travelled all round the world. I've lived life to the fullest. I've seen the edge and met with the best and drunk with the best and fought with the best and climbed with the best. Shit, I've had one hell of a life."

Bill March, more than any single person, sparked my own Everest dream. I wanted to go to Everest as a journalist. In spite of the fact that I had no high-altitude climbing experience, he wholly and completely supported my dream. We would chat at great length about the hazards of mountaineering. I would lay bare my deepest fears for him to see, and he always accepted me. His support was unconditional. We connected.

In October 1990, we were to climb together in the Andes of Ecuador. From my point of view, it was like being invited to play at center ice with Wayne Gretzky. I was absolutely thrilled.

But on Saturday September 8, 1990, at the age of 49, Bill March suddenly collapsed while walking down a trail in the Canadian Rockies. A full autopsy was performed, but mysteriously, no cause of death was ever determined.

So it was that the world lost a remarkable man. I lost an incredible friend. He is now, and will remain, a kind of

17

myth for me; a man who was not only my mentor and hero, but an inspirational figure.

I went to Everest this year as a journalist. While there, I often got the feeling Bill was with me. The place had such power and presence. Yes, he was there all right. And he's in these pages, too. To read them is to feel his force. You may never have met him, but you are about to come to know some of his personal philosophies.

If I write from a position of strength, part of that strength has come from Bill March. He will never leave me. I hope some of his lessons will never leave you.

Introduction

Tracing the Uncommon Thread

Back of every noble life there are
principles that have fashioned it.
– George H. Lorimer

20

"**O**ne step higher, one step beyond." That's how Laurie Skreslet described his last, agonizing steps onto the roof of the world on October 5, 1982. It was a day that would leave its mark in history – the day the first Canadian stood atop Mount Everest.

To reach that pinnacle, Skreslet and the other members of his expedition retraced the snowbound steps of Sir Edmund Hillary and Tenzing Norgay, who first reached the roof of the world almost 30 years before them. Laurie and his companions overcame leech-infested swamps, torrential monsoons, four deaths, sledgehammer winds, rarefied air and the mountain's worst avalanche in a decade. And they achieved their goal.

Perhaps better than any others, the words "one step beyond" capture the essence of adventure and achievement over the past millennium. From as early as a thousand years ago, when the Vikings first set foot in what is now L'Anse aux Meadows on Newfoundland's coast, to the adventurers of the human spirit today, achievements have come about because of certain attitudes and principles contained within the human character: courage, persistence, curiosity, teamwork and endurance.

These principles can be developed and integrated into our basic character. When we strive to achieve that integration, we will have attained our own pinnacle of success.

Just as this process of development is never-ending,

ADVENTURE IS IN THE MIND

Adventure isn't hanging on a rope on the side of a mountain. Adventure is an attitude that we must apply to the day-to-day obstacles of life – facing new challenges, seizing new opportunities, testing our resources against the unknown and, in the process, discovering our own unique potential.
-John Amatt

In the process of researching this book, I got to know the achievers in it very well. They have shared their doubts and dreams with me, their failures and successes. The thing that struck me most about all of them wasn't what they were on the outside. None of them were super athletes or brilliant intellects. In fact, they appeared ordinary in every way. They had fears and weaknesses just like all of us. They were human. The only differences I could find were in how they perceived the world.

Sharon Wood: "The way I perceive my environment is the only thing that makes me different – nothing else."

Laurie Skreslet: "It s not what you go through in life that makes you what you are, it's how you react to the world you're going through."

John Hughes: "It's not what you have. It's what you do with what you have."

All of this inspires us to a very clear, but propelling conclusion: that personal success and happiness is largely a matter of what we do in our minds.

21

Man alone, of all creatures of earth, can change his own pattern. Man alone is architect of his destiny. The greatest revolution of our generation is the discovery that human beings, by changing the inner attitudes of their minds, can change the outer aspects of their lives." – **William James**

22

neither have the possibilities for adventure stopped. In the last decade, adventure achievers have launched more than a dozen expeditions to retrace the routes of some of the world's greatest achievers – such as polar explorers Robert Peary, Robert Falcon Scott and Sir John Franklin; continental explorers Alexander Mackenzie and Jacques Cartier; and mountain men George Leigh Mallory, Andrew Irvine and Sir Edmund Hillary. In the process, they have taken themselves on epic voyages of personal discovery, beyond normal limits and, in many cases, beyond retreat.

Soon the calendar will turn an exciting new page – into the twenty-first century. Like that ocean of unknown and new world of hardships faced by the earliest explorers, the sea monsters and drop-offs of the future frighten many. Some of us turn back; some never start out. With the threat of environmental destruction staring us in the face, a global AIDS epidemic, over-population, mass starvation, terrorism, drug wars and untold economic uncertainty, there is only one thing certain for the next century: unprecedented global change.

John Amatt and I believe there is hope for the future. We believe that to collectively meet the challenge of change in the twenty-first century, we must rediscover the "adventure attitude" of the early explorers and learn how to integrate its basic principles of courage, persistence, curiosity, teamwork and endurance into our innate selves.

Adventure, by its very nature, involves overcoming

uncertainty, fear, obstacles, adversity and the unknown. The adventure attitude, particularly as used in the metaphors of the mountain or the sea of unknown, can be applied to our daily lives; it can be a powerful tool to use for achievement in the face of uncertainty.

I believe that we're all climbing our own mountains; that every striving individual or organization is climbing its own mountain in pursuit of its own goal.
– Sharon Wood

Our theory is this: Today's adventure achiever embodies principles and exhibits attitudes that have a long track record of success in times of uncertainty and change. These principles have been the thread that has woven the fabric of achievement throughout history. Somehow, somewhere, we have lost that once-common thread. If we can rediscover the principles behind the now-uncommon thread, and if we can pinpoint the elements of the "adventure attitude," we can use them to face our own approaching ocean of the unknown and ward off the "millennium shock" of the twenty-first century.

23

This book is about personal and professional success and how we all can achieve it in our own lives – today and tomorrow. It is an attempt to find the uncommon thread that runs through people who have achieved great feats. If we can find that thread, perhaps we can weave it into our own lives. There it will make the fabric of our lives stronger and more meaningful. And it will enable us to thrive on the uncertainty that approaches.

The Blueprint for Success

Successful people are like you and I. They may appear average, but they are far from ordinary. Over the years they have adopted a personal blueprint for success that is ingrained in their psyches. That blueprint is the "adventure attitude." The elements of this attitude are not restricted to adventure, however. They apply to the everyday goals of life: running your own business, raising a family, playing golf, or pushing the frontiers of science or industry.

A recent book, *The Entrepreneurial Mind*, pinpoints elements common to all successful, self-made business people. It lists a number of traits that help people to be winners: total commitment, determination, perseverance, an internal locus of control, calculated risk-taking, decisiveness, and a low need for status and power. The book concludes that attitude and outlook are the primary keys to success. It also says that these "entrepreneurial attitudes" can be learned.

In like manner, the "adventure attitude" isn't just about how to climb mountains or achieve in the outdoors. It is offered to you in this book as a practical and powerful tool that you can use and apply in your own life to become happier and more successful.

But a tool, as any skilled craftsman can tell you, is only as good as the person using it. The tool can be used merely to cut, or it can be finely honed and used to shape. This book is the tool. We hope your use of it will help you to shape your destiny and your dreams.

Nine Keys to Personal and Professional Success

The following elements of human behaviour and attitude pinpoint the key characteristics of people who have achieved personal and professional success in their lives:

A   Achievement internally; success is self-satisfaction.

D   Dream big and dream often; imagine the ultimate.

V   Value your values; be true to yourself.

E   Excel under pressure; cultivate courage.

25

N   Never say die; endure endlessly.

T   Trust others; be great in a group.

U   Understand your commitment; give it your all.

R   Risk-take carefully; plan meticulously.

E   Exude energy; triumph relentlessly.

To Get the Adventure Attitude

The following exercises are an expansion of the above nine key elements and are set out here to assist you in understanding the process of developing the "adventure attitude." They will also put the individual character profiles into perspective, so please keep them in mind while reading the peak performance profiles that follow in the main body of this book.

- Know Your Values. Know Yourself.

- Dare to Dream. Dream BIG!

- Don't Concern Yourself with Money, Material Wealth, Security, Fame, Fortune, Power or Position.

- Do Concern Yourself with Contentment, Self-Satisfaction, Freedom, Independence and Happiness.

- Decide on Your Dream. Know Why It's Important to *YOU*.

- Assess the Risks. Develop a Plan.

- Step Out from the Crowd. Step Up in the World.

- Learn through Experience. Experience through Learning.

- Cultivate Courage; Fight Fear.

- Display Tenacity; Have Capacity.

- Focus Ferociously; Endure Endlessly.

- When You're Challenged, Fight. When You're Wavering, Ignite.

- Forget Failure; Remember Resolve.

- Adapt Instantly; React Instinctively.

- Push through Pain; Parade Past Skeptics.

- Wonder at the World. Wander its Heights.

- Be Enthusiastic, Persistent and Tough. Being Driven is Not Enough.

- Turn Obstacles into Opportunities, Failures into Successes, Disappointments into Direction.

- Support the Team. Never Doubt the Dream.

- Be Ultimately Accountable to Yourself. Be Ultimately Appreciative of Others.

- Produce Under Pressure. Refuse to Crack.

- Don't Hesitate, Activate.

- Make your Effort Absolute. Make Your Will Resolute.

- When You've Given It Your All, Stand Tall.

For yourself, and for others, may this tool give you a new beginning. All that remains is for you to take the first step.

Five Peak Performers

This book is structured around five peak performance profiles:

Laurie Skreslet, of Calgary, Alberta, the first Canadian to climb Mount Everest; a manifestation of courage.

John Hughes, of Halifax, Nova Scotia, who sailed solo around the world and past Cape Horn with only a makeshift mast; the personification of persistence.

Mike Beedell, of Ottawa, Ontario, who was one of two men in history who made the first traverse of the Northwest Passage powered only by the wind; the culmination of curiosity.

Sharon Wood, of Canmore, Alberta, the first North American woman to climb Everest; the triumph of teamwork.

Laurie Dexter, an Anglican minister from Fort Smith, Northwest Territories, who was a member of the joint Soviet-Canadian Polar Bridge Expedition that skied from Siberia to the North Pole and on down to Ellesmere Island in the Canadian Arctic; ultra-marathoner; the epitome of endurance.

These profiles are designed to do the following:

1. pinpoint the uncommon thread of attitude of all these adventurers; their "adventure attitude;"

GO BIG . . . OR GO HOME

Those with the "adventure attitude" not only dream big, they think big – very BIG. First they make gigantic mental leaps of faith. Then they make equally quantum leaps in reality. This capacity to think far beyond the realm of "reasonable," separates great achievers from aspiring achievers.

2. add insight into "...why plumbers and poets, soldiers and suicides, millionaires and family men and single girls, do these amazing things (*The London Observer*)" and how they achieve them;

3. expand on the metaphor of the mountain, and show there is no distinction between it and the everyday; and

4. show how the "adventure attitude" can be applied to success in the 1990s and assist in the transition from the known seas of the twentieth century to the unknown oceans of the twenty-first.

If you start something, you might just succeed. But you'll never know until you start.
– John Amatt

ONE STEP BEYOND: Rediscovering The Adventure Attitude tries to find the common threads, recurring themes, philosophies and attitudes that occur in every one of these remarkable individuals. Each profile is set off in its own chapter. The chapter heading highlights the primary principle, or "element of excellence" that contributed to that achiever's success: "The Calibre of Courage," "The Power of Persistence," "The Capacity of Curiosity," "The Triumph of Teamwork" and "The Excellence in Endurance."

The final chapter looks back over all the profiles and traces those elements of excellence common to all. It goes on to describe how you might be able to use these elements to become happier and more successful in your own life.

The result, we hope, is a book which not only provides insight into excellence, but can be a tool which you can use to achieve your own dreams in the twenty-first century. It is intended not only to motivate and inspire, but, more importantly, to provide a hands-on blueprint for success in the 1990s and beyond.

29

Reaching the summit is not the significant thing, because you learn nothing on the top. It is during the journey to the top that the learning takes place. The important thing is to digest the experience, to learn what it was that got you there. Then you can apply this new knowledge to the future.
– John Amatt

30

The Ideals At Work: John Amatt

Obviously, not every high-achieving adventurer could be featured here. It is our hope, however, that this book will lead to future editions in which other great adventure achievers will be profiled.

Joe Girard, an American who has been called "the world's greatest salesman," was once asked what was the most important value of a book. His reply was that the people who produced it should live the ideals – and ideas – developed in the book. John Amatt is such a person.

John is unknown to most North Americans, but for almost five decades he has devoted his life to adventure and achievement. In his youth he was one of three people who made the first ascent of the world's tallest granite wall, the 1,500-metre-high north face of the Troll Wall in Norway.

The Troll Wall had a terrible reputation. "Experts" said it was smooth and holdless for a vertical mile. It was a full 600 metres higher than California's El Capitan in Yosemite National Park, and much steeper. In fact, it was overhanging. Many of the world's best climbers dismissed it as impossible. Others called it suicide. But in July 1965, John and his two companions silenced the skeptics by making an 11-day ascent.

"The scariest thing was the night before, lying at the bottom of the climb and trying to sleep, knowing that the next day you'd be going up. You camp at the bottom and look up at this bloody great precipice going into the sky and wonder what it's going to be like up there. But you don't know.

"That's the time when you're most tempted to turn around and go home. But you know if you turn around that you'll never know if you're up to the challenge. Your pride says you've got to try. So you do."

The only limiting factor to our achievements in life is our fear of the unknown.

– John Amatt

John's ascent of the Troll Wall shook the climbing world. Chris Bonington, the world's foremost leader of Everest expeditions, called it the single most important feat accomplished by British climbers in a decade. Virtually unknown in British climbing circles prior to that climb, John Amatt, as one magazine put it, "flashed through the climbing firmament like a meteor."

The ascent of the Troll Wall marked the first time John had really experienced true personal success.

31

"When you come back down, you begin to think about what you did," John remembers. "When you're doing it, you're too consumed with what's going on to appreciate anything. But when you come back down, you relax and consider. Then you start to think: if I could do that, I can do anything. But if we had turned our backs at the bottom and never gone up, we would never have learned that lesson.

"You learn that nothing is impossible. From there it becomes, What's the next challenge? How do I grow?"

Through climbing, John gained significant insights into the nature of effort and achievement. He also recognized that the challenges faced when climbing could be applied to everyday life. Mountaineering, he discovered, could be used as a metaphor for life. They both contain struggles, setbacks, triumphs and peak experiences.

"Mountains have always been significant for me. I think

my entire personality has evolved through my experiences in the mountains," says John. "I was brought up in England in a very protective environment. It wasn't necessary to take any risks at all when I was very young. Because of that, I had no way of developing self-confidence and I was very shy.

"Climbers always feel some element of fear on a climb. Success lies in testing your mental resources in overcoming this fear. It is this success that will ultimately lead to what might be called courage. Courage is not an innate quality, but one that is developed by facing up to danger and overcoming it. As the German philosopher, Friedrich Nietzsche, said: 'The secret of knowing the most fertile experiences and greatest joys in life is to live dangerously.'

"The challenge I find in climbing is that if you take it one step at a time and work out the sequence of moves, you can make the impossible become possible."

Three years after his success on the Troll Wall, John immigrated to Canada. After becoming a Canadian citizen, he began conducting management seminars through The Banff Centre for Continuing Education. His focus was to show others how the lessons of adventure are actually the lessons of life.

The seminars were a huge success. Consisting of a combination of rock climbing, mountaineering and outdoor challenge, together with intense personal growth discussions, their goal was to examine and reduce the effects of stress. The participants were largely high-level business executives from all over North America. They met at a secluded cabin in the heart of the Rocky Mountains.

Each seminar ran for 10 days. John was responsible for coordinating all outdoor activities, while one of his colleagues, Dr. Layne Longfellow, handled all the in-depth group discussions. Layne was a leading psychologist with the Menninger Foundation of Topeka, Kansas. He later became a successful professional public speaker.

Without adversity, without change, life is boring. The paradox of comfort is that we stop trying.
– John Amatt

John and Layne were a powerful team. While John was concerned with the "outer journey" of the mountain challenge, Layne worked with the "inner" psychological journey.

"Our objective was to develop the whole person," John recalls. "It had a dramatic effect."

At the conclusion of one session, a physically and emotionally reborn participant wrote:

To my wife and children: Your Dad has been away from home for nine days, but he's been gone for a long, long time. He's home now. Your Dad's really come home.

33

One of the highlights of the seminars was a 24-hour camp-out in the mountains – alone. During the solo, one participant wrote:

As I was shaping my walking stick to fit my hand, I started thinking that it resembled my life. I could start over at the top or, better still, I could start at any place I chose. Just as the wood was shaped many years ago in its rough, original form, so was my life shaped many years ago. I am able to...smooth out the rough edges...and perhaps reshape them to fit my new phase of life just as I am cutting and reshaping the stick to fit my hand. It appears to me that as long as you have a good base to work with, you should be able to reshape that base to fit whatever you want. But be careful not to over shape it. Leave some of the original character of the base, something solid you can recognize.

With my walking stick, there was some danger from the

knife as the rough parts were smoothed. I had to be careful. I am sure that I will have to be just as careful in smoothing and reshaping my new life. It will take time. I must not hurry.

"We don't have the right balance between our personal lives and our professional lives. The desire to achieve professionally has overcome the recognition of the importance of having a family structure and a life of our own."

While in Banff, John also founded the world-renowned Banff Festival of Mountain Films, the second largest festival of its kind in the world. It has been flourishing for over 15 years and features films about the mountain environment and mountain sports such as climbing, kayaking, rafting and hang-gliding. Every year submissions pour in from all over the world. Productions compete for awards in international film making.

In 1979, John was asked to be a climber and the business manager for the first Canadian expedition to Mount Everest. He accepted.

"I was determined that the '82 expedition would happen. My priority became to make sure the expedition had the optimum chance for success. Climbing to the summit would not be my priority. I realized that my climbing objectives had long since moved away from being on the summit of Everest. I became involved strictly to make sure the expedition was properly financed and properly organized."

For the next two and a half years, John approached hundreds of companies from coast to coast in an all-out effort to find sponsors for the climb. His salary was a scant $250.00 a week.

Along the way, he came face-to-face with a personal

fear many times greater than anything he'd ever faced while climbing: the fear of rejection.

The only failure in life is when you fail to learn the lessons from your experience.

– John Amatt

"What kept me going through all the "maybes" and "nos" was an intuitive sense that I was doing the right thing. I think intuition is a very important part of achievement. It gets you through the tough times. Just knowing that what you're doing is right and then committing all your resources to it is what makes things happen."

When he started, the expedition's only revenue was $25,000 earned from the sale of newspaper and magazine rights for coverage of the climb. By the time John finished in 1982, he'd recruited some 200 companies and private individuals and had raised $1 million.

35

"We realized the importance of reaching the summit. That was what people wanted. They didn't want failure. What we needed was a success story." Early in the expedition, four climbers died in two tragic accidents in two days. In the aftermath, John had to answer to the world on national television. He became the expedition's official spokesman. While he was taking the heat in front of the world's press in Kathmandu, Nepal, his colleagues were challenging Everest. Eventually, the team put six people, including two Canadians, on top of the world. It was one of the most courageous comebacks ever recorded.

"We faced death, deterioration and despondency on Everest. We were forced to dig deep. In the process we discovered that we were capable of more than we had ever thought possible; that we had the resources to keep going no matter what the setbacks.

Achievement is the constant process of going one step beyond your previous experience.
– John Amatt

"Life is a series of ups and downs, from valleys to peaks and back down again. We attain goals; we suffer setbacks. The art, I think, is to remember what we felt on the heights when we are down in the valleys.

"The lessons of Everest are lessons for us all: accepting the challenge, preparing, working as a team, treating people as equals, adapting to changing conditions, facing inner fears, setting goals that stretch us, coping with setbacks, recognizing the need for support, and remaining open to the next horizon – and the next and the next.

"We are all climbers. We all have our impossible dreams. We all have the potential to stand proudly on the summit of our lives."

After Everest, John's philosophy of achievement evolved even further. He formed a company called *One Step Beyond*. It grew from his desire to go "one step beyond" the Everest experience and apply the lessons of Everest to the challenges of corporate, professional and personal life. The "adventure attitude" has since become central to his psyche. Today, he is one of North America's most popular speakers. Somehow, he has grown from a small boy so shy he wouldn't even get out of a car to ask directions, into an individual capable of regularly addressing hundreds – sometimes thousands – of people many times a month. It has been a miraculous transformation.

John has spoken to some of the continent's largest companies and organizations, such as IBM, AT&T, General Foods and the American Dental Association. To date, he has made presentations to over 800 corporate and professional groups and an estimated 500,000 people. In 1984, he was the closing speaker for the 57th annual

36

meeting of the Million Dollar Round Table, a prestigious international life insurance organization. At that engagement he spoke to over 6,000 people from the famous Radio City Music Hall stage in New York City.

As we move forward, it will be the spirit of the adventurer, the intelligent risk-taker, that will make it possible for us to achieve ultimate success.
– John Amatt

John Amatt has a sincere belief in the content of his presentations. They touch on such concepts as vision, courage, commitment, endurance, resourcefulness and teamwork. These represent some of the lessons he has learned through his climbing experiences. One of his missions in life is to communicate the importance of these concepts to today's aspiring achievers. This is the reason for this book. It is his hope that we will all be able to apply the "adventure attitude" in meeting our own challenges of the future.

37

From Gymnast to Journalist: Alan Hobson

Like John, I also have a background in adventure and achievement. I was a competitive gymnast for 11 years and experienced the achievement process first-hand. During my gymnastics career, I was fortunate enough to be a member of six U.S. national championship-winning gymnastics teams and was named an "All-American" nine times, even though I am Canadian. It was during the endless hours of gymnastics training, the painful injuries and exhilarating victories that I, like John, began to learn critical lessons. These lessons included everything from learning how to fight physical and psychological fear to maintaining focus, evaluating risks and dealing with defeat. The biggest lesson I learned was what it took to achieve at a very high level. It was always uncomfortable, usually lonely, but, ultimately, extremely rewarding.

When I retired from gymnastics, I began to apply some of the lessons I'd learned to my new life in the working world. After university, my first job was as a junior reporter in the newsroom of a major Canadian daily newspaper. I soon discovered that I was actually a glorified "copy boy." Whenever an editor at the news desk yelled "copy!" I'd have to hustle off to the photocopier. Another of my responsibilities involved getting coffee and snacks for the entire 40-person newsroom. I had to bring back exact change to each person.

It was here, during this demoralizing introduction to the journalism field, that I remembered my gymnastics training. I set myself a goal. I wanted to be happy.

After almost two years at the paper, during which time I gradually took on more and more challenging assignments, I left to become a full-time freelance writer. This meant aggressively marketing myself to potential clients and working for several customers simultaneously.

TAKE CONTROL OF YOUR LIFE

We CAN be happier and more successful. We CAN achieve our dreams. The power IS within our control. It's not some arbitrary set of circumstances, fluke or chance that molds great people. Great people are the product of what's in their heads and hearts. Provided we have been raised in an environment which gives us the basic tools to choose, we can excel. In fact, we can dream, and realize our dreams. Perspective is power.

Wings are not only for birds; they are also for minds.
-Toller Cranston

When I left the paper, I had only one job lead: a possible story with a local magazine. My parents and friends were aghast. How, they asked, could I be so stupid? Why leave a promising job with long-term potential for the complete insecurity and unknown of the freelance world?

I skate to where the puck is going to be, not where it's been.
— Wayne Gretzky

For me the decision was the right one. My first year I netted $6,000, but I was infinitely happier than I had ever been at the newspaper. For the first time in years I was directing my own life. The sense of empowerment was exhilarating.

The next two years were also very difficult financially. I wondered where the next month's rent would come from. To keep my overhead to an absolute minimum, I rode a moped to and from meetings with clients. It got 110 miles to the gallon and cost 25 cents to fill the tank. My briefcase was a backpack. My office was the living room of my one-bedroom apartment.

Although the financial stress was severe at times, I never regretted my decision to leave the comparative security of the paper. My happiness became based on increased freedom and self-satisfaction, not on whether I could afford a home or a nice car.

Within just a few years, my range of experience broadened exponentially. I went to Europe and covered Canada's national teams prior to and following the 1984 Summer and Winter Olympics. I reported daily to *The Globe & Mail*, the Canadian Broadcasting Corporation, the national print wire service of Canadian Press and the national broadcast wire service of Broadcast News.

Then came the 1988 Olympic Winter Games in Calgary. Since I had specialized in amateur sport as a journalist and broadcaster for many years by then, I applied for a position as author of *Share the Flame*, the official retrospective book of the 1988 Olympic Torch Relay. I was accepted.

I firmly believe that each of us is capable of achieving our dreams, no matter what they are. In my public speaking presentations on the Olympic Torch Relay, I attempt to convey this message. My dream has been to become a full-time adventure author and public speaker, specializing in achievement. This quest has led me to participate in such sports as rock-climbing, ice-climbing, mountaineering, whitewater kayaking, parachuting, bobsleighing, luge, hang-gliding and marathon running. Far from fanatical, reckless activities, these adventures have brought me immeasurable rewards. I have cried tears of joy in my hang-glider as I soared thousands of feet above the Canadian Rockies at sunset, stood breathless above the clouds on the summit of Alaska's Mount McKinley, the highest mountain in North America, and kayaked with the "crazies" in the awesome power of the Ottawa River.

There is no such thing as "crazy," I've discovered. There is only inexperience with the unknown. The more we confront fear and challenge the often inaccurate perceptions of our own psychological limits, the greater our sense of self-confidence and personal satisfaction. The emotional and spiritual return is euphoric. It can send our spirits soaring.

This book is not just a collection of profiles of great achievers; it is a book about achievers, for achievers, by achievers. As producers, John and I are more than just a visionary and a visioneer, respectively. We are as committed to realizing our dreams as you are to realizing yours.

We want to help you realize your dreams. *ONE STEP BEYOND: Rediscovering the Adventure Attitude* will be a success if we can help to light just one candle in the darkness and light the way to the future.

Our dreams for the future CAN be realized. We CAN live happier, more satisfying lives. There IS hope. We don't need to live in fear or self-doubt. If we can spawn courage from fear, produce strength from weakness and feel hope amid uncertainty, we will succeed.

The twenty-first century will be a time of unsettling change. We can meet its challenges with frustration and fear or with courage and creativity. The choice is ours. But the answer, oddly enough, is not an external one. As Winston Churchill said: "The empires of the future are the empires of the mind."

May your mind and heart find meaning in the pages that follow. The uncommon thread unravels. Our adventure begins.

41

Are you in earnest? Seize this very minute.
  What you can do, or dream you can, begin it.
  Boldness has genius, power and magic in it.
– Goethe (*Faustus*)

Chapter 1
THE CALIBRE OF COURAGE

Fortune favours the bold.
– Juvenal

Profile on
Laurie Skreslet
of Calgary, Alberta

First Canadian
To Climb Mount Everest

To Wayne !

Cheers :-)
Laurie Skreslet

The Warrior Soul

So as long as I can see I will keep looking,
As long as I can walk I will keep moving,
As long as I can stand I will keep fighting.
– Walter de la Mare

"**G**od secure me from security, now and forever, Amen."

The words rattle in my brain as I sit bolt-upright in the passenger seat of Laurie Skreslet's shiny new sports car as it tears west from Calgary. The first Canadian to climb Mount Everest says the words with such quiet assurance that I cannot quite grasp their meaning.

I have other, more important, things to think about. I am white-knuckling the dashboard, or at least I would be if I could summon up the courage to get my hands there. They are clasped tightly in my lap, clinging to the fabric of my jeans as if it were the thread of life itself.

Our speed is typical of Laurie's ever-present impatience. When he plots his route from point A to point B, he seldom does it on the basis of distance; it's usually based solely on time and the number of stoplights between where he is and where he wants to go. He abhors inaction to such a degree that when he must wait at a stoplight, he's like a thoroughbred dying to blast out of the gate.

"Skrez," as he is known, does few things in halves. He travels fast, he walks fast and he talks fast. He reads books from back to front because he wants to know straight off what it all leads to. He waits for few things in life to come to him; he goes out after them.

As we barrel past yet another herd of beef cattle grazing on the rolling Rocky Mountain foothills, he lights up a cigarette. I find it hard to believe. So, apparently, do the thousands of people he now addresses every year as a professional public speaker.

Physically, I believe we're all basically the same. It's what you do with what you've got that makes the difference.
– Laurie Skreslet

"You can climb Everest even if you're a smoker," he says matter-of-factly. "I stopped smoking when I got to 20,000 feet, so I don't recommend it, but I'm not a clean-liver. I still stay up late, abuse my body, don't get enough rest. Sometimes, I eat or drink or smoke too much, but I don't use it as an excuse for why I don't achieve things."

What Skreslet has achieved since climbing Everest is astounding. Formerly a habitually reclusive, self-proclaimed loner, pauper and climbing junkie, he was petrified by the very thought of speaking to any group larger than one. But the moment he stepped onto the roof of the world – at 9:30 a.m. on October 5, 1982 – his life changed forever. From a shy, under-confident schoolboy plagued by self-doubt and strict protection from his parents, he has evolved into one of the most sought-after motivational speakers in the country.

Since returning from Everest, he has made major presentations to half a million people from coast to coast and pumped up the employees of more than 600 North American companies, including IBM, Northern Telecom, Exxon, Nestle, etc. His enthusiasm is contagious; his message

I know that if I want to keep going higher, to see the ground I've come from in a better light, with a better view, I've got to let go of things in the past and go for new things.
– Laurie Skreslet

riveting: that he is nothing special and that we can all achieve our dreams if we want them badly enough.

For Skreslet, the speaking circuit has been more than a career. He believes passionately in what he says, and strongly resists any allegations that he is living off Everest. That might have been true for the first two years after the '82 achievement, he points out, but now, years later, there is more to it.

There is more to him. He has since married. His wife Monique, an Air Canada flight attendant, and he have a daughter, Natasha. Together, they live on the same riverside lot Laurie grew up on as a child. His parents' house has been torn down and in its place sits a custom-built home of great beauty.

"If we had had to choose a Canadian who would be the first to the summit of Mount Everest, Laurie is the ideal person," says John Amatt, the business manager and one of the climbers on the 1982 Canadian expedition to Everest. "Laurie is very articulate and introspective. He's done a lot of thinking about the philosophy that goes into these kinds of achievements and he's able to communicate that philosophy well to people. I like his enthusiasm, his *joie de vivre*, and his whole attitude. He's just a neat guy to be with. Being with him uplifts you."

The late Bill March, leader of the 1982 expedition, agreed: "Laurie has really matured and carried that responsibility of being the first Canadian to the top of Everest in a manner that makes me feel proud of him as an individual. I think that's an awesome responsibility and he's handled it very well to the credit of himself and the country."

Today, Laurie and I are headed to one of what he calls his "power" places: a 365-metre-high monolith of limestone that juts from the foothills on the far eastern ranges of the Rockies. It's called Mount Yamnuska, or "Yam" in climbing circles, and is considered a mecca by local climbers. The two-kilometre-long mammoth is covered with dozens of routes, many of which Laurie has tried. He will be in his element.

The day had started like most climbing days do with Laurie: a little late. Three-quarters of an hour after our scheduled 8:00 a.m. departure, Laurie appeared from the shower, hair still wet, apologizing profusely for his tardiness and scrambling to put on his golf shirt, shorts and running shoes. He looked tired, the way he often does after an 18-hour day of packing a thousand tasks into a time slot that can only handle ten. He got through another yesterday – at 1:00 a.m. – when he finally finished sanding and staining the upstairs sundeck on his house after a writer had kept him preoccupied for most of the day.

After tearing out of the house, we got halfway down the block before we had to return home for a knife. It seemed he had to cut his right toenail so it would fit into his tightly fitting climbing shoe. The toe had been frostbitten in earlier years of ice climbing in temperatures near minus 40° C. Since then, he has had to take special care of it.

That task taken care of, our second stop was the equipment rental shop where he returned the belt sander he'd used on his sundeck the night before. Finally, after a third stop for breakfast at a fast food restaurant, we were on our way.

Now, at 10:00 a.m., I am relieved when Laurie suddenly slows down and turns off the highway onto an unmarked dirt road. Moments later we pull into a small, grass-covered parking lot surrounded by forest.

His jet-black BMW is completely out of place. So am I. I wonder where in God's creation Skreslet is taking me. He's on another of his adventures and I'm caught up in it.

You enter the sacred space of Laurie Skreslet, curiously enough, not through a mountain pass or along a wind-blasted ridge with the elements tearing at the foundation of your soul, but along a winding mountain trail. This one started at the base of Yamnuska and twisted and turned its way to the base of the cliff. Here, the rock towers over you like some giant, proclaiming its supremacy over the surrounding land. It's not hard to understand why Laurie calls this one of his power places. You sense a spirit here, an unspoken strength. It almost oozes from the rock through its thousands of cracks and crevices.

Overhead, ravens soar by, suspended on the ever-present updrafts that sweep up the cliff. The whole place has a

REMAIN FOCUSSED

"Disciplined focus," as one achiever said, "is what distinguishes those who make things happen from those who watch things happen."

All of our achievers have the ability to focus intensely. They know exactly what they want to do and they go after it.

"Your moment of strength is when you have the greatest amount of singleness of purpose," Laurie Skreslet says.

Adventure achievers focus on their goals, but they also keep a watchful eye on the world around them. This peripheral vision is what keeps them alive. They have the direction of a thoroughbred, but they do not wear blinders. Focus must not be achieved at the expense of awareness.

Once the dream is conceived through positive dissatisfaction and followed up with action and experience, it must be kept alive through constant focus. It is easy to lose sight of your goal.

character all its own, impressive, but intimidating. It has more than power. It has presence. It is here, flanked on his left by the Rockies and on his right by the rolling foothills and prairies, that Laurie is most himself.

"I love the big sky, the prairie and the wind," he says as his long, dirty-blond hair tumbles over his eyebrows. "This is where I disappear from the world."

He takes few people here. To get to this place you must make more than a journey out of town. You must enter his closely guarded inner space, gain his trust and prove you are worthy of seeing a part of him few people get a chance to see. It is Laurie at peace.

Sometimes, he admits, he doesn't even climb when he comes here. He just hikes for miles through the quiet rolling forest or lies in the sun, soaking in its warmth and gazing in delight at the ever-changing character of the clouds passing overhead.

49

When the objective is to climb the cliff, however, his concentration becomes tightly focused. Although Laurie may appear frantic and pressed in the "real" world, he is everything with his climbing that he often isn't in the work-a-day world: directed, highly organized and precise. In the mountains these qualities are his hallmarks.

Within minutes of parking the car, Laurie is talking about yet another of his passions besides climbing: war. "Studying battles has led me to better understand what conflicts are all about," he says, as he wraps a purple bandanna around his creased forehead and prepares to start up the trail. "Those conflicts can teach us things about ourselves."

Laurie is far from a superstar athlete or an Einstein intellect. He is a self-proclaimed absent-minded, often inefficient, and frequently intolerant character with an

It's not what you go through in life that makes you what you are, it's how you react to the world you're going through.
– Laurie Skreslet

obsession for the battle of life. He is a warrior. He loves a fight, especially one that pits him against himself.

Laurie's interest in war began as a child growing up in Calgary. He was raised in a small house on the banks of the glacier-fed Bow River, which winds its way swiftly through the city. At a little army surplus store not more than four blocks from his home, Laurie, then 11, bumped into former veterans and military experts.

50

"He used to drive me crazy with all his questions," recalled long-time friend, the late Glen Wells of Calgary, a former employee of the surplus store who first met Laurie there. "He was fascinated with military history. He saved his money from a paper route to buy a gun. When I fixed it up for him, he was so happy that I've never been able to get rid of him since."

Within a few years of discovering his fascination with war, Laurie became a military expert. He read everything about it that he could get his hands on. He went to trade shows and became completely captivated, not only with the inner workings of war, but with the inner conflicts of the people involved in it. He wondered why the recollections of some soldiers were so painful while those of others were full of fun and laughter. "'You put the horror out of your mind,' they would tell me," says Laurie, " 'because if you let yourself focus on that, it would twist and destroy you.'"

It would be a lesson he would apply on Everest years later, when four of his colleagues would be killed, six would choose to leave and he and seven others would keep climbing.

"During the three-week walk in to Everest, I cut the ties with the world I was leaving behind and hardened my heart, my mind and my soul to the hardships I might face on the mountain."

One of the hardships the team faced was the deaths of three Sherpas in a sudden and massive avalanche early in the expedition. Laurie respected the Sherpas, the mountain people of Nepal. They are known for their imperturbable sense of humour, courage and loyalty, attributes Laurie holds in highest esteem. That's why he was confused and disillusioned with himself when he couldn't seem to feel any empathy for the dead men during what should have been a painful period of mourning.

"I remember sitting up at night beside the only body [one of the three Sherpas] we were able to dig out of the avalanche and thinking, 'Why can't I feel anything?' All I could feel was something I was ashamed of: Better him than me, because I'm going back up there."

Since Laurie is a compassionate man, this made no sense to him. In their own way, however, it may have been the Sherpas' indefatigable spirit giving him the strength to continue. He'll never know. All he knows is he only felt resolve.

"It seemed to me that although someone died, it didn't mean it had to be over," he says as his finger stabs at you. "And I'm afraid that came from the war stories I'd heard as a kid. I remember being told that when you're preparing for battle, everyone's talking bravado, sharpening their knives and describing how they're going to stick the enemy. Then, when it starts getting down to it and you see the terror in people's eyes, some people freeze. Soldiers would tell me how you can't let that happen. You've got to know that when the horror begins you've got to stay fluid.

You gotta keep moving. Because when you stop, it's too difficult to start moving again.

"I wasn't afraid of losing my mind on Everest. I was afraid of losing my concentration and my composure. I thought we were there to do something. I felt like we were on a mission, and the mission was to do it."

Laurie is an only child of two Norwegian immigrants. His parents had to struggle and suffer greatly, both physically and financially, as they were growing up and they didn't want Laurie to have to endure the same hardships. As a result, they were very over-protective and discouraged him from taking the most natural boyhood risks.

When both of Laurie's parents died in his early to mid-20s, he became free to explore new potential within himself. Ironically, he evolved into exactly what his parents wouldn't have wanted: a consummate risk-taker.

"As a kid, my first dream was of climbing a set of stairs that never ended. I didn't know what it meant. But looking back, I think it had to do with what life's about. Life is an upward struggle, and I will be satisfied in this life as long as I stay on those stairs."

When he was still a youngster, a boy challenged Laurie to a race up the cables of a suspension bridge near the zoo. The bridge spanned the Bow River near Laurie's home.

"He said, 'Go!' and man, I pulled myself up, flipped my feet up and went blasting toward the top. I was concentrating and concentrating until I got about two-thirds of the way up. Then I started to get tired."

Wondering how his competition was faring, he glanced down only to discover the other boy was still standing down on the ground.

"What are you doing?" Laurie asked.

"Ah, I don't wanna," the boy replied.

Laurie was enraged. Raised on the principle that a commitment to try is cast in stone, he couldn't understand why someone would renege on their own challenge.

"I looked down and started to make a few moves to come down, but I realized it was closer to go to the top. So, I kept going.

"As I got higher, more and more people stopped and started watching. Then I heard people asking: What's going on?

"Ah, there's some stupid kid hanging from a wire way up there, someone said.

"You don't want to let go because it's a helluva long way down. But then I heard somebody say, 'I hope the stupid kid falls and kills himself.'"

When Laurie heard that, something inside him changed. In spite of his fear, it hardened him to the desire not to give the doubting Thomas the slightest degree of satisfaction.

"What kind of a person says that? I had no enemies. I had nobody who didn't like me. So I thought: Well to hell with you! I was scared, but I went to the end of the cable and I remember looking down in just enough time to see the person who made that remark turn in disgust and walk away."

This incident drove deep into Laurie's psyche and slowly started to wedge open the door to his real potential. Until then, that door had been locked by his perception of his own limitations.

"When I look back on it, that incident reminds me of what I've always run into in the future: when some people see you doing something they think is risky or that they wouldn't do, they wish for your downfall. I knew there would always be people like that; some people will always be against you when you try to achieve something, whatever it may be."

Whatever Laurie is, you will see him more clearly if you look at his brilliant, brown eyes. There is an intensity there, the kind that makes his stare burn. It's not hard to visualize him in the heat of battle, attacking a horrendous piece of overhanging ice with his only weapons: his ice axes and his ambition.

Behind the intense eyes there is a kind, compassionate man. "Sometimes, it's overridden by his energy," says Wells, who for more than 25 years had been the brother

DARE TO BE DIFFERENT

If we can endure the discomfort of being different, we will garner a new-found sense of strength and self-worth. Independence is empowering. It unlocks many doors to greater achievement because it gives us the confidence to know that we can depend on ourselves. No longer are we burdened with the weight of self-doubt and the goals of others.

I took the [road] less traveled by, and that has made all the difference.
– Robert Frost

If you know who you are, you can dare to be different. However, it is sometimes very difficult to be different. Anyone who has tried to step out from the flock understands that to do so involves a measure of personal sacrifice that may cause criticism from others, self-doubt and isolation.

All of our adventure achievers experienced some degree of difficulty before they saw their ultimate objective and stepped out from the crowd. But they overcame their frustrations and grew to achieve an independence that empowered them.

Laurie never had. "I would give my life for Laurie, as he would do for me."

Wells was one of Laurie's "allies." It is of special significance this word, "ally." While it has military connotations, the way so many of the words Laurie uses do, it is analogous to "brother" or "sister" to him. To be called Laurie's ally is to have been chosen for his regiment. He will stand by you to the last; it's part of his unwritten code. "In this life, defending a friend is more valuable than anything," Laurie says emphatically.

People mean more to Laurie than peaks. In fact, their importance to him goes to the core of his character.

"I remember meeting him once at the base of a climb, after I hadn't seen him for about two years," recalls Sharon Wood, of Canmore, Alberta. Sharon is one of Laurie's understudies who, in 1986, became the first North American woman to climb Everest. "Immediately, he just lit right up and gave me a huge warm hug, and I felt that feeling, that very powerful feeling I always get from Laurie. It's like you're completely enveloped and this guy really believes in you."

Though he displays a remarkable caring for others, Laurie, like all of us, is far from faultless. He is often late, sometimes to the point of infuriating Monique, his friends and his associates. He is sometimes lazy and, at times, domineering.

Whatever you may say about him, Laurie is a complex character. Described by others as odd and eccentric, he is an enigma; a people-person juxtaposed with one who has a powerful fixation on war. At first glance, the two aspects appear to contradict each other. On one side, love; on the other, war. In Laurie, they are complementary because underlying them is a code of the highest principle. It

55

permeates everything he does; from his interest in the military to his climbing to his flair at the podium. He has a value system and set of principles so strong they cannot be broken, even in moments of greatest stress. These values include a strong sense of justice, brutal honesty and an unbending loyalty to those he loves and to those challenges to which he commits himself.

Although he has never been a member of the military, he perceives its discipline as necessary to survive in wartime and in life. Indeed, for Laurie Skreslet, one of the initial attractions of the '82 Everest expedition was the prospect of being part of a team – a regiment – that would wage war against the highest mountain in the world. Though he has never been a soldier, he saw the expedition as his opportunity to serve his country. It was his way of seeing action.

"It's the identification with a common principle, of not retreating, of loyalty to one another, of 'together we are stronger than the sum total of us as individuals', of taking diverse elements and putting them together in a cutting edge. These are some of the reasons why the military fascinates me."

On the physical, emotional and psychological edge while on Everest, some of Laurie's values would be tested to the limit. It was because of his value system and belief in others, he says, that he maintained the attitude that eventually helped him get to the summit. The key moment occurred, he says, when the body of cameraman Blair Griffiths was being evacuated. Blair had been crushed between two falling blocks of ice in the deadly Khumbu Icefall, which guards the doorstep to Everest. While the evacuation was in progress, Laurie was clearing a passage to enable the remaining climbers to get safely down the mountain.

"I was being pressured to hurry up and get off the mountain," he recalls. "I looked back up the icefall and saw seven more people coming down. I remembered what it was like on Mount Rundle in the Rockies near Banff when I was climbing just before I left for Everest. My partner was anxious to get off the mountain and, in his haste, left me behind on the descent. I didn't like that, and I told him so when we were off the mountain. I thought there was an unspoken pact that if you go up together, you come down together. You don't break that contract until you're off the mountain.

"There I was, on Everest, ready to go down and I thought: I'm not scared. But maybe the last guy is scared. So I radioed that I was going to wait until everyone was off the mountain before I descended."

The last man got himself tangled in a rope in the middle of a ladder bridge across a crevasse and, in the process of trying to free him, Laurie was knocked off his feet. He fell four and a half metres into the chasm and cracked three ribs on his right side. Somehow, he managed to extricate himself, but a Sherpa had to help him down to base camp. There, while two weeks of bad weather made safe climbing impossible, Laurie recuperated. When he was well enough to walk, the team doctor, Stephen Bezruchka, advised him to hike to the nearest hospital four days away so he could get a more complete diagnosis of his injuries. While walking to and from the hospital, Laurie was able to recover during those eight days, but his colleagues had gone back to work on Everest. While they were weakening from the debilitating effects of the altitude, Laurie was getting stronger at the lower elevation, eating good food and getting proper rest. One day, he ate 16 eggs, half a kilogram of garlic and a small pile of potatoes. When he finally rejoined the team, he was stronger and more fit than his fellow climbers. The eight days of rest and recovery and their resulting improvement in his physical and mental condition led to him being chosen for the first team and put him in position to make a summit attempt.

"When I look back at it, I couldn't have planned it better," he admits openly. "But I didn't do it consciously, and I wouldn't have done it consciously even if I'd had the opportunity. My accident was the key. The reason I had the strength to go to the top was because I'd had eight days less deterioration than the others.

"It was a fluke, but the fluke happened because of the pact I'd made with myself. Once in a while I think it was luck, but it was almost like there was something that kept saying, 'You just keep doing your part Skreslet, and things are going to fall into place.'"

The part Laurie doesn't tell you about is the pain he endured from his cracked ribs. It was his constant companion for the balance of the climb. He tried to subdue it with painkillers, but with the respiration rate and depth of inhalation required just to walk in Everest's rarefied air, it was difficult.

"It hurt at every breath, but I tried to overlook the pain and focus instead on the goal. Pain is sometimes part of the price you pay in mountaineering. Besides, it seemed pretty insignificant compared to the deaths of Blair and the three Sherpas."

It was never Laurie's goal to be the first Canadian to the top. He had vowed to take the climb one step at a time, one day at a time, and to give it better than his best every day. The rest he left to fortune. Whenever summit aspirations entered his head, he consciously dismissed them.

"I've always known that anger is the result of unmet

expectations," he says. "Every time I saw myself pulling onto the top of the mountain, I'd cancel it. To me, that's not the way. This was too serious to daydream about."

When you run away from fear it gets bigger, but when you move toward it, it shrinks.
– Laurie Skreslet

As a child, Laurie daydreamed a lot. Unfortunately, his father quashed many of his son's ambitions. Jacob "Jack" Skreslet had grown up in Norway in a poor family north of the Arctic Circle. For financial reasons, he had been forced to join the Norwegian Army at an early age just to help his family make ends meet. It was an experience he did not enjoy, but instead endured out of necessity.

At six feet, six inches tall and 250 pounds, Jack was more than just a huge man. He was an imposing figure in Laurie's life. Discipline was strict. Fortunately, Laurie's mother was not so rigid. Instead of dictating, she was aware that Laurie's boyishness was a natural part of him and his exploration of life. As she saw it, Laurie should be allowed to play like any other child.

He did. When his father wasn't looking, he'd steal away to a forbidden tree at the end of the block.

"One day, some kids in the neighbourhood challenged me. They said, 'C'mon, let's go climb!'

"I said, 'No, I can't. My dad says it's too dangerous' and they made fun of me.

"I didn't go up until they left. I just stood there beside this tree at the end of the block and looked up at it. Then, I started wondering: they climbed it and they didn't die. So, I climbed it. I went very high up. I remember sitting up there, recalling that suspension bridge at the zoo and thinking to myself that just like then, if I watch where I put my hands and feet and I think about it, there's no reason

I have to fall. You only fall if you make a mistake, if you take your mind off what you're trying to do. That made me start wondering if it wasn't my dad's fear that was preventing me from doing things."

Like the roots of that tree, the climb at the end of the block began to establish the roots of Everest in Laurie. They started shallow in the soil and from there went deeper and deeper as he explored himself and his world.

After downing something to drink, we start up the trail. It is a superb July day. With the temperature of the mid-morning air hovering at about 24° C, we know that by mid-afternoon it's going to be a scorcher. Overhead, there is a brilliant blue sky, a few scattered clouds and a cool breeze from the west.

The trail is steep. Within minutes we are both puffing and panting through the forest. Once above the tree line, we are greeted with the warming rays of the sun. We sweat.

Laurie comes up behind me, slowly but steadily, not like the jack-rabbit or mountain goat you might imagine, but like a cross between a bull and a tortoise: determination coupled with patience. He rarely stops to rest. Instead, with his hands in his pockets, he resigns himself to the task.

It's been a while since Laurie went climbing. With a speaking schedule that would make your head spin and a bustling home life, there is often little time left for himself. In a way, he has become a victim of his own success: the harder he works, the more people want to hear him. Since Everest, it has been an Everest he could not have imagined.

As we climb higher, the view of the Bow River Valley and surrounding foothills becomes breathtaking. It is more than the rock face that produces the power of this place. It is the entire environment, from the pristine waters of the surrounding lakes and plush green forest to the majestic summits that grace the sky. We stop little to enjoy the view. Alone in our worlds, the slog continues. Higher and higher, hotter and hotter.

Up by the face you can see the ravens soaring just a few metres from the rock, gliding effortlessly in the air, dancing in the late morning sun. The birds seem such a separate reality from us, two earthbound humans grounded by gravity and, with every step, fighting against it.

At last we arrive at the foot of the cliff. But like two bullets bent on a target we do not pause, and instead fire off down the trail for 10 more minutes to the start of our route. When we finally get there, it is well past 11:00 a.m. Laurie drinks a litre of a sweet mixture of electrolytes and water. I drink straight water and prepare the gear.

61

In spite of the heat, he dons wool knickers, baby blue knee-high wool socks, a red sweatshirt, a harness and a red helmet. As the temperature is now pushing 27° C, it's astonishing. I'm wearing only shorts, a T-shirt, my harness, climbing shoes and helmet. "If you've ever fallen on limestone, you know why I'm wearing all this," he says, sensing my disbelief.

I keep quiet, but Laurie's comment does little to bolster my confidence. I begin to think I may be climbing with a creature from the past bound in the present. All his gear looks brand new and there isn't a scratch on it. The only hint I have that I am climbing with a veteran is his age-old alpine hammer, which has clearly seen its share of 20-hour days and epic, high altitude adventures. It alone reassures me.

Noon: Laurie starts up. As neither of us has been out climbing in many months, we have purposely chosen an easier route. I learn quickly that my hesitancy is unnecessary. Everything Laurie does, every move he makes, is safety-oriented. To begin with, he climbs tied into two ropes instead of one. The additional weight of an extra rope might be a concern to most climbers, but Laurie is not like most climbers. He has stayed alive all these years by focusing on intelligence and intuition. First, he uses his intelligence to control those elements within his control. Then, he uses intuition to tell him when, where and how to move. It's a bit like watching a woodcutter chisel his way through a piece of rock-hard mahogany: first he makes sure he has all the tools he needs – both physically and mentally. Then, he uses feel to produce a product that is a stunning combination of skill and sensitivity.

For much of his teenage and early adult years, Laurie had been anything but focused in this way. In 1967, frustrated by school and angered by his father's over-protective nature, Laurie quit school at 16, ran away from home and headed for Florida. There, he signed on for an Atlantic crossing as an able-bodied seaman aboard a privately owned four-masted sailing ship. For a short time at sea, he relished the words of James Joyce he had found in a book:

He was alone and young and willful and wild-hearted, alone amidst a waste of wild air and brackish waters and the sea harvest of shells and tangle of veiled grey sunlight.

Laurie's sense of freedom would be short-lived. After the crossing, he sailed the world for two years; literally floating through life, reassured only by the feeling that he was happier in action than in inaction. There was no direction, only directing.

In the course of his travels, he experienced storms off the coast of Mozambique and Madagascar, and saw camels silhouetted against the setting sun in Iran. For most people it would have been the adventure of a lifetime, but for Laurie it left only an aching pang for purpose.

In Iran it occurred to him that he was in Asia, and he should go and see Mt. Everest. He decided to make a pilgrimage there, but got robbed on the Afghanistan-Pakistan border. Using a resourcefulness that later became one of his greatest assets, he sold a few litres of his own blood and hitchhiked out with just enough money to eventually get him back to North America. Once there, he returned home.

When he got home, he remembered something about an organization called Outward Bound. He'd read about it in *Reader's Digest* once. The headline to the story had said, "You'll Never be Afraid to Try Again."

Travelling hadn't given him what he'd been searching for, he thought to himself, so maybe Outward Bound would. He got himself to Colorado and enrolled in a 26-day course. That was in 1970.

Laurie could not have known how significantly Outward Bound would affect his life, and eventually contribute to his success on Everest. In the strictest sense, there could not have been a better organization for him at that moment.

Outward Bound was founded during World War II to train merchant seamen how to survive. When merchant vessels taking war supplies to Great Britain were sunk, it was noticed that a higher percentage of the younger men died compared to the older ones. When the ship, the symbol of security for the youths, was taken away, their sense of self-confidence apparently sunk with it, along with their will to survive. It became Outward Bound's goal to reverse this trend through the medium of outdoor adventure, not only at sea, but in the mountains, jungles and deserts of the world. The organization's founders wanted to force people to stretch beyond the security of their known limits into the unknown world of their true potential.

By the time Laurie reached Outward Bound he was 21 and had been a merchant seaman for two years. He understood the rigours of life on the ocean and the ideals to which the organization aspired.

CONTROL YOUR FEAR

Fear in all its forms – physical, emotional, spiritual, financial – is one of the biggest barriers that stands between us and our dreams . Fear is a four-letter word. It simultaneously terrifies and immobilizes. Yet to confront fear is to flourish.

"When you run away from fear, it gets bigger," Laurie Skreslet says, "but when you advance towards it, it shrinks." Someone once said that there are three barriers to success:

1. Fear of failure.

2. Fear of being ridiculed.

3. Fear of the unknown.

John Amatt agrees: "The only limiting factor to our achievements in life is our fear of the unknown. "

Adventure achievers have a unique way of dealing with fear. First, they acknowledge that it is there . John Hughes is not some fearless fighter. He is an intelligent strategist – and self-analyst . Rather than letting his fear control him, he channels his energy into achieving success. Rather than focus on fear, he focuses on what he must do to overcome it.

"Fear must be dealt with," he says. "There is no option. If you don't stay in control, then you can be in serious trouble . You have to suppress fear and cope."

After just 26 days of seeing him operate, *If you want to* officials at Outward Bound hired Laurie on *master your* the spot as an assistant instructor. The secre- *situation, con-* tary in the Colorado office observed one day *trol your fear.* that he was the only instructor who never **– Laurie** complained. Endowed with a mental and **Skreslet** physical toughness borne from years of self-searching, he was the embodiment of their motto, "To serve, to strive, and not to yield."

These attributes never became more clear than a few months later. It was a Sunday in September, 1971, halfway up Yamnuska. Laurie was out for a climb with his friend and mentor, Eckhard Grassman. About a kilometre west of where we were climbing that day, they had been forced to take refuge from a thunderstorm. Eckhard had been 45 metres above Laurie when suddenly lightning struck the monolith. Both were knocked off their stance. They were anchored to the face by their ropes, but they were badly shaken. Shivering, disoriented and afraid, they huddled in their places for more than an hour. Gradually the torrent subsided. Laurie decided to move. When Laurie reached his friend, Eckhard announced he could lead no longer. He was too shaken from the lightning strike.

Laurie had never led a climb of this difficulty before. Forced to confront his fears, the rock face and the weather, he took his first terrifying steps back out onto the cliff. His heels hung straight out into space, a wafer-thin edge his only purchase. Slowly the rain turned to sleet, the sleet to snow, the snow to hail and the hail to more snow. Darkness was gathering.

Soon, both were showing signs of hypothermia, a condition in which the temperature of the body's inner core begins to drop. If it falls more than a few degrees, death can

65

To progress, you have to leave something behind.
– Laurie Skreslet

be imminent. They were far too high to descend to the bottom now. The safest and fastest escape was to keep climbing.

Damp, soaked to the skin, and grappling with the numbing effects of the cold, Laurie pressed on. The wet snow continued to fall, streaming down his face and making every hold slippery and insecure. He could feel panic begin to grip him in his guts. It wound its way up into his stomach.

Beneath an overhang, he needed to make a difficult series of moves, but he couldn't seem to get their sequence right. He was terrified, cold and alone at the end of an 11-mm-thick rope and he knew that if he fell, he would plummet 18 m and pendulum wildly into a sheer wall to his right. The results could be disastrous.

"I'm running out of strength, so I try to go back. I realize I can't reverse my moves. So I try to move up again and I can't. I feel trapped."

It's hard to describe the feeling of helplessness you get on an exposed rock face when you just can't seem to find the key to open the door. Although the rope has the strength of steel, you anchor it as you climb, and your partner has you secured, there is a feeling of utter isolation, that you will be there for the rest of your life.

To progress upwards you must bend and contort yourself to fit into every new shape of the stone puzzle you encounter. Movement can be painfully slow, and miles are measured in inches.

Regardless of how high above the ground you are, however, your world is only as big as you can reach. When you've reached as far as you can, when you're at wit's end and you know you're about to come off, there can be a paralyzing panic. If it isn't instantly checked, the result is inevitable.

66

Your mouth goes dry. Your arms and legs begin to shake uncontrollably. Your eyes become as wide as saucers. Your body's natural fighting instincts take over.

Failure is saying you don't have the strength to try again. Failure is folding. **– Laurie Skreslet**

"I started to cry because I knew I was going to fall. I was losing it. Then pride kicked in. I said to myself: Well, if I'm going to fall, it's not going to be while retreating and it's not going to be from doing nothing. It's going to be from trying to get out of this."

At that moment, instead of just reaching upward, he also reached inward. As if by a miracle, he made the move. And he kept moving and moving and moving; flowing up the rock face like the water flowing down it. It was one of those rare but exhilarating moments of peak performance in which fear kicks out and fluidity kicks in; the moment when mind, body and soul move together as one, regardless of the risks.

By the time they reached the top, it had been dark for several hours. The moon had come out and it was starting to snow again. As Laurie pulled up on the last hold, he entered a curious winter world. The mountain was about a metre under snow. The wind was howling. At the edge of the cliff – and his energies – Laurie dragged his body face first into the snow. After panting there for several seconds, he stood. "I let out this yell like I'd killed something awful, like I'd slayed a dragon and was holding the bloody sword above my head."

After Eckhard made it to the top and they were walking down the back side of the mountain together, Laurie couldn't stop laughing. In a rare moment, the euphoria of their achievement overwhelmed him. He hugged Eckhard over and over again.

"It took years for me to understand that I did slay

When the situation starts saying: Lose your cool! Pack it in! Call it quits now! Better go home 'cause now it's going to get really difficult, that's when something comes up inside me and says, 'Ah, now it's getting interesting.'

– Laurie Skreslet

something that day. The thing I slayed was the fear inside me that had said I couldn't do it. I learned that I can do it. Over the years and the countless climbs we did together, that's what Eckhard taught me. He taught me never to give up."

This was another key turning point in Laurie's life. That day, he cut away not just a piece of his own fear, but a piece of his father's.

Sadly, Eckhard would perish a decade or so later while attempting to climb the north face of Mount Edith Cavell near Jasper. Before he died, he left a lasting impression on Laurie and provided critical building blocks to his character.

A few years later, Laurie was hired by Outward Bound Canada in Keremeos, British Columbia, a town in the Okanagan Valley about 50 km southwest of Penticton. It was there that he had another important revelation.

"We'd had three courses of all guys when, all of a sudden, it was a course of all girls," recalls Laurie. "Who did I have? A pretty blonde girl and a less attractive, slightly overweight girl. From the beginning, I was talking and interacting with the pretty girl more, but trying to treat them both the same. We did the first climb. The good-looking girl just breezed up. She was a natural. The other one had a difficult time with almost every move. But toward the end of the morning, the attractive girl re-injured an ankle she'd twisted the day before, so she had to sit out the two climbs in the afternoon.

"Well, the climbs took a long time to do. The slightly overweight girl struggled with all the problems, but something happened inside me that made me feel uneasy. I realized I was beginning to enjoy her company more, and that I liked her more."

At this point in his description, something begins to stir in Laurie. You see it in his eyes. They begin to glass over. His voice starts to crack and the warrior starts fighting back the tears.

"Why did I like her more? Because throughout the day, she never once said, 'I can't'. Every time I explained to her what to do on the rock, she tried. And invariably she'd be able to do it. Sometimes she slipped and fell, and maybe she would cut her knee, but she never asked for sympathy.

"By the end of the day, I had so much respect for her because she had been willing to try. It didn't matter to me anymore what she looked like.

"That girl taught me something: that the willingness to try has a beauty that outweighs physical beauty. Effort alone demands respect from me."

Eight years later, Laurie would apply the lessons of Yamnuska and Outward Bound again, this time on his way to the top of Everest.

September 24, 1982: The deadly Khumbu Icefall is a frozen tongue that licks its way over a huge rock ledge to the base of the world's tallest pyramid. A solitary figure stood in its midst.

The day before, most of the team had reached Camp 1, above the icefall. For safety reasons, Bill March had closed the Khumbu to any further climbers. Laurie was there anyway.

"When Bill told me they'd closed the icefall, my first thought was: Wait a minute! Not after what I've put into this trip. Too much of me was there. My feeling was, 'I don't belong down here. I belong up there, where the battle is. I'm not here to sit in base camp. I'm here for the fight. We're here to get up this thing, if we can; to do battle with it. So let's do battle. Let's go for it.'"

Laurie was going for it that morning, but he'd never been in a battle like that before. Only weeks earlier, four members of the expedition had been killed in the icefall in less than two days. Three had been buried in the biggest avalanche on the mountain in a decade. The fourth had been crushed between two huge blocks of ice. Now, Skreslet was there alone.

70

It is impossible for most of us to imagine the Khumbu Icefall. It descends from a height of about 7,300 m down to about 4,900 m over a distance of 20 km; part of a truly massive glacier, tumbling slowly, often unnoticeably, from

---

BECOME ULTIMATELY ACCOUNTABLE

"Ultimate" accountability is just that – ultimate. To put your life on the line for what you believe is not only the ultimate sacrifice, but ultimately empowering. As Laurie Skreslet discovered when he crossed the crevasse in the Khumbu Icefall, "I looked around and it was like a blanket had been taken off me. It was clear what I was here to do. For the very first time in my life, as I moved away from that bridge, I realized that if you're lucky, once in your life, you come to a place where you realize you must make manifest what you profess to believe."

If we profess to believe that we can succeed in the future, we will need to commit completely and be ultimately accountable. If we do everything else right, we should be ultimately successful.

the flanks of Everest down to its foot. As it moves over a rock ledge at the rate of about a metre a day, it groans, creaks and wails as deep crevasses open and close inside it. In a ghastly way, it seems alive.

When it's serious, that's when you make the biggest advances in your life. That's when you learn the important lessons.
– Laurie Skreslet

Along with crevasses, enormous ice blocks split into shape. As the beast gouges its way downward, massive collapses of ice towers the size of tractor-trailers can occur. The final moments for many climbers come when the tremendous pressures, like anger built up inside the behemoth from the man-made assault, release in a terrifying and completely unpredictable surge of many metres in a single second. It is a bit like playing high-altitude Russian roulette. You never know when the bullet is coming.

71

The psychological stress of this deadly game is severe. As the huge ice blocks teeter on the brink of disaster around you, your life hangs in an equally precarious balance. You can try to forget, but you always know where you are. It is purgatory.

On any other mountain, the icefall would simply be left to its own deadly devices, but on Everest it provides the only access to the mountain's upper reaches from the southern, Nepalese side. Thus, with heads down and hearts racing, climbers endure its relentless tension, lured by the challenge of the summit beyond. They have no other choice. If they want to get to the top, they must risk being permanently entombed in ice.

This is where Laurie found himself that morning. Surrounded by the corpses of the Khumbu – the old snow stakes, shredded ropes and twisted ladders – he slowly worked his way through much of the maelstrom. So that his fellow expedition members would know where to find him in the event of an accident, he called out the numbered ladder bridges on the radio as he crossed them.

Then he came to a 30-metre-deep crevasse with no ladder and only a single strand of 10-mm polypropylene rope dangling from the other side. It was a one-and-a-half metre jump and he was carrying a 30-kg pack.

"I backed off and tried to find another way, but there was no other way. It's like so many things in life. You know the move you've got to make, but you look to see if there's some other option. After 10 minutes, you realize the only option you've got is the only one you knew you had at the beginning."

Using all the ingenuity and knowledge he had accumulated in 12 years of climbing, Laurie carefully hooked up a makeshift system of two anchored ropes that might hold him in the event of a fall. His plan was to jump across, plant his axe immediately in the ice on the other side and "hope like hell that if I didn't make it, the ropes would hold."

It was a prospect few men would even contemplate.

"It all came down to the question: What are you here for? I knew what I was there for. I was there to give it not just my best, but more than my best – 110 percent, 150 percent, 200 percent – every day. Then, even if we failed, there would be no dishonour.

"Either way, I was going to be a winner. I didn't want to be a loser. It was like in this battle, even if we don't win, I'm not coming back dragging my shield behind me. I'm going to come back proud. I was terrified, but it was simple."

Emptying his mind of everything but the goal, his heart began to pound; his respiration quickened. He took a few steps back. Then, he powered to the edge and launched himself into space.

Eternity was over in an instant. Like some animal clawing for its existence, he planted his ice axe, stabbed his free fingers into the snow and drove the points of his crampons into the ice with everything he had.

Obstacles are like a nutshell that, once cracked, reveals meat inside that nourishes you.
– Laurie Skreslet

Straining on his axe, and for one split second suspended only by his feet and his free hand, he yanked the pick from its purchase and with one clean, clear stroke, hammered it higher into the snow. His feet followed with equal ferocity, pounding into place, beating back the hands that seemed to reach up and want to haul him into the crevasse. Then, puffing and panting, and with adrenalin coursing through his body, he slowly stood triumphant on the other side.

He never looked back.

"As I started moving, I looked around me and it was like a blanket had been taken off me. It was clear what I was here to do. It was clear. I knew that all I had to do was give it my best. That's it. That's the conclusion. For the very first time in my life, as I moved away from that bridge, I realized that if you're lucky, at least once in your life you come to a place where you realize you must make manifest what you profess to believe."

Until then, Laurie had thought he believed in himself. Now, he knew he did.

"Life is such a waste when you're in that confusion where it's all self-doubt. To hell with that. Cross the bridge and get moving. It's the momentum that carries you over. The thing to remember, too, is that if you stop and get into self-doubt and start rolling backwards, momentum works in both directions."

There was only one direction Laurie was headed in now, and that was up. He had made more than a leap from

73

one side of the crevasse to the other, he had made a gigantic leap of faith. It propelled him into another dimension of confidence and commitment. The momentum of that single act helped carry him up the mountain.

Within minutes, Laurie has come to the end of his ropes. After anchoring himself to the rock, he gives me the call to come up.

The climb proceeds uneventfully, smoothly, the way you wish climbs always would but sometimes don't. Today it would be no epic in the altitudes, but instead two friends out for some peace and tranquility in the warm summer sun. Except for feeling like fritters baked in a vertical frying pan, there are few other obstacles.

On top, we shake hands. There is nothing like the elation many people imagine. Instead, there is a straightforward realization that the climb is finished and a touch of sadness in its conclusion, like the last pages of a good book. Because Laurie has family commitments back in town, we call it a day.

Laurie seems relieved. On the way down to the packs, he pauses to admire the view on the back side of the mountain and to soak in the scenery, majesty and magic of the place. With his bandanna, tanned skin and square features, he looks like an Indian brave, a warrior pausing for a quiet moment of contemplation after a brief battle.

Ten minutes later, we are back at the base of the cliff. There, Laurie finishes off more liquid. Then, by some appropriate coincidence, a lone army officer happens by. He is training in the area and is enjoying a hike on his day off. Immediately, Laurie launches into volumes of "militarese," asking him what kind of weapons his regiment is using, how they're training and why.

By the time the young corporal leaves 20 minutes later, he has no idea he has just bumped into something of a military expert, or, for that matter, the first Canadian to climb Everest. Laurie does not mention the fact. It happened years before and he is proud of it, but he does not broadcast it. He has gone on with his life.

When you can convey to your children the positive qualities of character that will allow them to choose and serve this world and themselves well – that's success.
– Laurie Skreslet

We sit there for a long while after the officer leaves as Laurie lights another cigarette and talks casually about life as it is.

"The biggest challenge I've faced in my life hasn't been Everest," he says. "It's the one I'm involved in right now: learning how to make a family work, how to become a social person, because I tend to be a loner. It's harder than anything I've ever tried to achieve.

"I remember one time when I was a teenager. I was climbing Mt. Andromeda and I got hit by rockfall. It cracked my shoulder blade and was so painful that with each swing of my axe, I'd scream. When I got to the top, I lay there, face down in the gravel, groaning in pain and fear. I thought I might not even make it off the mountain.

"Then I asked myself how this compared to the pain of breaking up with my girlfriend (a girl he'd been with for three years). It didn't even compare, not even close. And I laughed with my face in the gravel.

"The agony of relationships that don't work overpowers the agony of effort. The pain on a mountain is just physical. It doesn't hurt like affairs of the heart, like when your soul's at war with itself. But you don't give in. You can't give in.

"I gave in once. I got to the point where I was on my

75

Do you really want to get to the summit? Do you really want to get to your goal? Well, there's a process. It involves one step at a time, and it involves patience.
– Laurie Skreslet

hands and knees in a corner, crying because I couldn't figure out what was wrong with me. How come I couldn't love someone? How come I couldn't make it work? I couldn't figure it out. The thing that preserved my sanity was climbing. I kept going back to the physical things that I could ground myself with."

Some of the answers to Laurie's painful questions about love and relationships didn't come until months after Everest. Days after returning to Canada, the team was received by the Prime Minister. On a flight back from that reception, he met Monique, his wife-to-be.

"I remember this tremendously handsome guy dashing up to the door of the plane," she recalls, "late, as usual for Laurie, and thinking to myself, Who the hell is that? I couldn't look at him for some reason. I was too nervous. I thought he was a skier, all tanned and athletic-looking. Then somebody said they thought he had something to do with Everest. It wasn't until about two hours later that I discovered who he really was.

"It was his strong charisma I remember most," says the tall, blonde, attractive French-Canadian who has become the business brains behind Laurie's speaking success. "It pulled me to him. Then he started talking about dreams and how he had made one of his come true. We can all relate to that. That's where it started."

Monique and Laurie have been married since 1985. His wedding ring is a melted down mixture of a piece of rock from Everest and remnants of a silver ring from a veteran of the French Foreign Legion. While he can be scattered, disorganized and impulsive at times, Monique is efficient, effective and highly disciplined. Together, they are a powerful team.

"I sometimes call him the tornado," she says. "He has tremendous energy. But if you get caught in his tornado, look out. I bring him stability and he brings me excitement."

Above all, there is love between them, a love that endures the possibility that one day, Laurie might not come back from the mountains.

Success to me is that sense of deep satisfaction you get when you're doing what you love. Money is a side issue.
– Laurie Skreslet

"If he didn't, at least he would go doing what he loves to do best," Monique says. "To ask him to do otherwise, to stay at home, or to just work, would destroy the person he is.

77

"I love to watch him in the mountains," she says, as a smile appears on her fine-featured face. "That's his world. He's effective there and he's meticulous.

"We all have places in which we feel comfortable, whether it's with the kids, in the garden, on the golf course, wherever. But he's himself when he's out there. He can be tired in the city, but once he gets into the mountains, the energy and the power fill him up."

There is a strong spiritual side to Laurie that not many people aside from Monique get a chance to see. He believes deeply in reincarnation and, in fact, has been told by a Nepalese lama that in one of his former lives he lived in the shadow of Everest as a Tibetan monk. Whether or not you believe it is not important to Laurie. What is important is that Everest is more than a mountain to him.

"I feel an energy there," he says. "It's a power place. I'm drawn to it. I remember the first time I saw it during the walk-in to base camp. I looked at it and thought: Oh, BIG

If you want an adventure like Indiana Jones goes through on the screen, well it has its price... Don't throw the dice if you can't pay the price.
– Laurie Skreslet

sucker! Ya, definitely BIG.

"Then, as I got closer, I thought to myself, Jesus, that's big. That's a BIG mountain. How the hell are we going to get up this thing?"

The dimensions of Everest challenge the imagination. Its base alone is over 16 km across and, at an elevation of 5,500 m, it's almost as high as Canada's highest mountain, Mt. Logan, in the Yukon. From this prodigious foundation, three separate ridges five kilometres long stretch skyward for three kilometres.

The first time Laurie set eyes on the mountain, he knew he needed a plan – a big one. What it came down to was simple: one step after another, after another, after another.

This formula was nothing new to Laurie. He had applied it hundreds of times in his climbing career. One of the first times occurred on a frozen waterfall in the dead of a Canadian winter.

Located on the edge of the world-famous Lake Louise, Louise Falls in winter is a stunning cascade of water frozen in time; beautiful, blue and luminescent. Towering 100 m above the lake, its hardest section is a 10-m vertical pillar of unconsolidated ice that has turned back more than its share of experienced climbers.

Over the course of the winter, Laurie had failed to scale the pillar seven times. On his eighth attempt, and by the light of the moon, it happened.

"As I was climbing it, there was such a sense that 'this is right'. It was a sense throughout my whole body. There didn't have to be a reason. I just knew it. But I didn't know where it was headed."

Finally, that need he had felt since he left home started to be met.

"The feeling of rightness is the feeling of the moonlight; the gleaming of the crystals that night on the snow. Everywhere you looked there were diamonds – the luminescence of the waterfall, the acknowledgment of your partner that there was magic in the air tonight, the sound of the metal on your bodies and the symbolism of trying to conquer something you can't really conquer."

Effort is everything to Laurie. He has returned again and again to places of previous failures. In a world obsessed with being first, in a country that idolizes him because he was the first, he puts effort first. It means more to him than accolades or wild applause. It is the essence of his excellence.

"In the western world, a lot of people believe that achievement is what matters, not the effort involved. That works for a while, until you begin to look at life with an eye that's just a little more sensitive, and you see that effort does count. In the end, effort is what it's all about. Effort is what allows you to get to the point where you can gain enough experience through failure that you can start to succeed."

Another important facet of Laurie's character is something he calls "the price." This concept permeates every part of his life, from his home life to his business, even his climbing. It is the idea that nothing is free.

"Everything in life has a price. When you're in a situation that's going to demand a lot more – a lot more hardship and long-suffering, patience, or endurance – that's the price you pay if you want to succeed in a situation that might turn a lot of people back. But the reward is great, too, because that reward is shared by few.

And the fewer who share in the reward, the more valuable the reward is.

"That always confused me, seeing those adventure movies and seeing people so excited by them. Then you get them in the wilderness and they complain. So what if the pack's heavy? If you want all the comfort that's in the pack, you've got to carry it...People want it all, but they don't want to pay the price. There's nothing wrong with wanting it all, if you're willing to pay for it."

2:15 a.m., October 5, 1982: After only two hours of fitful rest in a tent perched on top of the world's highest mountain saddle, the South Col, Laurie awoke bleary-eyed in his nylon shelter. It was minus 44° C. Outside, the wind was gusting to 80 km an hour, buffeting the tiny tent and slamming the paper-thin membrane of its walls, transforming them for those inside into the skin of a booming base drum. It was impossible to get any proper sleep. It was like being in the middle of enemy attack with artillery shells exploding all around you.

Two hours later, after fellow climber Dave Read of Vancouver, helped him brew hot liquids, Laurie and the Sherpas were finally ready. Dave had been a pivotal figure in the expedition. He had come within inches of his life in the icefall, when two ice blocks headed straight for him had miraculously cantilevered against each other to form a protective roof over his head. Here at Camp IV, because of a shortage of full oxygen bottles, he had relinquished his spot on the summit team to allow Laurie to go alone with the Sherpas. He had personally tested each one of the bottles they were to take to the top and, once confident that the bottles were functioning properly, had drawn a happy face on each. With Dave's unselfish backing, moral support and strength behind them, Laurie and the Sherpas crawled from the security of their tents and outside into the wind-blasted darkness.

The gusts were still strong, but, fortunately, not over-whelming. It was dark and windy and cold. They were going.

The cloak of the night hung ominously around them. There was no way of knowing what the weather would be that day. It was like trying to find light at the end of a very long tunnel. It was impossible. All they could do was take the first steps and hope for the best. In the midst of it all, though, one thing reassured Laurie: the crunch of his crampons biting firmly into the ice and snow. That alone was familiar.

Unfortunately, the same could not be said of his breath-ing. It was such an effort just to move. Trying to function with two-thirds of the world's atmosphere beneath him, leaving only one-third of the air's usual oxygen for breath-ing, produced an instant headache. Added to that was the pain caused by his ribs when he was forced to breathe deeply. It made for significant discomfort. At last he and his two Sherpa companions, Sungdare and Lhakpa Dorje, got their oxygen sets going and some of the explosions in his skull stopped.

Together they set off, their steps guided only by the seven and a half centimetre wide beam of their headlamps and the Sherpas' relentless drive. For Laurie, it was unset-tling to know that he was in the land of the giants. Yet what he could see of this world was only a few metres wide. The vapor of his breath was instantly ripped away by the wind. Like all signs of life at this elevation, with every exhalation he was reminded of his own fragile mortality.

The climb began on ground that consisted of a structure

81

well-known to him: green-blue rolling ice as hard as rock. He knew it well from the Rockies. For the moment he felt at home.

The terrain curved gently up from the col, but soon became wind-crusted snow above. In a demoralizing slog, he was forced to wallow knee-deep in the stuff. Every five or six steps, he had to stop to suck the empty air.

Sungdare was setting an incredibly fast pace. Adapted perfectly to life high in the Himalayas by living at about 4,250 m year round, he was enjoying a 3,050-m advantage over Laurie, a Calgarian who normally lived at an elevation of around 1,200 m. While Laurie's steps were slow and laborious, Sungdare's were quick and continuous, like a high-altitude yak on two legs. It was impressive to watch, and almost inspirational to follow. Fortunately, it appeared that Lhakpa, much younger and less experienced than his fellow Sherpa, was also having some difficulty keeping up.

At times Laurie was forced to crank up the flow on his oxygen set. It helped him get over the steeper and more difficult sections. At the same time, it produced a nagging sense of uneasiness in his brain. He knew that if he increased the oxygen's rate of delivery too much he might literally run out of air only footsteps from the top. At this altitude and in these extreme temperatures, he knew that could be fatal.

Climbing at high altitude can be excruciating. Above 5,500 m – Everest base camp – the body can no longer adapt physiologically to the elevation. It becomes a race against the slow but inexorable deterioration of your own body, the weather and most importantly – time. The next 3,350 m becomes prolonged pain.

In its futile attempt to extract as much oxygen from the

82

air as possible, the body responds by producing more and more oxygen-carrying red blood cells, with the unfortunate result that the blood thickens significantly. Even in minor cold, the blood's increased viscosity can slow its flow through the fingers and toes. The result can be rapid frostbite. In cases of extreme cold common in the Himalayas, the potential for later amputation becomes high.

Sleeping can feel like suffocating. The involuntary mechanisms that make you breathe automatically are completely disrupted, as are your senses of hunger and thirst. In a terrifying moment you can awake in a cold sweat in the middle of the night, gasping for air. You constantly feel nauseous, dizzy and incredibly weak. A simple step becomes a supreme triumph of will, and the brutal rush of blood inside your head is relentless.

After you lose your desire to eat and your ability to keep anything down, the next step is slow physiological deterioration. The body, exhausted of all external sources of energy in the form of food, is forced to feed on itself. It is not uncommon to lose 15 or 18 kg during an expedition because, while you're unable to eat, the relentless and high energy demands of mountaineering continue at two to three times that of normal everyday life. The bottom line is that the energy demand far exceeds the energy intake and you come out haggard and gaunt on the losing side of life's critical equation.

This physiological stress combines with psychological stress. As your brain is forced to make life-and-death decisions on one-third the oxygen it requires, hallucinations are common. It has been written that some climbers talk to imaginary partners on their ropes and offer them food. Italian Reinhold Messner, widely acknowledged as the world's greatest living mountaineer and a man who has climbed Everest twice without the assistance of artificial oxygen, apparently experienced a strange moment high on the ramparts of the world's twelfth highest mountain, Nanga Parbat in Pakistan, when he lost his way. Although he was alone and his native tongues are Italian and German, he reported that he heard someone say in English that he should climb to the left, which he did, to safety.

There have been hundreds of others; climbers at 5,500 m in Peru, swearing they could hear a horse hauling a cart stacked with beer coming up the mountain towards them and expecting in all seriousness to down a few brew, then catch a lift to the top.

Add to this dehydration at the rate of up to six litres a day from breathing the cold, dry air, the scorching ultraviolet rays that fry the cornea within minutes and produce searing snowblindness; parched skin, lips and throat;

MOVE FORWARD FROM THE KNOWN INTO THE UNKNOWN

Successful individuals in the 1990s and in the twenty-first century will be those who learn to take courageous, calculated risks. They will move with courage but care from the known world of the present into the unknown world of the future.

Success for the next generation will mean cool-headedness. We'll need to have more entrepreneurs and gutsy business and political leaders to make it happen. All of us can prepare now by doing our homework: acquiring the skills, knowledge and experience needed to enable us to assess our risks and make those critical decisions.

Having done that, like Laurie Skreslet we must then have the courage to leap into the void if we are to reap the rewards. To do so may be contrary to our basic nature and nurturing, but our very survival may depend on it. Those who prepare their wings now will fly later.

diarrhea and vomiting; the high-altitude killers of pulmonary and cerebral edema, and the whole affair becomes an exercise in abject agony. There is nothing glamorous or romantic about it. It is exhausting, extreme and hazardous work. High-altitude summiteers do not pound up slopes with their jaws set squarely into the sun and with the wind in their hair. Sometimes they are forced to crawl on their hands and knees, and the only satisfaction on the summit is that at last they don't have to look up anymore.

This was the world in which Laurie and his companions had been moving for months. He knew things would only get worse the higher they went.

Thankfully, his oxygen set was working perfectly that morning, so he was still thinking clearly. That did little to change his image of the mountain the Sherpas call "Sagarmatha – Churning Stick in the Ocean of Existence."

"Everest can be brutal. It can be inhuman. It can be cold and just take you, or it can be kind to you in a way and make you feel very, very lucky. But you can't relax."

He didn't. He couldn't. Part way up Everest's lower south summit, he came upon the ghastly remains of the body of a German woman, Hannelore Schmatz, still frozen in the mountain. She and her partner had died three years earlier after a successful ascent, but had perished on the descent. Sungdare had also been on that attempt and had tried to save her, but her oxygen had run out and she had collapsed. In the process of trying to rescue her he lost four toes to frostbite.

Lying face down in the snow with her empty oxygen tank still on her back and wearing sunglasses and a wool toque, she looked like she'd just lay down the day before for a brief rest and slumped over into eternal sleep. It was the oxygen tank that stood out most; empty and devoid of

Your moment of strength is when you have the greatest amount of singleness of purpose.
– Laurie Skreslet

life, like the body to which it was strapped. In her silence, Hannelore spoke of the stakes of the game Laurie and the Sherpas were now playing: for every three or four people who reach the summit, one expedition member dies.

Laurie and his companions were determined not to join her. A few hours later they reached the summit ridge. Overhung precariously on one side by huge slabs of wind-blown snow, it looked deceptively stable. They knew it wasn't. To safely move across it would require intense concentration and extreme caution.

Everest's summit ridge is one of the most spine-tingling in the mountaineering world. Just a metre wide in places, it runs for 150 m to the summit. It is a deadly tightrope. On one side there is a 2,750-m, stomach-wrenching drop into Tibet. On the other is a 2,450-m dive into Nepal. To add to the lethal character of the knife-edge, jetstream winds of up to 150 km an hour sometimes descend on the line and can blast a climber into oblivion as easily as a hut in a hurricane.

There is more. The high winds drift the snow into ponderous overhanging slabs on the leeward side of the ridge, and it is sometimes impossible for you to know which side of the ridge you are walking on. Your tenuous toehold on the world – and on life – can fall away beneath you unexpectedly, and you can exit instantly through a hole in the snow. Within minutes the wind fills in the opening and quickly erases any evidence of the incident. You vanish. There are no clues.

It was onto this summit ridge that Laurie Skreslet and his companions stepped that historic day. He knew he was there thanks to every member of the expedition, the hundreds of sponsors who had backed the dream and the millions of people back home 24,000 km away who hung on his every step.

His parents were with him, too, and that spiteful snipe at the zoo, and the boys by the tree at the end of the block, and Glen Wells and the soldiers. They were all there with him as he began those final steps.

"One thing that kept me going on the mountain was the feeling that if we did it, it would be something we could give back to Canada." "I want to be able to go back home knowing I gave it my best," he had told a newspaper reporter before the attempt. "It would make me feel proud, regardless of whether we reach the summit, to know the others gave their best, as well."

87

"I remember that a few days before his summit bid we had to persuade Laurie to go for the top," recalls expedition leader, Bill March. "We had to sit down and put the points out why we wanted him to go. Initially, he didn't want to go, because he felt he hadn't acclimatized yet. He wanted more time. I found he was a quicksilver kind of person. He was up and down a lot. I think he's got an innate intelligence; he is his own man. He had tremendous energy, but it seemed to be unfocused. I felt my job was to get Laurie focused."

He was focused that morning. With the aid of their ice axes, the trio carefully determined the fine line on the ridge between stability and collapse. All the way up, Laurie drove the end of his ice axe as deeply into the mountain as his strength and the snow would allow. A few times he drove the axe clean through to daylight and into more than two kilometres of space beneath. Then he saw it: a tunnel view on his own indefinite existence. He took the warning and moved a few metres further down the ridge.

"We all agreed that if one of us fell on one side of the ridge," he later told a magazine, "the other two had to immediately jump off the other side so the rope would balance us."

The final obstacle was the 20-m snow and rock step that climbers call the Hillary Step, after Sir Edmund's first successful ascent of Everest on May 29, 1953. At sea level it would have been easy for any of the three climbers, but at 8,780 m and with the world at their feet, it was like wrestling a bear.

Clad in his heavy, one-piece high-altitude suit, his clumsy plastic boots, bulky mitts and oxygen mask, Laurie looked like a creature from another planet. His goggles were so badly fogged he was forced to peer out through a little window no bigger than an inch across. That window was encircled in ice.

His toque slid down over his eyes. His 14-kg pack pulled back at him like the invisible fingers of that doomsayer at the zoo. Thanks to his oxygen, for the moment at least, it was like climbing in the Rockies. He couldn't see very well, he couldn't move very well, but at least he could breathe.

The pain in his ribs had been somehow reduced. Perhaps it was the magnitude of what he was trying to do, but packed in all these clothes and equipment he still felt uneasy. He might just as well have been a circus performer. It was like trying to execute a delicate highwire act over eight kilometres above sea level in a space suit. There was no landing net. He couldn't even see his feet. So much could go wrong. One misplaced step and all or any one of them would be gone.

Somehow, they made their way over the Step. Then, for the first time, he realized they were going to make it.

"Everest was taking the support of the soldiers I'd talked to, the climbers like Eckhard and the students like that girl at Outward Bound. They were with me on the mountain; if not physically, in spirit, in prayer. I could feel them there. I wasn't just climbing for myself. I had their support. With all that support, how can you lose? You can't lose. That was the feeling I had."

Then, a magical transformation took place.

"The last few hundred feet to the summit was no effort at all. It was just like the hands of a thousand people lifting me up the mountain. It was the hands of all those people that made the trip work. It was real. I didn't imagine it. I consciously remember thinking that I could fall flat on my face and somehow I'd end up on the top of the mountain."

In an appropriate way, not even the last step was easy. The ice broke away under his feet twice while he struggled to step onto the summit cone, but finally, on the third try, he stood there.

It was magnificent. He could see to the horizon in all directions. He looked down on a postcard so beautiful it was indescribable. He felt something well up inside of him. It was a surge of liquid fire that raced through every vessel in his body. It created an internal warmth and strength he had not felt in a long, long time.

The top was just a patch of snow and rock about the size of a cafeteria table. For Laurie, the journey to that spot meant so much.

"One of my first thoughts was about Blair and the Sherpas, hoping that they were standing up there with us and hoping that they understood. I also thought about all those people who said we weren't going to do it."

In his own, understated way, another explorer by the name of Ed Hillary was there, too: "...going straight up this snow slope and Tenzing and I stood on the top of Everest...It was a pretty important moment to both of us. In a rather square, Anglo-Saxon sort of fashion, I just shook Tenzing by the hand. But this wasn't enough for him. He threw his arms around my shoulders and gave me a good hug, so I gave him a hug, too."

There was a lot of hugging and joy when Laurie got there, too – and the taking of photographs of the Sherpas. Sungdare would go on to become the first person in history to reach the summit of Everest five times. With the same cautious zeal he had displayed throughout the entire climb, Laurie decided not to risk frostbite to his fingers reloading the camera. Fortunately, he had a second camera along. He handed it to the Sherpas, but sadly, he had no way of knowing its batteries were dead. He never did get a shot of himself on the summit. He didn't know that then. All he knew was that there was happiness and sadness and joy and triumph.

Almost as soon as it had begun, though, it was over. Laurie checked his watch. It read exactly 10:03 a.m. They had been on top for 33 minutes. Before finally turning his back on the top, Laurie removed one of his oxygen tanks. As he placed it in the summit snow, happy face to the heavens, its bright yellow paint shone like a beacon from the pinnacle. He knew that because it still contained three-quarters of an hour of life-giving gas, it might save the next person to the peak. Barring some unforeseen disaster, he had plenty of gas left for the descent.

With this simple but powerful tribute to the teamwork that had brought them there complete, they headed down. The descent would not be easy.

In high-altitude climbing, almost 40 percent of all accidents occur on the summit day, as exhausted climbers retrace their steps. It is not enough to be able to attain the summit, you must have enough energy left to make it down alive.

"The night the Sherpas died, the sky over Everest was an ugly, dirty brownish red," Laurie remembers. "The next morning, it should have been a rainy, desolate, funereal day. Instead, it was the most brilliant day I've ever seen in the Himalayas. There was no way you could connect it to the day before when three men died.

"Everest is serious business and it can blow your life out in a puff. Like the war stories I'd grown up with, Everest was like those images of dead bodies on the Russian front with vehicles riding over them, not even paying a second glance at the bodies trashed under the treads of tanks. I knew that could happen to me.

"As soon as we got to the summit, my vigilance tripled. I wasn't going to lower my standards. No damn way. I knew that's how you died. There's no way you're equal to Everest. It's way stronger than you and it always will be. You don't conquer it."

Painstakingly, Laurie and his companions made their way down. By 12:30 p.m., they were back at Camp IV on the Col. As the entire team waited with near-bursting anticipation, Laurie announced the news on the radio.

It was like a cork had popped in Camp II. Jubilation reigned. Tears flowed, snowballs soared, and goggles and toques showered from the sky. Wasted climbers sprang like children to their feet, laughing and crying and laughing again. Even the iron leader, Bill March, couldn't contain himself. Together, they wept openly, freely, for the first time since the accidents, but this time with joy. From the tattered remains of an expedition in ruins and facing potential disgrace, they had resurrected the human spirit.

What made the Canadian assault even more poignant

was that Laurie's team's elapsed time of 8 hours, 15 minutes from Camp IV to the summit and back was extremely fast. Not only had they done what many said was impossible, they had done it in record time!

Two days later, following the footprints left by Laurie, a second Canadian, Pat Morrow of Kimberley, British Columbia, also stood beside that smiling face in the snow. A professional photographer by trade, his breathtaking pictures from the summit became the focus of the celebration of a nation.

Laurie found nothing but pride in Pat's photos. "It was fitting, in a way, because more often than not, people forget the second person who breaks the ground. It was a team effort."

To this day, Laurie acknowledges this team effort every time he signs his name. At the end of his signature is Dave Read's happy face. It serves as an ever-present personal reminder to Laurie that where he is now is a result not so

SEEK THE OPPORTUNITIES IN ADVERSITY

A key factor in excelling under pressure is the ability to see opportunities where everyone else sees only obstacles. Adversity, uncertainty and the unknown can be motivators, not deterrents, when attacked with sufficient resolve, creativity and adaptability.

Four deaths and the ensuing team rift could have scuttled the 1982 Everest expedition. But the team saw the opportunity for a renewed attempt and made a miraculous comeback. Likewise, the higher Sharon Wood climbed on Everest and the more conditions worsened, the more focussed she became. "I looked at the wind as just another test and if I could pass the test, I'd be better able to deal with the hardships ahead of me."

much of where he's been, but who helped put him there.

It wasn't until a few weeks after the expedition, when he was safely back in Montreal, that Laurie first learned about what had happened to his summit photos. In a moment that perhaps reveals more about the truly flamboyant and cheerful nature which exists side-by-side in his intense and complex character, Laurie only laughed. "It was such a joke. I'd struggled all this way and there was absolutely nothing I could do about it. It really didn't matter. I'd been there and I knew I'd been there. I didn't need them."

To most, it might seem like a loss and a shallow rationalization, but for Laurie it is truth. Throughout his long climbing career, he has consciously climbed without a camera to prove to himself that it isn't for others that he is climbing, but for the personal satisfaction of doing it. With or without a photo, his achievements have not been diminished. The memory of that magical moment on that most sought-after of all summits will be engraved indelibly in his memory.

On their return from Everest, some of the members of the expedition presented then-Prime Minister Pierre Trudeau with a rock Laurie had brought down from the top. "I would have preferred it to be the head of the enemy with us presenting it to our king, but I don't think Mr. Trudeau would have appreciated that."

On the way down to the car, Laurie seems more at peace than he has all day. He pauses along the trail, pointing out a marmot's home under a large boulder.

Lower down, he stands on a rock outcrop admiring the view. You can tell this really is a special place for him. With his mouth set and his eyes gazing straight into the afternoon breeze, there is a look of deep pride and strength in his face.

93

Moments later, he stops by the side of the trail, bends over and gently strokes the petals of a robust red tiger lily shooting stubbornly skyward from between the rocks. As his thick, powerful fingers run smoothly over it, he absorbs the sensation in an almost hypnotic trance. For a moment, man and nature seem to blend together as one, the way the mountains here seem to slide quietly down into the foothills, and from there disappear in the distance into the flat prairie of the horizon.

He crouches lower to smell it, gazing at it. It is the kind of intimately personal moment you don't want to disturb. Slowly, he stands, still looking at it, and finally turns to go down. Before he does, a serene smile lights on his face like one on a small boy relishing the delight of an ice cream cone.

94

Laurie practically skips back to the car. His smooth, quick strides seem to float over the ground, airborne for a moment in celebration.

It is at that moment that the real Laurie Skreslet steps forward: the little boy at play, the noble mountaineer striving for that elusive summit, whether it is the simple beauty of a mountain flower or the stronger statement made by a crampon mark in the snow on some windblown mountain top.

I couldn't help but be inspired by the boy and the man. He seemed so happy then, the way we wish it could always be in life, but which is usually just a temporary peak.

There would be other victories for Laurie, and I drew strength from his happiness the way his audiences do. He was just a kid, but he captivated you, grew on you, the way people who achieve great things do.

In the mountains, the warrior's weapons are his axes, his

ropes and his resolve, and the war he fought was against the mountain and, most importantly, against himself. Here, it was a battle just the same, and there was a point to shoot for. Yet there were still moments of peace, moments when the fight fell away and all that was left was simple joy.

Before entering the forest, he paused one last time. Looking out toward the prairies, his eyes grew softly sedate, almost acquiescent. "Once, while I was wandering out there by myself, I saw a lone coyote high on a bluff turning somersaults in the air and chasing his tail," he said quietly. "He was so alive, just celebrating life. That's the power of this place. It strips away all the things that aren't essential in life and reminds us of what we so often forget: that life can be a celebration. If we forget that, I think we've lost everything."

In spite of the fame and the accolades, and the often harried nature of his life, Laurie had not lost the real goal. It wasn't, oddly enough, the summit of a mountain or the top of a cliff at all. That's because the goal wasn't really a place, but a feeling. It was an emotion deep inside him, and inside all of us; a sentiment we all search for, but which always seems so elusive. The key to getting that feeling is somehow linked to reaching a point in life in which you can understand the outstanding achievement even in a flower. First, you have to endure the struggle with something greater. To appreciate the peace, you have to experience the war.

"This time, and for what I am and what I stand for in the eyes of my child, and in those who are my friends," he said, as a raven soared by and Eckhard's spirit came back to visit him. "Christ, I hope they remember me this way; that I'd never give up."

95

Chapter 2
THE POWER OF PERSISTENCE

Success seems to be mainly a question of hanging on when others have let go.
– Unknown

Profile on 97
John Hughes
of Halifax, Nova Scotia

First person to deliberately sail around Cape Horn with a makeshift mast.

Probable world record-holder for the longest solo sailing journey with a makeshift mast.

The Marlin

He absolutely will not give up.
– John Sandford

He didn't see the wave. It built up from behind him to massive proportions. Then, in one terrifying and explosive onslaught, it caught the solo sailor unaware. After 14 exhausting hours at the tiller, he was slumped over, sound asleep. At that moment, there could not have been a worse thing for him to be doing.

Suddenly, his world turned upside down. The frigid waters of the North Atlantic engulfed him. There was a deafening roar of water in his ears. Utter terror washed over him.

Totally disoriented, John Hughes instinctively flailed for the rudder. Thousands of litres of icy ocean blasted him with crushing force. He was knocked senseless, gasping for air. Swirling water, flashes of sail, lines flying everywhere. What was happening?

In a second, he knew. The boat came upright. Water poured down on him from the rigging. The only thing that had kept him from going overboard was his safety harness. That, and a great deal of luck, had saved his life.

Frantically reorienting himself, he began assessing his situation. Quickly, he realized what must have happened: The boat had gone broadside to the waves while surfing at 50 km an hour. How could he have been so stupid? For a man with ten years of commercial sailing experience, he knew what the sea could dish out.

Galvanized by fear, he scrambled to get the *Joseph Young* pointed into the wind. All around him, the storm raged. Waves slammed the boat like battering rams. Needles of rain stung his skin. The wind shredded what was left of the sail. The rudder was bent, the boom was snapped in two and the jib was fast becoming rags. He had to do something. Fast.

Fear must be dealt with. You have no other choice. If you don't stay in control, you can be in serious trouble and you very well might not come out of it. You have to suppress fear, and cope.
— **John Hughes**

99

"At that very instant, the only thing that kept me going was the fact that I had no option. When you've got 50-foot waves crashing down on you, you haven't got time to go call a cab."

As the next swell gathered its strength and built up behind him, he braced for the blast. It hit with tremendous force. Then came another – and another. After what seemed like an eternity, he got the sails down and his boat under control. With his heart racing and chest heaving, he collapsed on deck. He wanted to quit.

The nightmare had started so innocently. Six days off Canada's east coast and headed for England, he had laughed out loud at the thrill of being driven before the wind. This, he then thought, was the ultimate way to make his first solo ocean journey: not just sailing across the Atlantic, but flying across it. He had never gone this fast before.

But things had got out of hand. The weather in the

North Atlantic in October was predictably harsh. This year was no exception. Within a week of leaving port, the self-steering mechanism broke and he had been forced to man the helm, unable to reduce sail. When a storm developed, he found himself in trouble. If he left the tiller, the boat could turn broadside to the waves and capsize. If he didn't reduce sail, he would become five tonnes of lead and plastic careening out of control over the sea.

He had opted for the lesser of the two evils: leave the sails up, hang on and pray. If the storm abated before he ran out of energy, he could stood chance. He had to stay awake.

He didn't – couldn't. No man could take the stress of surfing in a twelve-and-a-half-metre boat for that long, especially at those speeds and through those conditions. He should have reduced sail sooner. He should have been smarter. He should have....

It was too late now. Now, he had to suffer the consequences.

"Why I decided to do it is still difficult to put into words. Whatever you do as a solo sailor, you have to take the blame or the credit. It's a double-edged sword. But it's also true that you find out very quickly what you can take and what you can't."

He found out. By deliberately setting out late in the year, John had played with the odds and entered into a kind of Russian roulette with the sea. In his mind, it was a risk worth taking. Ever since he had been a child, he'd dreamed of sailing around the world. This was his qualifying journey for a round-the-world race that was to begin in less than a year. If he didn't complete the qualifier, the dream would die. This, and his desire to survive, had forced him to push the limits of his boat and himself beyond reason.

In truth, it was not entirely his fault. He'd only taken delivery of the yacht a few months before. To wait for spring, he knew, would not leave him enough time to fine tune the craft before the start of his round-the-world epic the following fall. This unfortunate set of circumstances, and his inexperience, very nearly cost him his $140,000 boat; maybe even his life.

"The race was a way to find out if I could handle it. You either perform or you die. It was my opportunity to find out if I had whatever it is that people are supposed to have to make them whole."

He nearly ended up in pieces. Cursing his stupidity over and over again, the 25-year-old sailor from Halifax, Nova Scotia, slowly made the necessary repairs. It was cold, sodden and frustrating work. Every time he tried to stand, a wave would knock him off his feet or the sea would slap

---

TAKE PERSONAL RESPONSIBILITY FOR YOURSELF

While few of our everyday actions have life-threatening consequences, our achievers show us the great potential of the human spirit . Theirs is a simple but prepotent rule: ultimate accountability can produce ultimate success.

This adage seems distant from life as some know it today. We live in a sue-happy society in which millions of hours and dollars are spent trying to prove the other guy was at fault. In the end, the only winners are usually the lawyers.

"It seems to me more and more that nobody wants to take responsibility for what they do," says John Hughes. "If you lose your job, you got fired because management was at fault. If you have a car accident, there is insurance. Almost everything we do is insurable. And it's always somebody else's fault if bad luck comes our way. I'm not saying that isn't true in some cases, but it never tests you."

him in the face. It seemed as if the sea was punishing him for his arrogance. How dare he toy with nature!

Hours later, as the storm began to abate, he was finally able to retire below. He had no energy left to remove his foul-weather gear or safety harness. He simply crawled under the chart table and fell asleep.

The weather cleared a few days later. Three frustrating days of calm followed, then things improved. Finally, John approached his final destination: Falmouth Harbour, England.

The port had special significance for John. As a small boy growing up in Britain, he had spent every holiday here at his grandparents' home, "Sea Horses." It was a quaint little cottage overlooking the bay. In every direction you could see ships from around the globe – coming, going, or just lying at anchor. He had delighted in peering through his grandfather's telescope, trying to read the names of each vessel and marking them off in a log. He'd wondered where they all came from, where they were going and, most of all, what adventures they'd had along their way.

John had had a close relationship with his grandfather, Joseph Young. He had instilled in John a sense of respect for others and for life, which the boy would carry with him into adulthood.

"I think he was one of the last of the real gentlemen," John says. "He didn't have a particularly exciting life, but he was a very considerate, gentle man. I think we share a lot of the same character traits."

What John and his grandfather shared more than anything else was a genuine love of the sea. Through books written by the likes of Sir Francis Chichester, who set a record for the single-handed passage of the Atlantic in 1962, when John was still an infant; Robin Knox-Johnston, another British sailor who completed the first non-stop circumnavigation of the earth in 1969; and others, Joseph Young whetted his grandson's appetite for adventure. Together they passed many a day adventuring in boats, swimming, playing on the beach or just sitting and watching the ships go by.

"My Dad looked after John because John tended to be a bit difficult," says Mary Hughes, John's mother. "It grew from there. Dad liked making things: boats, gardens, soapbox cars. He was just a nice quiet man who let John get on with it."

Get on with it, John did. Whenever he could, John would escape from his sometimes stifling city life deep in central London. His sanctuary was the sea. He had no way of knowing that one day he would become the only person in history to deliberately sail through the worst stretch of ocean in the world: Cape Horn, with only a makeshift mast.

103

"One of John's early ambitions was to sail down the English Channel and have Dad look out through his telescope," Mary recalls.

John never got to fulfill that dream. In 1979, when John was 19, Joseph Young died of cancer. John took it hard. It was no surprise, therefore, when John named his boat after his grand "old man of the sea." John had fallen in love with the boat the first time he'd seen her at a boat show in Toronto. She had no heating system, no hot water and no shower, but, like her namesake, she had simple strength. She was, as John put it, "a goer"; she could weather the storm.

All John's childhood memories and emotions that he associated with his grandfather came flooding back as he approached Falmouth Harbour that dawn in October 1985. He had not sailed into that bay since his early teens.

As was often the case off the south coast of England, it

was misty and wet. That did little to dampen the power of the moment. As the sun came up, the sky slowly brightened and "Sea Horses" ghosted into view. Tears began to run down John's face.

"It was very emotional. I tried to picture that he could see it happening and I tried to imagine what he'd be thinking and feeling. I knew he would have loved to be with me. It was a great shame that he wasn't around to share in it."

Perhaps he was; perhaps he wasn't. John had no way of knowing. There was one thing he did know: his around-the-world dream was possible. Although the moment of arrival was tinged with the sadness that his grandfather couldn't be with him, there was happiness too. John had achieved his goal. He didn't want the crossing to end. He just wanted to savour the satisfaction.

"When I got to England after that three weeks, it was a

ACT ON YOUR DREAMS

Dreams are not enough. Positive dissatisfaction must be channelled into action. The dream, or vision, must be internalized as a motivating desire. Then a plan must be prepared, executed and constantly modified in the face of a changing world. In this way, the dream goes from the head to the heart and out through the hands and feet. In short, it goes from an internal idea to an external action.

Central to this process is the ability to take that first step. Without exception, all of the adventurers in this book have had the faith and the courage to do that. Once taken, it leads to successive steps which eventually lead to the realization of their dream.

"If I'm different," says Hughes, "it's maybe that I'm just a thread less cautious than most at the start."

fantastic feeling of having won something. It wasn't a race. There were no screaming crowds. I had done it just for myself. It felt good. I won self-confidence and self-respect, and a better understanding of what I could do."

John's adventuresome spirit began with the introduction his grandfather gave him to life at sea. From there, John continued to pursue his love for the ocean. When he was seven years old, his family moved from England to Thunder Bay, Ontario. Up to that point, John had lived in a lower-middle-class neighborhood in downtown London. His father, a teacher, had struggled to make a better life for his family, but it was time for a change. He chose Canada, accepting a job as a professor of physics at Lakehead University in Thunder Bay.

105

The highlight of John's trip to North America was an 11-day trans-Atlantic voyage aboard a cruise ship. "I didn't care where we were going – Canada or Timbuktu. It involved a sea voyage and that was a real thrill."

Once settled into Thunder Bay, John delighted in watching ship after ship arrive at the Lake Superior docks, load or unload, and then disappear over the horizon. He longed to know what lay beyond his view. In the end, it was curiosity more than anything that fueled his ultimate dream.

"As far back as I can remember, I was fascinated with single-handed sailors. They would just get on a sailboat and vanish off to places I've never heard of. I was captivated by that. I wanted to know more."

At 11, John and his family returned to England, this time for a two-year teaching sabbatical for his father. John didn't mind. It was another opportunity for an ocean voyage; this one was nine days long. He got seasick during

You do adventuresome things to find what you're capable of, what you can be pushed to do and what you can push yourself to do. It's a self-test.
– John Hughes

the journey, but that didn't bother him. "Talk about fun. So what if I was sick? To me, this was great stuff. It was a real adventure."

While on board, John got a chance to visit the engine room and the bridge. He thought the ship's officers were next to God. Within five years, John would join their ranks.

When his father's sabbatical was over, John, his parents and his two brothers David and Tom, returned to Thunder Bay. It was here that he began to chart the course that would eventually lead him to the BOC – the British Oxygen Challenge, a gruelling solo race to circumnavigate the globe by sail. By 14, he already knew what he wanted to do in life. It was not a sudden revelation, but a gradual evolution. He wanted a career in the merchant navy.

"I think I was very lucky. I really sympathize with people who don't have any idea what they want to do. It must be very difficult to focus on anything and feel good about it."

At 16, John got a job as a caretaker in the local church. It paid just $200 a month. That was enough for him to save up to build his first boat, a $1,200, 4.8-m racing dinghy. He ordered away for the plans and over the course of a year built the boat from scratch in the church basement. While the parishioners were praying upstairs, John was praying downstairs that his boat would float.

"In high school, most kids want to be hanging out with the gang. But I was happy down in this dingy, crappy old church basement – a pretty spooky place – building a boat."

Finally, the moment of truth arrived: the summer of '76.

"The day I launched the boat was probably the worst

day in my family's memory. I distinctly remember that at the last minute I couldn't fasten one of the little rigging screws that hold the mast up. I think I used some of the foulest language, threatened to kill people, whole families."

If I'm different, it's maybe that I'm just a thread less cautious than most at the start.

– John Hughes

Finally, after overcoming his technical difficulties, John pushed his boat into the wide expanse of Lake Superior – a real inland sea. Much to everyone's amazement, the boat floated. An immense sense of satisfaction moved through him. A smile lit-up his face. He had done it.

In celebration of the moment, he took it for its maiden voyage, a 30-minute spin around the harbour. For the rest of that summer, every spare moment was spent on the water, driving out through the waves, feeling the wind in his hair. It was fabulous.

107

Although John's boat was a "racing" dinghy, he had no desire to compete. To him, beating someone in a race was not the biggest lure. The biggest lure was to test himself. It was his primary motivation then, as it was in the BOC – and still is.

"It seems to me more and more that nobody wants to take responsibility for what they do. If you lose your job, you got fired because management was at fault. If you have a car accident, there's insurance. Almost everything we do is insurable. It's always somebody else's fault if bad luck comes our way. I'm not saying that isn't true in a lot of cases, but it never tests you."

While he was sailing, one thing kept taunting John: the horizon. He knew there was an ocean of adventure beyond it. Beyond that? Who knows? He longed to cross that line. He wanted to do it alone.

Don't pretend that other things are stopping you from reaching your goals. They only stop you if you let them.
– John Hughes

"Whenever you go out for a sail, in the back of your mind you know you could just keep going. You're not constrained by how much fuel you have in the tank."

After high school, John enrolled in a three-year marine navigation course at a college in southern Ontario. He was the youngest applicant. The dean of the school, dubbed "Dead-eye Dick" because he had a glass eye, told John he wouldn't last two weeks. John was incensed.

"I knew he was wrong. He didn't know me and I knew myself better than he did. I was thoroughly pissed-off with him to have the audacity to say that to somebody he had never met before."

The course was exhaustive. Half of the year was spent at sea and the other half at school. There were no holidays, not even at Christmas. To graduate, you had to be totally committed, whether it was at sea or on land. The attrition rate was 70 percent. Four weeks after graduating from high school in Thunder Bay and with only a 10-day orientation course to prepare him, John reported aboard his first ship.

"The first six months were hard," John recalls. "I almost quit."

John stuck with it in the manner that has become his hallmark. Once he gets his teeth into something, he never lets go – ever.

John graduated at the top of his class. The dean was amazed. "I didn't do it to prove him wrong. I just knew what I was going to do."

John was 19. He had laid the foundation for some of his strongest character traits; he preferred to work alone, he never listened to "Doubting Thomases" and, once started, he remained absolutely committed to his goals. As time went on and as he gained more ocean experience, these character traits became stronger. "He's got the ability to look at something squarely, decide what to do and get on with it," says his mother.

The value of adventure is self-satisfaction and self-confidence.

– John Hughes

John's ocean experience came in the merchant navy. He began as a second officer and gradually moved up the ranks. This did not occur simply by putting in time. Every spare moment ashore, John worked to formally upgrade himself, studying hard.

It was not all work and no play. There were many adventures along the way. John worked on ships sailing everywhere from Africa to Europe and from the Mediterranean to the Caribbean. For two years he hauled grain in and out of Leningrad (now St. Petersburg).

109

When he was back home, John wrote exam after exam until he finally reached what he considered his one professional goal: to be captain of his own ship before he was 30. In 1984, at just 24 and after seven years of effort, he received his Master Mariner's certificate. He got the highest marks in Canada. Soon after, he realized his goal of captaining his own ship, a tugboat that serviced offshore oil rigs.

Suddenly, at 24, John began to feel empty. He had a steady, well-paying job with a major oil company, lots of time off and he loved what he was doing. For most people, it would have been Utopia. It wasn't for John; he was missing something. He was missing a goal.

"Some people are content with cruising. I'm not. I like to set a goal and go do it. When it's done, I set the next one; that's the way I like to operate. There has to be some reason why we're here. I'm still looking for the reason... I'll tell

You make your own luck to a great degree in life. If you just take that first step, the next one will naturally follow.
– John Hughes

you after the next race." John's whole life has been nothing more than setting a goal, going towards it, achieving it and instantly setting another one. Without a goal, he seems to drift aimlessly. Eternally restless, he is most at home with the wind in his sails and the objective just beyond the horizon. Life for him will always be a race to the finish because, in the end, there really is no finish. It's always just out of reach.

The next challenge for John Hughes began with a single-paragraph announcement in a sailing magazine he was browsing through one morning over coffee. His eye burned through the words: the BOC. It was the ultimate test.

He turned the page. No, he thought, it was impossible. He didn't even have a boat, let alone a sponsor. And, he had no solo ocean sailing experience.

"I started to think that this was crazy even to contemplate," he remembers. "But wouldn't it be fun to at least find out about it?" So he wrote away for information. That, believe it or not, was the step that led him to the next, which led him to others and eventually put him on the starting line.

About this time John began seeing a woman named Vicki. They met in a bar in an historic quarter in downtown Halifax where the famous clipper ship *Bluenose II* docks. She was a waitress there. "I'd seen him for a year before that," she recalls. "Because of his accent, I thought he was Australian. He was quiet, a loner. He was often by himself and I didn't think much of him except that he made me nervous. He kept watching me."

It took many months before John got up the courage to say hello. Then, one evening, Vicki got off work early. John offered to walk her to her car, then asked her out for coffee.

Four hours, four slices of cheesecake and 10 cups of coffee later, he dropped her off at her car.

"There was a magnetism, a definite attraction from the first time we spoke," Vicki recalls. "John would walk into the room and my heart would flutter. I'd hear his voice on the phone and I'd want to be with him. He was very honest and didn't try to impress me. We were friends for a long time."

Eventually, the two started dating. From there the relationship blossomed. John told her of his dream of sailing around the world. "She pictured somebody sort of cruising around the South Pacific with a pina colada and a bathing suit," John says laughing. "She had no idea what I was talking about." She soon found out.

111

Vicki will never forget August 30, 1986. For John it was the beginning of the realization of a life-long dream. For everyone it was a gut-wrenching experience. "It was horrible. You just knew this was it. It was the end. It was all race. Saying goodbye was almost a chore to fit in. He was nervous. He went over things, over and over again."

That day in the waters off Newport, Rhode Island, 25 men from the world over gathered for what has been called the Everest of all sailing races: a circumnavigation of the globe – alone.

John had known from the beginning that there was no way he could win. There were two classes: "A" Class for 60-foot boats and "B" Class for 50-footers. Generally, the longer the boat, the faster. The *Joseph Young* was just 12.5 m (41 feet) long. Even if he sailed brilliantly, his chances of winning were next to nil. The only way he could win would be if everyone except him dropped out.

"Once we checked out each other's boats, you realized very quickly that there were some 50-footers there that were built specifically to win that race. It was patently obvious to me that my class wasn't a collection of people with the same goals." John's goal became to finish the race, whatever happened.

The field included the likes of Phillipe Jeantot of France, the holder of the record for the fastest solo circumnavigation; Harry Mitchell of England, who at 62 was the oldest competitor; and an elite group of some of the boldest and best-backed sailors from around the world. Jeantot alone, who sailed a 60-foot custom-built racing machine, was financed for about $1 million by a French bank.

Hughes, by contrast, was the ultimate underdog. He was self-financed with his life's savings. He had no sponsorship, no professional support crew and no million-dollar yacht. Aside from ten years of ocean experience on big ships, he had relatively little solo sailing experience. He had the smallest boat. And, at just ten days past his 26th birthday, he was also the youngest competitor.

"I thought it was the wrong boat for what he was trying to do," recalls fellow competitor, Mark Schrader of Seattle. "It looked like it was designed more for inland cruising than for ocean sailing. I was absolutely amazed. It looked like it would be wet and cold and inconvenient to live in. I couldn't even get down below without banging my head or knees. I wouldn't have wanted to sail that boat for two days, let alone 200. It was obviously a shoestring effort."

For the record, the *Joseph Young* was 2.6 m (8-feet, 9 inches) wide and cost $170,000 fully dressed. Its hull was made of bullet-proof plastic and lead that had been specially reinforced by the manufacturer for the race. Although it was the most spartan of the boats in the competition, it was all John could afford. When all efforts to secure a sponsor had failed, he had been faced with the decision to self-finance his dream or see the dream die.

"Some guys had showers and CD players. I had a bucket for a toilet and my sink drained into a plastic tub. You have to adapt your goals to the resources available. But I don't buy lack of money as an excuse."

If the reason you're doing something is to get famous and make lots of money, you're deluding yourself. You won't finish because the motivation has to come from within.
– John Hughes

There was very little about the *Joseph Young* that would qualify it as a yacht. It was more like a plasticized prison, a sea-going cell built for solitary confinement. There were no comfortable chairs, lavish dressers or fancy furnishings, just the basics: a flat, hard berth about two feet wide, with belts that buckled you in for the night. On one side of the cabin there was a small gas stove. On the other there was a radio, not the entertainment kind, the communications kind. The only real luxury was a tape deck.

To buy his boat, John had spent his life savings on the down payment of $50,000. The rest he had either borrowed from the bank or worked extra hours to earn. To cut corners, he shared an apartment with his older brother, David. It took all he had just to get to the starting line.

"I set sailing around the world alone as a goal to establish what sort of a person I was," John says, as his tall forehead tips forward the way it does when he's serious about what he's saying. "Even today, people say that with the money I dumped into my boat I could have paid for a house and be living on easy street. Maybe I could, but

113

In order to be good for the people around you, you first have to feel that you have a sense of self-worth. You have to be happy with what you're doing and who you are. If you're not, you're not going to be any good to the people around you.

– John Hughes

that's not so important to me. That solo sailing goal was more important to me than anything."

The dream began badly at the starting gun. John zigzagged his way through the masses of boats peppered all over Newport Harbor. It took him five hours just to get out of the Sound.

"I was almost puking from the physical exertion of trying to get out because the wind was against us. There were hundreds of boats and I had to dodge every one of them. It was a zoo."

If he felt ill, there was far more to it than sheer exertion. In the days and hours leading up to the gun, his life had come into tight focus. Besides the looming challenge of the race, there was the reality that he would be leaving his family and friends behind.

"Everything that happened in the end, I was afraid would happen in the beginning," Vicki says. "We would fall in love, he would go away to sea and I would be left at home worrying."

"I thought the voyage would drive Vicki and I apart. I knew that no matter what the outcome of the race was, she was going to go through some pretty tough stuff before she said, 'I can't handle this anymore' or 'No, I'm going to hang in there.' Either way, it wasn't going to be easy. So I felt a lot of guilt. But if I had said 'Scrap the relationship' to Vicki, neither one of us would have made it."

These were the thoughts that dogged John that morning. Although he was focused intensely on the start, in the back of his mind his fears were as ever-present as the wind.

"Eventually, he became just a speck on the horizon. You wondered what was on the other side," Vicki recalls. "It was a fear of the unknown. I said goodbye and I didn't feel it was enough. I felt sick to my stomach. I didn't even have the energy to wave goodbye. It was very sad."

The reason you go off on adventures isn't really to escape as much as it is to find out. And once you've found out then that applies to whatever you're doing.
– John Hughes

Ahead of them lay a nine-month separation. That would have been difficult even under normal circumstances, but these were not normal circumstances. Everybody knew John might not come back.

"I guess it's a selfish thing to do: sail off and leave your loved ones back home with the possibility you might not come back. I don't know how to rationalize that."

115

John did not know it then, but the pain of that parting would furnish his biggest sustained challenge of the journey. Though he would face tremendous physical hardship, it would pale in comparison to the emotional heartache he would suffer from the separation. As he pulled away from the dock, tears ran unabated down his face. Although they eventually evaporated, they were always there – inside him.

Vicki watched him finally disappear, swallowed up by an ocean of uncertainty, and by the future. Slowly, she turned and walked away. She didn't want to talk to anyone. She just wanted to be alone.

That night, as she got into bed red-eyed and exhausted, she found a little note pinned to her pillow. It said: "Thanks. I miss you already. The time away will make our love grow stronger. Until I see you again, I love you."

Perseverance is the only way.
– John Hughes

There was something special about John Hughes. We met in the April darkness at 6:15 a.m. The Dartmouth Yacht Club, across the harbour from Halifax, was completely deserted. A single street lamp lit the quay.

At precisely the appointed hour, John pulled up in his red Canadian Coast Guard car. Toting his ever-present cup of coffee, he shook my hand and bid me a polite good morning.

It was not the greeting that struck me. It was ordinary in every way. It was, instead, those two steely-grey eyes that peered out at me in the darkness. They were like cat's eyes, cold and mysterious. They gave me goose bumps just looking at them. I discovered later that they changed colours depending on his mood. When he is calm, they are grey. But when he is excited, they become a deep sea-blue.

If there is an ocean persona for John Hughes, it is the marlin. When excited, particularly just before they first sense the bait, marlins light up. What begins as a dark blue on the back and silver on the sides momentarily transforms into a brilliant silver with gold bands. They are legendary fighters, the greatest sport fish known. Capable of swimming strongly even after 12 hours of violent fighting, they are among the most solitary of all ocean creatures.

"John absolutely will not give up," says John Sandford, long-time friend and fellow sailor. "He hates a plan that doesn't work."

"I just don't like to be stopped," John says flatly.

Since completion of the British Oxygen Challenge (BOC) round-the-world solo sailing race in 1987, John Hughes has worked as a ship safety inspector with the Canadian Coast Guard.

116

"I quite enjoy the job," John says in his deep, slightly hoarse voice spiced with an English accent. "But I'd rather be sailing. Failing that, I'd rather be working at sea." John's working days are spent scrambling in and out of vessels assuring that everything from the pitch of the propeller to the size of the stern post is up to snuff. He also examines skippers, officers and fishermen on sea standards. It is a job that requires a precise attention to detail, something John has in spades.

"As a sailor and as a person, he's very, very thorough," says Sandford. "Everything is checked and double-checked; there's no room for error. He has a sense for the sea. He inspires confidence." Sandford played a critical role in John's solo success. They met at the yacht club.

"Hughes showed up with this racing boat. No one had even heard of John, let alone the BOC.

"He was very quiet and unassuming. That really impressed me. He came across as this natural, normal person who was going to do this incredible feat. I took to him because he was the underdog. He was low-budget and low-profile. He just wanted to do it." While John was at sea, Sandford would work every day until 1:00 or 2:00 a.m. coordinating fundraising, keeping track of John's position and arranging for the replacement and shipping of worn-out gear.

"That was my life," says Sandford, himself an understated, humble man of English origin who, like John, tries to maintain the classic British stiff upper lip, get-on-with-the-job attitude. "Every day he was out there, there was a bit of me out there, too."

Sandford was not alone. The members of the Hughes support committee at the Dartmouth Yacht Club were also central to John's success. They raised money through lobster raffles, T-shirt sales and other enterprising ventures. The funds went toward the costs of John's ongoing equipment needs.

By his own admission, John has gone through a "hellish adjustment" since returning from the BOC. He has had to adapt to a high local profile and all the publicity resulting from a book he wrote of his journey. Increased demands on his time and financial debts left over from the $250,000 cost of his race have left him strapped. Now, he's married to Vicki and they have a young son. All of these changes have been significant, especially for a man who was a self-appointed loner for the longest time.

"He still has a problem with a large number of people, even driving in heavy traffic," says Vicki. "Life is just not as it was before he left. You can't really talk to a lot of people about that kind of experience; so few have lived it. So he holds it inside."

John often keeps his emotions inside. He has a quiet, soft-spoken nature that conceals an inner sensitivity. It is difficult for him to articulate his deepest emotions. When personal issues are touched upon, the result is sometimes silence.

Alongside this sensitivity there is also a volatile temper. "He had temper tantrums when he was little, and what he does now is the equivalent," says his mother, Mary. "Not long ago, he was a very angry man. He saw that there was a lot of grey in the world and I think that frustrated him. Everything is either black or white with John; there's very little grey in his life. Yet he's very tender-hearted."

It is this contrast of a quiet, kind exterior with an intense, explosive interior that is the core of John's character. He's a bit like the sea on a calm day. On the surface, all seems serene, but just beneath there is an underlying wave that can instantly well up and spring sky-ward. He is the kind of man with whom you can relax, yet he is one around whom you tread carefully. It is not fear that causes your uneasiness; as it is with the ocean, it is respect.

"I still have a volatile temper, but I'm a lot more relaxed than I was before I went away," says John. "If you know what you're capable of and how bad things can get, then petty, everyday hassles are meaningless. You're much more relaxed with yourself. The biggest lesson I learned from the trip was patience."

Every person has to measure themselves to success. If you've done your best and triumphed over obstacles, then I think you'll be self-satisfied.
– John Hughes

John is a man of few words. He is a man of action – driven and disciplined. He hates disorganization, tardiness and too many things to do.

119

There is more to him than sailing. He plays piano and at one time played the bass guitar. His passions include curried chicken and the TV show "Star Trek." His vices include chocolate, coffee (not just by the cup, but by the pot), impatience, periodic intolerance and cigarettes. Yet he never smokes at home. "I find it amazing that he smokes," says Sandford. "It's hard to believe that somebody with his kind of incredible will power couldn't seem to quit."

"Although John is something of a household name in the province of Nova Scotia," continues Sandford, "he is largely unknown in the rest of North America." Hughes was not the first Canadian to sail solo around the world. That distinction belongs to Joshua Slocum, who was born in Nova Scotia. Slocum was not only the first Canadian, but the first man in history to sail single-handed around the world. He did so from 1894 to 1898.

Hughes' claim to fame is that he is likely the first person in history to deliberately sail around Cape Horn with a makeshift or jury-rigged mast. He's probably also the solo sailor who has recorded the longest journey under jury-rig: some 7,000 km. Historical records are incomplete.

Although John's efforts have earned him tremendous respect in the sailing fraternity worldwide, he has not aggressively promoted himself outside of Atlantic Canada. That is because he is a humble and fiercely independent man with little desire for public acclaim. "He's understated and undemanding," says Sandford. "Money's not what's important to him; satisfaction is what counts."

For the moment, John is satisfied with being at home. He lives in a modest two-bedroom, two-storey Cape Cod style house on a hill in a quiet suburb of Dartmouth. It's within a stone's throw of the harbour. Like the man, it is quiet and understated on the outside. The white aluminum siding and black shutters give no hint that anything but the ordinary is inside.

Home for John Hughes is only a temporary on-shore leave. His real home is at sea and his latest goal is to enter the BOC race again, this time with the hopes of winning. So, when he isn't working for the Coast Guard, he is laying the plans for his next voyage.

"I'm happy at home and I enjoy being at home. But if I don't get the opportunity to do this race again and go to my grave this way, I won't go to my grave a happy man.

"As a whole, people in our society have moved away from testing their mettle to measuring everything by accepted standards: the size of your house, the number of cars you have, your income, etc. I'm not saying those aren't nice to have, but I don't think they should be what we as individuals measure ourselves by. Unfortunately, we tend to be a little more concerned with how we think other people view us than with how we view ourselves." In a way, you believe him, but when you actually see him at home, you don't.

If there is a meaning to John's life after his trip around the world, it is his family: his newborn son Benjamin and Vicki, his wife. "He's an adventurer," says Vicki, the vibrant woman who is as much his wife as his antithesis, "but there was always a sad air about him when he was alone. He likes the stability of a relationship." Born and raised in Halifax, Vicki is a stabilizing force for John. Her gentle, kind manner makes her immediately affable. Socially at ease with others and spiritually at peace with herself, her smile radiates the contentment of a person who has endured much for what she wanted in life.

121

"I am very lucky," John says, and his eyes show his sincerity. "She's great. It's her attitude towards things that's one of the reasons why I love her so much. We hold the same things dear, the idea that people are what matter. The money and all that stuff is not really important."

Vicki and John are a study in contrasts. While she is rarely on time, he always is. She is gregarious and warm. He is quiet and seemingly aloof. The differences do not end there. She expresses her emotions openly and easily. John does not. "I'm very black and white in a lot of ways, and she has a little more of a grey tinge around the edges. We get along fantastically."

During John's voyage, Vicki went through hell. Phone bills totalled a staggering $10,000 dollars – ship-to-shore connections cost money. In order to make financial ends meet, she often worked 12 hours a day, sometimes seven days a week. "One month, I couldn't make it," she recalls. "So the support committee kicked in."

On top of the financial stress, there were emotional pressures, too. "In the middle of the night, the phone would ring and I would jump for it," she recalls. "I'd sometimes cry afterwards. I questioned why I was doing it. But I'd have a good cry and go on."

Anyone who has cried alone at night in the darkness of their room will know what the pain is like. For Vicki there was the pressure of never knowing what the next phone call would bring. It was like being regularly patched-in to a war front. It was usually John's voice on the other end, but she dreaded the night when it wouldn't be.

"Going through the race taught us a lot about each other," says the dark-haired, blue-eyed beauty, who weathered her own share of personal storms alone. "We wanted for so long to be together."

If there was a key to John's sailing success, a big part of it was Vicki. She was like a beacon guiding him home. More than anything, she gave him a reason to continue. He knew that every mile brought him closer to her.

Throughout his passage around the world, John called her on a regular basis on the radio and wrote to her once a day. Although there was no way, of course, to mail the letters from mid-ocean, John still found it reassuring to imagine that she was there aboard with him and that they were having a private conversation. He had a photo of her to look at when things got rough.

"There's a real difference between being alone and loneliness. I have honestly been much lonelier on land than I have ever been at sea by myself. To be surrounded by people you don't know and who don't particularly want to know you, that is lonely. But to be by yourself and to know that there are people who care about you and with whom you can get in touch, that's not being lonely, that's merely being physically alone for the present. I never feel lonely at sea."

Vicki and John are the quintessential young married couple: outwardly open in their expression of mutual affection and very much in love. Considering what they have been through together, it's no surprise. When you have dealt with the ever-present danger of death, you don't tend to fight a lot about who should change the baby.

If you discuss a decision too much, there will never be a right time. You have to take that first step.
– John Hughes

If you are searching for the soft side to John Hughes, it's when he's with Benjamin that you'll see it. Born the day after Christmas 1989, Ben has become something of a surrogate ship for John to sail safely through life's seas and bring, as he always has, safely back to port. Ben's cradle sits in the living room beside the piano and fireplace. A grandfather clock stands in one corner and, on a table top in the other, the photo of John's grandfather that John took with him all the way around the world.

123

As a cold rain falls silently outside, there is warmth inside. After rocking his son to sleep in his arms after a diaper change, John gently places him in the cradle, covers him quietly with a blanket. As he does so, a slight smile appears beneath his neatly-trimmed red moustache. At that moment, the inner intensity disappears – but only momentarily. Gone is the explosive action and fighting spirit of the marlin. Instead, it is replaced with a peaceful serenity that registers all over John's face. It is John Hughes unmasked.

"I used to think I'd live all my life alone," he whispers, "and that didn't bother me. But then I met Vicki. We sweated a lot about whether or not to have kids, then finally decided to try. Now, I can't believe it. When I first

The most important thing is to be happy with what you do.
– John Hughes

saw him smile at me, that was it."

Slowly, John placed Ben's rattle beside his son. Then, ever so gently, he bent and kissed him. "That little being is our flesh and blood. And all that he is now and all that he'll become depends on us."

John awoke to a terrible crash. Jack-knifing up in bed, he came close to knocking himself unconscious on the roof above.

Ahead of him, through the darkness, he came face to face with his worst nightmare. Even in the darkness, he knew what had happened: the mast had broken. It had sheared off flush with the deck, hopped off its mount and come smashing straight down through the cabin like a half-ton pile driver.

Water was pouring in. Shattered pieces of the deck were everywhere and the cabin was in chaos. For the first time in his life, John Hughes tasted real terror.

"I had an immediate fear for the boat and, by association, my life. I knew that if the top half of the mast went over the side and punctured the hull, the boat would sink."

Clad only in his boots and underwear, John scrambled on deck. The entire upper part of the mast and all the rigging was lying in the water at right angles to the boat. It was like looking at a bird with a broken wing.

2:30 a.m. February 6, 1987: He was 2,880 km east-southeast of New Zealand and 5,280 km west of Cape Horn, the southernmost tip of South America. At perhaps the furthest point from land of anywhere on his 44,800-km journey, John Hughes was facing the greatest of all seafarer's fears: adrift without a mast and completely alone.

As he stared incredulously at the tangled mess, John was overwhelmed with disappointment. Amid this emotional deceleration he struggled to sort out the jumbled destruction before his eyes. Where to start? He didn't have time to think. He had to react.

He grabbed the bolt-cutters and started cutting everything in sight. Slowly, like some crippled creature with a hundred arms, the whole mess slid off the deck and plunged into the water. As it went, it made a spine-tingling grating sound, like chalk across a blackboard.

John held his breath. He waited, frozen in fear for the crash of the mast punching through the hull. Nothing...nothing.

Suddenly, there was a sound like a gunshot. John's heart skipped a beat. His head snapped forward. The bow wire holding the whole mess below the boat had sheared in two with the weight.

Slowly, like someone beside a grave, John stood up and peered into the depths. In the rolling swell of the night, he watched dejectedly as his mainsail silently drifted deeper, deeper and deeper. In a moment it was nothing but a shrinking shadow. Then it was gone. He crumbled into a heap on deck. His dream had died.

"I'd had nightmares and premonitions about this before," he recalled later. "It was a feeling of total nakedness out there. Here's this boat and I've got no way of moving it. What if I get into a storm tomorrow morning? I'm dead."

Stripped of his only method of getting back to land, and ultimately, his life, John wallowed in the swell. Without the huge weight of the mast above deck, the *Joseph Young* tossed violently from side to side. It was like one of those inflatable punching bags that always comes back to center; every movement of the vessel was whiplike and jerky. It had no resemblance whatsoever to the usual motion of a craft at sea. What was once a sleek dart knifing through the water had become a lifeless tub in the middle of nowhere.

John struggled to collect himself. He was trembling. He knew that if he let his emotions bottom-out with the mast, he would be in even more trouble. Instead of panicking, or perhaps to suppress panic, he steered his thoughts into more practical matters; he had to repair the hole in the deck. Water was still streaming in and if he didn't get that fixed soon, he would sink. If he couldn't control his craft, at least he could control his mind. He channeled his fear into action.

"The main thing was to take it one step at a time. First get rid of the mast. Then patch the hole."

What made John's situation even more serious was that with the mast had gone his radio antennas. Now, he realized, not only was he a lame duck in an endless pond, but there was no way of telling the other competitors or race organizers what had happened. If he didn't hook up something soon, they would assume he was in serious trouble, or worse.

John hurried to attend to these two primary tasks: repairing the deck hole and rigging up an antenna. Using a resourcefulness born from years at sea, he managed to rig a spare guywire for a makeshift antenna. Twenty minutes before the scheduled 7:00 a.m. radio check he had both challenges accomplished. But he had no way of knowing if the antenna would work.

At 7:00 a.m., with great trepidation, he turned on the radio. To his complete surprise, no one seemed to notice any change. Now at least he could share his grief with someone. That was a huge relief.

"I remember asking him how he was doing," Mark Schrader remembers. "He said, 'Not so good Mark. I lost the rig last night.' But he said it so matter-of-factly it was incredible. I don't think any of us grasped what had to happen next."

What had to happen – and what did – was that John set about constructing a jury-rigged mast. But before he did, there was such an outpouring of sympathy and so many offers of help from his competitors that John was almost overwhelmed. Mark, who was the nearest competitor at about 240 km distant, offered to sail over and take him aboard.

When things are very bad and the chips are down, if you give it that last little kick, you can make things better. **– John Hughes**

"I was relieved that John was okay, but then as it sunk in, I realized I was losing a friend. No longer would he be able to keep up with the rest of the fleet. I became really depressed." The only person who should have been depressed, but wasn't, was John.

"There was this incredible outpouring of sympathy for my predicament. It was a pretty tremendous feeling to know these guys were all out there pulling for me."

John refused all outside assistance. To accept any, he knew, would mean he would be disqualified from the race.

"Right off the bat I knew there was no way I was going to abandon ship. That would have been insane. The boat was not going to sink anymore than it had been yesterday. The problem was that I had no means of moving it. But I had lots of water, lots of food, a radio, two spinnaker poles and a few sails. I'd figure something out. I told myself: 'Just make a few calls, let people know what's happened. I'm okay. Don't push the panic button.'"

In John's view, the only reason to quit a race would be if your boat sank. There were no other acceptable excuses in his book. "Nobody wants to die," Hughes says. "It's something we're all afraid of. It's the final wall, isn't it? To try and feel the wall and take a risk that is life-threatening

127

When you come to a wall, either you climb over it or you go back. But once you've given up, you can't go back and re-do it. You only go around once.
– John Hughes

is amazingly exhilarating. Every hour that you're alive, you appreciate it more." Another man might have pushed all the buttons, accepted outside assistance and packed it in. Everyone on the ocean and on land would have understood why. But at the moment when John Hughes was most threatened, he became the most resolved. The pragmatic tactician inside him emerged, and the marlin began to fight.

128

Instead of hurrying headlong into the process of building a makeshift mast, John took an hour out to clean and dry the boat, have something to eat and, of course, have a few cups of coffee. Considering the gravity of his situation, it was a remarkable response and one which, in the end, might well have saved his life.

"I was shaking like a leaf at this point. The adrenalin was just pumping and I hadn't had anything to eat or drink for 10 hours. I needed to get some sugar and fluid into my system.

"There was no immediate danger," he insists stoically, "no need to panic. I knew I couldn't afford to screw up at this point. I knew I needed to take time out to relax, sit back and think about it."

Carefully, and with meticulous attention to detail, John developed a blueprint for his makeshift mast. "I didn't want to make a mistake with the new jury-rig. I knew I had only one chance."

Using the only two spare poles that had somehow escaped unscathed in the destruction and subsequent burial of his mast, he patiently and methodically lashed together an A-frame structure. Securing the bases of the poles with hose clamps, he flattened a couple of coffee cans and positioned two pieces of plywood under each pole. These "feet" of wood and tin would prevent the poles from being driven down through the top of the cabin. At the apex of the "A," he fastened the poles together using hose clamps and rope; then, using more rope, he hoisted the whole works into a near-vertical position. Finally, he raised a small storm sail in the middle of the triangle. The whole process took about five hours.

> *It's not what you have. It's what you do with what you have.*
>
> **– John Hughes**

"All the time that I'd been on ships at sea during many crises," he later remarked, "and all the training I'd had, taught me not to lose my head. There are ways to approach things. Whether there's a fire on board or a crew member with a broken back – whatever – you stay cool. People are looking to you for guidance. Besides, there's no point in freaking out; that's not going to change your situation."

The only person looking to him for guidance was himself at that moment, but he knew that things could change. If the weather suddenly got bad and the rig didn't hold, it could all be over. He threw those fears overboard. "When the mast went over the side, after I got over the absolute terror that I was going to die, I got things fixed up and was able to realize that it was all pretty good.

"Life is relative. If you're starving to death, suddenly roast rat looks pretty good. But if you're sitting in a restaurant, you wouldn't order it."

Soon, word arrived back home of John's plight. At 6:00 a.m. Vicki was stirred from sleep by yet another disturbing phone call. "I was shocked," she recalls. "I just couldn't believe it. Just the thought that he'd gone through this hell and I hadn't known about it until afterwards was unbelievable."

129

"I thought it was dreadful that he might not come home," says his mother, Mary. "But I sensed somehow that he would."

The key to his coming home was John Sandford. He got the news from one of John's support committee members at the yacht club. He immediately called BOC headquarters in Newport.

"At first I thought, 'I've got to talk to him.' There was no doubt in my mind he would jury-rig something. He's not the kind of guy to cry wolf and jump ship. I was concerned, but actually, I was more concerned about how he was going to react to it. I could just picture him there in mid-ocean totally upset."

The first thing Sandford requested was a complete list of what Hughes would need. Sandford's plan was to somehow get a new mast and rigging to him when he reached land. Through a fellow competitor who relayed the message, and at a cost of $10 a minute, Sandford got the information he needed. He laughed when he heard that one of the items on John's list was – of all things – lettuce.

After Hughes' successful Atlantic crossing from Halifax to Falmouth, Sandford had volunteered to join him on the return home. Before their departure from England, Sandford's mother had fed them lettuce sandwiches and salads every day. This became something of an inside joke. "Not lettuce again," they would snipe.

Fearing that her "boys" might not eat enough green vegetables on their way home, Sandford's mother had secretly stowed away several heads of lettuce on board the *Joseph Young*. Halfway across the Atlantic they had discovered several plastic bags filled with a foul-smelling, wet and gooey black substance.

"So when I heard he wanted lettuce, I knew things

weren't too bad," Sandford recalls. "He still had his sense of humour."

From that moment on Sandford worked day and night for six weeks, spearheading the efforts of a small army of volunteers to raise money for a new mast, arranging for its purchase and ultimately its shipping. It was a huge logistical challenge that involved people in half a dozen countries on both sides of the Atlantic. In the end, the bill came to some $30,000.

Less than two days after disaster had struck, John Hughes was sailing again. Progress was slow, but at least he was moving. He had no way of knowing that ahead of him lay an even greater challenge.

Somewhere along the line you ask yourself, 'What am I doing here?' It is then that you must think back and remember that it was the right thing to do at the start. Therefore, the right thing to do is to carry on and finish whatever it is you've started.

– John Hughes

131

Three weeks after the dismasting, John was faced with the most difficult decision of his life. For 21 days he had either drifted aimlessly under no wind, or had been forced to creep along at an agonizing pace under steady rain. As the days and weeks passed, his psychological state progressively deteriorated. Gone was the victory of having survived the dismasting. What replaced it was an overwhelming cloud of despair, depression and utter solitude.

Although his initial goal had been to head to Chile, he slowly began to realize that because his progress was so sluggish, he might run out of water or food – or both – before he got there. Worse still, he might lose his sanity.

For a "type A" personality like John – an ambitious, often impatient achiever – there are few punishments worse than slow progress toward a goal. One of the things

If you quit before you've given your all, I think it takes a toll on your self-respect.

– John Hughes

132

about sailing that appeals to John is the concept of speed. He lives for a freshening breeze and bursting sails. He dies with inactivity.

"To me, the most important thing was that I had to finish what I'd started out to do. It didn't matter that the race was lost.

"The thought of not completing the race started to depress me so badly that I began to see why people commit suicide. Not that I was contemplating it," recalls John of those draining weeks of fickle winds and frustrating progress. "So, I said, Hey! This is crazy. I've got to convince myself that anything is better than not finishing this. Finishing first is important to other people, but I hadn't gone into this to prove to anyone else what I could do. I was there to see for myself what I could do. If you don't finish what you start, you're only letting yourself down. Nobody else is going to care. If I hadn't finished, that would have been unbearable because I would have been beaten by something I should have been able to overcome."

As the days dragged by, John was almost overcome with dejection. "He was getting crazier and crazier as the days went by," Vicki recalls. "I could hear the bang, bang, bang of flapping sails over the radio, and could just imagine the cold and the sun. He was so depressed, and he sounded like he had nothing to look forward to."

During a radio call to his mother, John declared: "I don't know what's going to kill me first: cold, boredom or hunger."

Slowly, John began to feel more and more like sailing around Cape Horn was his only option. His competitors were anything but supportive.

"I thought he was off his rocker," recalls Mark Schrader, who over the months had become his closest friend and confidant. "A boat without a mast just rolls around horribly. I knew he could tumble around Cape Horn, but definitely not sail around it."

What complicated matters was the issue of time. Race regulations specified that if you fell too far behind the other boats, you could be disqualified. At some point it simply becomes too difficult for race organizers to handle the complex logistics of having the whole fleet in one place and one boat thousands of kilometres behind. The support team can't stay at stopover points forever. Sooner or later, they have to move on. And once they do, the door for lagging competitors closes behind them.

John knew this. He also knew that to continue on his present course was futile. Even if he did make it to Chile for repairs, by the time he was underway again, he would be disqualified. Even now, the majority of the fleet was either approaching the Horn, or already around it. Although they'd all threatened to withdraw if John was disqualified, John would soon be out of radio contact with them. Then he really would be completely alone. "One by one, they sort of dropped off the edge of the world. All of a sudden, I was alone out there."

To understand the magnitude of what John Hughes was proposing to do, you need only pick up a history or geography book. A geography book will tell you that when the westerly winds hit the Andes in South America, they take the path of least resistance – around the Horn.

All of this power is funnelled through Sir Francis Drake's Strait between the island of Cape Horn and the South Shetland Islands, 800 km to the south. This is further

133

complicated by the fact that the winds in the Andes themselves have already been whipped into a frenzy by the mountain peaks.

It doesn't end there. The westerlies produce an ocean current from west to east which also channels itself through Drake's Strait. It's a bit like taking all the water in the Pacific and forcing it through an 800-km gap. The result is pure power.

Beneath this frothing current, the bottom of the sea becomes more shallow. The result is massive wave action. Rollers higher than five-storey apartment buildings have been recorded, and if the wind is blowing in the opposite direction to the ocean currents, the whole area begins to boil viciously. The final ingredients to the witch's cauldron are icebergs and pack-ice, which are pulled into the maelstrom from Antarctica.

That's a rather technical description of the waters around Cape Horn. The history books tell the real story: centuries of human tragedy. Francis Fletcher, the chaplain of Sir Francis Drake's ship *The Golden Hind*, recorded the horror of 56 days around the Horn in 1578:

...the storm being so outrageous and furious that the barque 'Marigold' with 28 souls, was swallowed up with the horrible and unmerciful waves, or rather mountains of the sea, which chanced in the second watch of the night, did hear their fearful cries, when the hand of God came upon them.

The tales go on. They speak of a vast and terrible cemetery of seamen and a monstrous supernatural magnet that draws everything on the surface to the icy confines of Davey Jones' locker. Richard Walter, a seaman, wrote the following in 1741:

...we had a continual succession of such tempestuous weather as surprised the oldest and most experienced mariners on board, and obliged them to confess that what they had hitherto called storms were inconsiderable gales compared with the violence of these winds which greatly surpassed in danger all seas known in any other part of the globe; and it was not without great reason that his unusual appearance filled us with continual terror for, had any of these waves broke fairly over us, it must in all probability have sent us to the bottom.

Success boils down to not being mentally encumbered by other people's ideas of what you should or shouldn't do. What it comes down to is what's inside of you.
– John Hughes

In short, Cape Horn is the most feared stretch of ocean in the world. Even big, fully equipped ships with large crews approached it with dread. To attempt it alone bordered on lunacy. To do it without a proper mast was akin to suicide.

This was the decision that faced that lone man, in that lone boat, on that lonely ocean. Essentially, it all came down to one thing: what John thought – and no one else. The arena was empty.

"The boat was still the same boat," he thought. "The only difference was that my rig was smaller. If I was going to get myself out of this, I didn't think I had much of a choice, really."

John's fellow sailors did not share his view. His greatest opposition came from the Finnish competitor, Pentti Salmi. Over the radio one day Pentti declared flatly: "The heroes I know are all dead."

John lost control. Squeezing the microphone as if he would crush the life out of it, he blasted into the void: "I'm

135

not doing this to be a hero, to you, or to anybody else. You're not here. You don't know what it's like. If I don't do this, in my own eyes, I'll be scum. So I don't give a shit about what you or anybody else thinks."

If he went for it, at least he had a chance. If he didn't make it, there would be no shame. He would die trying.

At noon on February 27, 1987, John Hughes turned the *Joseph Young* slowly toward the south. In the silence of the sea, no one cheered. John alone was witness to his actions.

Just then a slight smile spread across his face and his eyes became deep blue.

John saw it coming, but by that time, it was too late. In a flash he reached behind him and slammed the hatch. But in the adrenalin-powered panic of his reaction, the door flew to the end of its track, then rebounded a few inches.

That was all the space the sea needed. With a deafening roar and the force of a fire hose, the wave blasted through the gap. John was picked off his feet and slammed across the cabin.

When the water subsided, he struggled to his feet, disoriented and in shock. No sooner had he done so than another wave exploded into the cabin. Instantly, a chaos of swirling confusion filled John's tiny world. He felt the boat go over, then roll. He cartwheeled inside. Anything that wasn't bolted down joined him. Was he dead? Was he sinking?

One more time he tried to stand. Somehow he reached the hatch and closed it. Then he braced himself for another assault.

It never came. Instead, a wave of fear came over him such as he had never before experienced. My God! What about the jury-rig? He didn't want to go outside. He knew that another swell might strike him from behind and knock him unconscious.

There was water everywhere. It poured from the drawers and from the cabinets, off the radio and out of the stove. Books, utensils and tools were either floating around in six inches of icy cold water by his feet or were crashing to the floor of the cabin as the boat lurched from side to side.

But the mast! Was it still there?

He pried open the hatch. He had to look. In the gloom of the night, he peered wide-eyed into the void. By God, it was still there! It was still standing! It was a miracle.

Soaked and shivering, John returned below deck and began to sort out yet another mess. He had been lucky again. He wondered how much longer it would last.

March 12: He was less than 1,600 km from Cape Horn. Since turning for the bottom of the world, John's psychological condition had markedly improved. Unfortunately, the same could not be said of his surroundings.

The cabin was green and black with mould and mildew. The bread had run out and the eggs had long ago rotted. Everything below decks was cold, clammy and thoroughly miserable. The satellite navigator was on the fritz, his sleeping bag was a sodden, foul-smelling rag. He had a painful ear infection.

Above decks, the situation was no better. Every day the temperature dropped closer to freezing. There were frequent snow squalls and a steady increase in the speed of the wind. As he approached the bottom of the world, winter was descending. With hot liquids his only source of warmth, things were beginning to look grim. Then, the unimaginable happened. He began to run out of water.

"It was a sort of gradual deterioration," John recalls. "It was like a slow realization that this could be serious."

137

It was. He dug out his emergency water supply, – about ten litres. Then he got on the radio and asked what was the minimum requirement to sustain life. He was told a litre a day. He had ten days to round the Horn and put into the Falkland Islands. At the rate he was going, his chances looked fair. But if he got stalled by bad weather...

The next day, a gift came from heaven: hail. Rushing around on deck, John frantically collected the frozen water pellets in a saucepan. Then he melted them on the stove. That gave him almost an extra day of water.

Back home, the ordeal became a nail-biter. "It was really tense waiting," recalls Vicki. "It seemed so slow."

Gradually, John Hughes – sodden, alone, cold and running out of food and water – approached the Cape. A shiver ran through him, but it was not the cold.

Cape Horn is not, as some believe, a peninsula which juts out from the bottom of South America. It is, instead, a single island amidst an archipelago of dozens of landforms of varying sizes and shapes. Cape Horn itself is actually named after the Dutch village of Hoorn, the home town of sailor Willem Schouten, who first sighted the foreboding outcrop in 1616.

From any perspective, it is an ominous piece of geography. With steep sides that rise a sheer 150 m to 180 m from the sea, it looms up on the horizon with sudden and foreboding presence. Its cold climate and sparse plant life make it barren and bleak and, as one mariner once said, "One could hardly design a more suitable finish to a great continent."

This was the arena into which John Hughes sailed that day. He knew that because of the rigid position of his sail, there was no way he could turn back if he had to. Even if he could retreat, he knew he would run out of water before he reached land. There was no turning back. "It was sort of like going downhill in a car with no brakes," he recalled.

At 3:30 p.m. on March 19, through a cold drizzle, land filtered ominously into view. It was not the Horn, but he knew it was the beginning of the end. A pit formed in his stomach.

The wind was howling at 100 km an hour. Eighteen-metre seas were crashing around him. The drizzle had turned to snow.

Most sailors could never have done what John Hughes did next. Having determined there was no danger of running aground and with open sea in front of him, he decided after many hours that it was pointless to wait. At 10 p.m. he turned-in below decks. The quarterberth was pungent and soaked. He was beyond the point of caring. He strapped himself in and sloshed to sleep.

Suddenly, the bottom fell out of John's world. He had this terrifying sensation of falling, falling, falling. It was like the feeling you get in nightmares when you tumble off the side of the building. But he did not wake up before he hit bottom. He hit hard. "I woke up and there was an explosion of noise like a bomb had gone off. It was a noise like a train. Things were flying around the cabin. I put my hands over my face. Just noise – unbelievable noise. And then I hit and it sort of felt like I was bouncing down a road. I figured the boat was breaking up, or that I'd hit land or was in the surf. I was being bounced on rocks or had been run down by a ship."

The force of the impact knocked the wind right out of John. In the blackness of the night he frantically tried to breathe as objects of all description avalanched down on him. Strapped in as he was to his bed, there was nothing he could do.

139

He felt the boat roll again. Then the sound of breaking glass. "Then, all of a sudden, it was over. I was back up; the boat was back to its normal ungodly motion."

His chest heaved, sucking in empty spasms. Finally, it eased and he was able to breathe.

"What the hell was that?"

When he had cleared the debris from his body, John scurried on deck.

"Nothing. The boat's just like she was when I went to sleep. Looking around, I expected to see the sails gone, but they were still there. Only the clear plastic shelter over the hatch was ripped away by the sea. Nothing had broken in the self-steering, so I was still in business."

John deduced what had happened: the ship had been blasted forward off a wave. In ocean swells, the way to stay upright and stable is to stay just ahead of the cresting waves. If you don't, in strong winds such as the ones he was experiencing, you were simply blown into the trough between waves. Bad luck had caught up to him.

"I was really scared at that point, so I got up, went up on deck and put on my safety harness. I steered by hand for the next eight to ten hours until the wind eased off a bit."

RESOLVE TO STICK WITH IT

Closely linked to physical endurance, persistence is mental endurance.

B.C. Forbes said, "Nobody can fight their way to the top and stay at the top without exercising the fullest measure of grit, courage, determination and resolution. Anyone who gets anywhere does so because they are first firmly resolved to progress in this world, and then have enough "stick-to-it-iveness" to transform their resolution into reality. Without [persistence], nobody can win any worthwhile place among their fellow men."

It was then that John realized he had rounded the Horn. After all he'd been through, it was a bit anticlimactic. He didn't complain. He'd paid his dues – and more. He'd earned the right to be there. "It was like going through the sound barrier."

Below deck, he hunted around for some means of celebration. To his delight, he discovered some old Christmas pudding that wasn't too mouldy and some rum-butter sauce. He threw it all into a saucepan.

Thousands of kilometres away in warm and sunny Rio, Mark Schrader and the entire fleet breathed a sigh of relief. For hours they had stared at the tiny dot that marked John's position. Now, they knew. "As he got closer and closer to the Horn, I really began to think he'd make it. Then, when he did, well...it was absolutely phenomenal."

Back home in Dartmouth, Vicki wept openly. For once, they were tears of joy and not grief. For the first time in months, it really looked like he was going to come home.

A few days later, a shell-shocked and beleaguered John Hughes crawled into Port Stanley on the Falkland Islands. In the spring of 1982, it had been the site of a war between Britain and Argentina. On that day, John was a solitary soldier returning from his own battle.

As his tiny craft cruised up alongside a sprawling British Navy ship, John stepped ashore and into his first shower in over two months. After 7,000 km and 45 days of sailing under jury-rig, he had done what everyone had said was impossible. More important than that, he had lived up to himself.

In the Falklands, the Canadian cavalry had come to John's rescue. Led by John Sandford and backed by many volunteers back home, Sandford and his team had arranged for the purchase and shipping of a new mast. For three days, he, John and a small support crew worked 20 hours a day installing the new equipment and making necessary repairs to the old.

"John looked pretty weather-beaten when I first saw him," Sandford recalls. "He had red, puffed up and salt-encrusted eyes. But he was just smiling. I gave him a hug. I was so glad to see him on dry land and in one piece. As for his jury-rig, it was bullet-proof. It would have taken a team of engineers a week to do what he did."

Thanks to Sandford and everyone who backed John's dream, the BOC's last competitor left the Falkland Islands in better shape than when he had left Newport. Only one major goal remained: to finish in time for the awards ceremony on May 30.

142

The voyage home to Newport was anticlimactic. Although there were the usual daily challenges of equipment repairs, navigational difficulties and the like, the real hurdle was past.

At 3:00 a.m. on May 26, John Hughes lay down in his berth for the last time. All that he had been through and all that he wanted to come true danced in his head that night, less than 110 km from the culmination of a lifelong dream.

It seemed like he'd been away for years, not just months. It was as if his life had somehow sped up while the rest of the world turned at the same consistent rate. If there was anything consistent in his thoughts that night, it was that he just wanted it all to end. The anticipation was unbearable. John wrestled with mixed feelings of elation, relief and exhaustion. As always, Vicki was there with him, if only in spirit.

Within hours he knew that at last they would be together again. That, as much as his relentless desire to finish what he'd started, had driven him onward these many months. He knew she would be there for him. There was no doubt in his mind then that he would ask her to marry him.

When he awakened, he cleaned himself up in preparation for arrival. He had a shave and a wash, and put on freshly pressed clothes which he'd kept for the occasion since being in the Falklands. Now all he needed was some consistent wind and he would be able to sail smoothly to the finish.

The self-confidence you get from accomplishing a very difficult goal will make the rest of your worries seem insignificant. It's worth a heck of a lot – millions. It's priceless.
– John Hughes

143

It was not to be. Since he'd begun sailing, John has always had a problem with landfalls. For some reason, the sea never seemed to cooperate; it hadn't coming into Falmouth Harbour, not on his return to Canada, nor when he arrived in Cape Town or Sydney. "Landfalls hate me," he says. "I get near land and everything goes to pieces. Weather-wise, it's phenomenal.

"I used to look at the videos of races and see these guys coming in with the sails up and a nice steady breeze, flat sea and sunshine. I thought, 'You lucky guys. When I get there I always look like a bag of dirt and smell like one, too.'"

On this day at least, he would be clean-cut and shaven. But just as he was within striking distance of the finish, the wind shut down completely. It was as if the ocean would not release him, that she, and not Vicki, would have him, at least for one long, final day.

John cursed his misfortune. "It was the ultimate cruel joke."

At dawn on May 27, Newport Harbor came into view. Mark Schrader appeared in his boat and shouted greetings over to John. They bantered back and forth playfully.

"I can remember feeling very close to him at that moment," Mark recalls. "I was just so proud of him."

Vicki came out twice in the committee boat to see where John was. It was fabulous to see her, but painful to be able to look and not touch. Across the water their minds and hearts met.

"He looked incredibly well," Vicki remembers. "It looked like he'd just been out for a sail around the harbour."

Gradually, a small flotilla of boats appeared. And more gradually, inch by inch, foot by foot, he drifted to the line.

144

KNOW WHY YOU'RE DOING IT

Our adventure achievers don't commit themselves in a casual way. They commit with their heart and soul. But before they do, they thoroughly think through what it is they are proposing to do, what sacrifices it will entail, what heartaches and what pain. Most importantly, they know why they want to do it. Then, if and when things get difficult, they don't waste time and energy in the paralysis of self-doubt. They know why they're there and they want to be there – regardless of how difficult the challenge becomes. Of course, since they are human, they will occasionally feel hesitant, but that hesitation is never long enough to significantly stop their forward movement.

Those with the "adventure attitude" seem to be of one type of mindset: circular. They set out from the start and when they encounter a major obstacle, their minds return automatically to "go." Here, they re-affirm their reasons for starting, draw again from their original motivational well and continue.

At 4:44 p.m., after 224 days, 13 hours, 55 minutes and 24 seconds of racing, John Hughes realized his dream. To a flurry of horns, whistles and cheers, he stood, shook his head in disbelief and raised both arms in silent celebration. With fists clenched and head down, a wave of emotion swept over him such as he had never before experienced.

Human potential stops at a point somewhere beyond infinity.
– Toller Cranston

It was a warmth and satisfaction unparalleled in the everyday and one which he knew could never be equalled.

In seconds, the committee boat was alongside. Vicki jumped on board and leapt into his arms. They squeezed each other long and hard. The tears flowed freely.

Somewhere, someone played the national anthem. Champagne was cracked. John soaked in the celebration. He reveled in the relief.

145

Everyone was there: Vicki and Mary, his brother David and Mark. There were two notable exceptions: his grandfather and John Sandford. With his last nickel long spent on the support of Hughes' goal, Sandford had been forced to stay behind in Canada. At the yacht club back home, he got the news through the pay phone in the lobby. There, the big, burly and stoic man who, as much as anyone, had been the architect of the achievement, shed a quiet tear after he hung up.

"I didn't feel left out," he said as he tried to buoy-up what little English exterior he had left. "It wasn't the celebration I was interested in. It was just the fact he'd done it. But I wish I could have been there to shake his hand."

Three days later at the prize-giving, race-winner Phillipe Jeantot declared humbly: "John Hughes won this race." It was the ultimate compliment to the man who had finished three months after Jeantot and weeks after the penultimate competitor. John's fellow competitors voted him the sailor who best embodied the ideals of the BOC: perseverance, tenacity and sportsmanship amid adversity. He was awarded a special "Spirit of the BOC" Trophy, the first time it had ever been presented.

Sandford got to say his piece to John about two weeks later, when John sailed into Halifax Harbour to a true hero's welcome. On that Sunday in June, an explosion of emotion greeted John. Thousands poured onto the shore and dozens of boats decked-out in flags formed one of the biggest flotillas in the city's long maritime history. Not even the fog and drizzle of yet another classic Hughes landfall could dampen it.

In the middle, John stood silently in the stern of the *Joseph Young*, no longer facing the waves, but the stirring music of a city-wide celebration. A huge banner erected on one of the buildings on shore said it all so succinctly: "Ahoy, John" it proclaimed in huge letters. "Welcome home."

"To me it meant that I'd set out to do the hardest thing that I could think of doing, and I'd done it. Whatever else happened in my life, nobody or nothing could ever diminish that for me. I knew what I was capable of, I suppose, and I'd proved it."

Fifteen months later, on Sept. 2, John and Vicki were married aboard the famous Atlantic clipper ship, *Bluenose II*. It was a perfect day for sailing. The sun was shining and the wind was blowing at a crisp clip over the Atlantic. For two hours, 88 people frolicked on and below its decks. John and Vicki stood arm in arm at the stern as the ship heeled over in the wind.

It had rained the day before and it did the day after, but on that day, John's landfall was the best in years.

"It was perfect," Vicki recalls. "John wasn't the one sailing."

The story of John Hughes' solo sail around the world says as much or more about his character than any personality portrait ever could. It couldn't have been written better if it had been scripted: Man sails off alone in search of his dream, has numerous close calls with death, makes history thanks to his own bulldog tenacity and the support of his friends, and finally limps home to a hero's welcome and his bride.

When John finally crossed the finish line, there was barely a dry eye in the harbour. But the tears did not come just because he'd come home. They came because he'd touched home.

His mother, Mary, perhaps, said it best: "I hope these things that he does mean more than just sailing around the world. Already, I, for one, have learned that I can – we can – control our lives."

In this world that measures success in medals, material wealth and mergers, John Hughes gave us cause for pause.

He wasn't the first, or the fastest, or the best, or the biggest. In fact, he finished dead last. But although he may have been out-distanced, out-financed and out-sized, he was never out-classed.

John's success had nothing to do with a race. It had everything to do with winning – and mostly with believing.

147

Chapter 3
THE CAPACITY OF CURIOSITY

Don't keep forever on the public road, going only where others have gone. Leave the beaten track occasionally and dive into the woods. You will be certain to find something you have never seen before. Of course, it will be a little thing, but do not ignore it. Follow it up, explore all around it; one discovery will lead to another, and before you know it you will have something worth thinking about to occupy your mind. All really big discoveries are the result of thought.
– Alexander Graham Bell, 1914

Profile on
Mike Beedell
of Ottawa, Ontario

Member, Qitdlarssuaq Expedition, one of the greatest dog sled journeys of the century.

Member, Polar Passage Expedition. Along with Jeff MacInnis of Toronto, made the first-ever sail of the Northwest Passage using only wind power.

The Joyous Journeyer

I have a sane level of lunacy.
– Mike Beedell

Caught with his pants down beside the iceberg, Mike Beedell tried valiantly to protect his hindquarters as twenty ravenous sled dogs moved in for a meal. "Inuit dogs have a voracious appetite for human excrement. There I was, out in the middle of the ice, flailing a whip in the air trying to keep them at bay."

Every morning on the Qitdlarssuaq (pronounced KIT-LAR-SUE-ACK) dogsled journey, Mike's routine was the same. He would emerge from the team's igloo and head out onto the ice. As he did, a pack of sled dogs would look up with joyful anticipation on their faces. Mike would glare back at them with a look containing both humour and dread.

"This was serious business. You could lose your family jewels very quickly if two or three of them got to arguing too close to your tail end. Sometimes, I'd have to hit them over the head. I had a few favourites that I trusted not to get carried away. They got the treats on a daily basis, while I flailed at the more dangerous lads."

The Qit dogsled journey was the greatest adventure of Mike's life. It had everything he dreamed of: history, culture, character and direction. And, it had laughs.

On April Fool's Day that year, 1987, Mike entertained the dogs and his four companions with a classic return to nature. With the temperature a crisp -34°C, he stripped to his birthday suit and ran around the nearest iceberg.

"The other guys were looking at me, saying, 'Holy shit! He's crazy.' Well, I started laughing my head off. I was frisky and elated."

"Mike's a real fun-loving character," says expedition leader, Renee Wissink. "When you're on a trip in the Arctic, there has to be comic relief. Every day you're under a lot of pressure, living in very intense circumstances."

The Qit journey was Wissink's brainchild. A northern school teacher, he had a passion for polar adventure. His idea, in essence, was simple: to re-create a century-old Inuit migration from Baffin Island – high in the Great White North – to Greenland, using authentic Inuit methods. Those methods included Inuit sleds, or komatiks, Inuit clothing, including caribou parkas, pants and boots, and traditional Inuit food, such as seal, caribou and walrus meat. The team even navigated using wind direction and the pattern of the snowdrifts.

At night the five men, including three Inuit, would nestle together into their cozy igloo or tent. In the morning they would move on. If they were lucky enough to get some hunting in along the way, they lived off the land. Otherwise they fell back on modern freeze-dried and boil-in-a-bag food. The only flat-out concession to modern life they made was for safety reasons; they carried a radio.

The logistics of the expedition were intriguing. The route from the tiny community of Igloolik, just southwest

151

of Baffin Island, wove 2,880 km northward and eventually finished in Qaanaaq, on Greenland's northwest coast. While both communities could, at best, be described as nondescript, what happened between them was not.

The Qit expedition became one of the greatest dogsled journeys of this century. The trip took some three months to complete. Its goal was to retrace the route of the 19th-century Inuit spiritual leader of the expedition's namesake: Qitdlak the Great.

Qit had had a colourful life. As a religious leader, or shaman, he had led the last recorded migration of the Baffin Island Inuit to Greenland in the 1850s. In the early 1830s, he and a band of 50 or so followers had left their Baffin Island home. Some 30 years later, they had turned up in Greenland, where they joined the polar Inuit.

Although Qit was a spiritual leader, he was far from a white knight of the day. In 1832, he killed a man and became a fugitive on an endless search for escape. But he was a charismatic and influential member of the community. When he began his exile, he convinced dozens of others to join him. His followers believed he could commune with the spirits. On one occasion, as legend has it, Qit turned himself into a polar bear. The bear magically transformed water into ice so a young companion could escape in mid-ocean from an approaching storm. When Qit travelled at night, they said, a curious, surrealistic glow encircled his head. In short, he was a type of Arctic Superman. When he died of mysterious stomach cramps off the coast of Greenland in 1875, he was elevated to the status of legend.

This was the man whose route they wished to follow. He would accompany them in a fashion: the three Inuit members of the expedition were his descendants.

Mike Beedell has always had a "sane level of lunacy." To understand why anyone would deliberately face the hardships of a three-month polar journey by dogsled, you need to return to a hillside in Sudbury, Ontario.

Located about 400 km north of Toronto, Sudbury is one of Canada's most important mining communities. Behind the apartment in which Mike lived with his parents there was a steep rock drop-off. To Mike it seemed huge, the way things always do when you're small. But it was this "cliff" that became his first introduction to a life of adventure, risk-taking and mischief.

"There was this old lady living nearby. She would rant and rave every time we'd go near the place," Mike recalls. "She was always scowling at us. But we had a great time frolicking up and down the cliff, clambering around. I remember her always there, wagging her finger at us.

"I can remember excitement and a bit of fear; I'd say exhilaration. It was a great kind of surging feeling of adrenalin produced by the challenge that we were exploring something."

Mike's exploring instinct expanded from the cliff into all manner of activities. Slowly, these activities began to foster in him a wonder of nature. He learned early that in addition to being exciting, nature could also be dangerous if you didn't treat it with respect.

When he was young, his parents forbade him from going over the fence by the cliff into the neighbour's yard. But in the true rebel nature that would increase in him as the years went on, he deliberately disregarded the rule. On a dare from a friend he climbed the tree overhanging the fence and, while swinging and cackling in delight, fell and broke his arm. "I remember landing, getting up and flailing with my arm to try to get back over the fence so my parents wouldn't be mad at me."

153

Before he started kindergarten, Mike received his first tricycle. Because his family lived on a hill, his mother wisely established boundaries for his safety. But it wasn't long before Mike was blasting through them, yearning to know what secrets were contained on the other side.

"I remember thinking, 'Wow! What a whole new world I'm seeing.' It was a feeling of pushing the limits. That was very exciting. I would keep that a secret until later when I was able to say, 'Well, I went that far and everything was okay. So what's the big deal?'"

When he was 5, Mike's family moved to Ottawa, the nation's capital. His father, John, was going through teacher's college and training as an Olympic canoeist. His mother, Ann, worked part-time as a telemarketer to help make ends meet. Along with his two-year-old brother, Jeff, the family struggled financially.

Mike had many friends when he was a child. He was active in cubs, hockey, band and choir. But he was not interested in all the usual things of young boys, like baseball and football. Even as a youngster, he was a little bit of a nonconformist. He was fascinated with animals, all kinds of them.

CULTIVATE CURIOSITY

Mike Beedell's enthusiasm is coupled with a curiosity that enables him to achieve. In fact, enthusiasm and curiosity, more than physical or photographic ability, have been two of the keys to his success. He's like a kid in a candy store. Everywhere he looks there's something new to taste, touch, feel or experience.

Although all our achievers are adults, they have not lost their childlike curiosity. They are far older than their years in many other ways, yet this part of them seems to be forever locked in the past.

"My family had a menagerie," he remembers. "We had pet foxes, owls, baby sparrowhawks, ravens, turtles, snakes, iguanas; even rabbits, guinea pigs and fish. At one time I had about 15 animals."

One of Mike's favourite pastimes was watching tadpoles turn into frogs. Using a magnifying glass, he would wait patiently for hours beside his aquarium while the little critters transformed themselves before his very eyes.

Another of his major interests was the praying mantis. He had one as a pet and would take it for walks. "I had a little thread that I could put around his neck and I would take him around the area feeding him flies and so on. It was so incredible to watch. He'd always eat his prey head first. I would watch him in my magnifying glass.

"I wasn't a scientist, I was an observer. I always wanted to do things that gave me a sense of enjoyment from within."

155

While a young child's attachment to a praying mantis might seem bizarre at best and insignificant at worst, the reason why Mike was captivated by it reveals a critical early clue to his eventual character.

"I liked him because he was such an aware hunter, and he was so incredibly patient. He would sit and wait, totally still, camouflaged for the exact right moment. Then he was lightning fast. I had great respect for his abilities and he seemed very respectful of me. He was gentle and never aggressive. He just seemed to have such a great character."

In the years that followed, Mike would acquire some of these same characteristics. As a photographer, he developed incredible patience, waiting for hours, sometimes days for the perfect shot. Most of all, like his praying mantis, he was gentle and never aggressive.

"Mike's an easy guy to like," says Renee Wissink. "He's outgoing, he's friendly, he's sort of a go-with-the-flow type of guy. He's a pretty hard guy not to like."

If there was an early, but important influence in Mike's love of nature, it was his father, John. He was the 1956 North American canoe champion in doubles and fours, and he competed in the 1960 Olympics in Rome. As a youngster, Mike delighted in going down to the local canoe club to watch his dad – trim, tanned and superbly fit – tear up and down the river in a canoe. Surrounded by athletes like his father, Mike gained an early appreciation for physical fitness that would be essential to his success – and survival – in later life.

"I remember looking up and seeing these guys at the canoe club doing one-arm chin-ups," Mike says. "Dad was incredibly muscled, too. I was so proud of my Dad because he was the best. As a little guy, that swelled my heart with pride."

"I suppose there was the perfection that I sought that Mike picked up on," John says. "But I never tried to make him do anything. I just exposed him to it."

John's second level of influence was perhaps even more significant. As a biology teacher and canoe trip leader, he introduced Mike to the out-of-doors.

One of Mike's early adventures in the outdoors was at the local ski hill. His father was a ski patroller there and he loved to have Mike, then 7, accompany him. But as usual, Mike had to be different – and daring. He went off a ski jump, got too much height, fell and broke his femur.

Around this time, the family was able to move to a middle-income neighbourhood in another part of Ottawa. Mike's new home bordered on 20 hectares of field and woods. This became his playground. Mike reveled in every new discovery. On one occasion he watched a dragonfly nymph pull itself out of its shell. Minutes later, on its maiden flight, it became food for a passing bird.

Everybody has to seek their dreams if they want to be fulfilled.
— **Mike Beedell**

"Mike was crushed," his mother, Ann, recalls.

Mike's summers were spent investigating everything from insects to earthworms or selling frogs to fishermen at his grandmother's house a few hours drive from Ottawa. At school, although he excelled in reading, he spent much of Grade 1 daydreaming.

"I was a great daydreamer. I dreamed like crazy – and in technicolour. Half my school life was spent daydreaming. But I believe that helped establish my visual sense for photography. I was able to "pre-visualize" everything. Now, when I do my photographic work, I "pre-visualize" what I think's going to happen. Then I'm able to go out prepared and tuned-in to capture those images. That visual sense became incredibly well-tuned in school. I still spend at least a few hours of every day of my life daydreaming. On journeys, I create visions every day. I call it "visioneering." It's a way of tackling a challenge.

"Most of my daydreams have come true. The power of my belief in a vision becomes so solid that it overtakes my being and gives me the drive and ability to concentrate on making it a reality."

"As a child, he sort of wandered," Ann says. "He was a dreamer."

One of the things Mike daydreamed about was performing mischievous schemes and pranks. He was a bit of a show-off. He would often act these out and usually ended up on the wrong end of the strap because of it.

When Mike graduated into high school, things were not much better. It seemed impossible to contain him in a

157

Too much self-doubt destroys the foundation of the dream.
– Mike Beedell

structured environment. While attending Grade 12 at Ashbury College, a private high school for boys in Ottawa, he got a zero in algebra. He was so frustrated, he refused to write the exam. He had difficulty with chemistry and math, but not surprisingly, he excelled in biology. If the subject was technically structured with rigid rules, he had no interest in it. But if it went by nature's flowing order, he poured himself into it. Mike Beedell was not a hellion in school. He did buck the system, but he was never a bully or a spoiled brat. He simply hadn't found his niche.

"I was not cut out to be in the standard education system or to pursue standard things. I knew I had to pursue something in the outdoors. I just had different perceptions, I guess, of what was important in life."

In high school, Mike developed a strong sense of camaraderie with his chums. One frigid February day as the temperature outside hovered at -34°C, he sat naked with three of his buddies in an idling car outside Elmwood School, an exclusive private girls school.

Donning masks and bolstered by a little Southern Comfort to help buoy up their courage, the four boys prepared to perform the ultimate dare: to streak before 350 innocent girls at the height of the noon-hour rush.

The whole affair was planned and executed with the precision of a bank job. First, there was the get-away car, a Volvo driven by a friend who'd "borrowed" it from his parents while they were away. Next, came the target, the Grade 12 girls. They were old enough to know what was going on, yet young enough to be flustered by the whole thing. Finally, there was the route of entry, passage and escape. To work, the whole thing had to come off without a hitch.

It didn't start that way.

"We were sitting there in the Volvo when suddenly a police car cruised by. We freaked out!"

Two minutes to zero hour: The first bandit-in-the-buff leaped out. Before he could get two steps, Mike and the others locked their doors behind him. As they bent over double with laughter inside the car, the solitary streaker ran in panicked circles around and around the car, protecting his privates from the cold, pleading to be let in. "Then, we all got out the car," Mike recalls. "We tore in through the front door. Everyone was in the midst of lunch, so we ran right through the lunch-hour traffic. The noise was incredible! People just lost it, fell off their chairs, bumped into each other. It was a scream.

"Then we ran through the plush center of the place, then into the gymnasium, where there was a gym class going on. "Everybody was doing handstands and they all collapsed. I leapt over one of the mats and went straight for the back of the school."

The Volvo was waiting. As the three puffing and petrified figures piled in wearing only their smiles, the car sped off, sending a plume of snow in its wake. In seconds, they were all laughing hysterically in the back seat, telling each other what they'd seen and how glorious it had all been.

The staff at Elmwood School for Girls was not amused. They called the police. The press got hold of the story and the episode exploded into something of a minor scandal. "The story that was published said a Volvo had been seen leaving the scene. My friend was terrified for weeks."

Eventually, the dust settled. They had got away with it, or so they thought. On the last day of school, one of Ashbury's teachers took Mike aside. Putting his arm quietly over Mike's shoulder, he looked the lad straight in the eye and declared in hushed tones: "Mike, that streaking

159

was one of the best things that ever happened around here. It was a great idea."

After high school, Mike enrolled in a recreation degree program at the University of Ottawa. Little changed academically. He had trouble with statistics and math, but excelled in the rest of his subjects.

It was at university that Mike first began to find his niche. He became director of the university's outdoor club and in 1978, at 22, he took the critical step. On a whim, he bought himself a camera and within a week had joined the university newspaper.

"The connection to the camera was so natural," he recalls, "it was as if I'd known it from another lifetime."

Mike's first photo assignment yielded less than dramatic results. On a 36-exposure roll, his emotions got away from him and he cranked off 45 frames, ripping the film from the spool. The photo editor was not impressed.

PURSUE YOUR PASSION WITH PASSION

All adventure achievers exude boundless enthusiasm. They seem like children in how they pursue their passions with fervour. Listening to Laurie Skreslet describe a challenging ice climb is as riveting as hearing Mike Beedell talk about an exciting photographic experience. You are immediately captivated.

Youth is not a time of life...it is a state of mind. Nobody grows old by merely living a number of years; people grow old only by deserting their ideals. You are as young as your faith, as old as your doubt; as young as your self-confidence, as old as your fear; as young as your hope, as old as your despair.

-Unknown

As always, however, Mike persevered. Although not technically proficient, he sensed immediately that photography was right for him.

"It was an extension of my being. It was a totally natural thing for me. Although I had no formal training, I photographed by instinct. There was almost a spiritual connection with it."

On weekends Mike taught outdoor skills, canoeing and kayaking. For practise, he began photographing the participants. To his surprise, by the end of the weekend, he would have 150 orders for prints. This is where his photographic business began.

Mike's involvement in the outdoors was the key to what would become a remarkable photographic career. He got a job with Trailhead, a local outdoors store, teaching whitewater kayaking and canoeing. The store's owner, Wally Schaber, was quick to pick up on Mike's affability with the public, his superb communication skills and his advanced outdoor abilities. He invited Mike to be an assistant guide on a trip down the Coppermine River in the Northwest Territories.

161

The Coppermine River flows from Lac de Gras, about 190 km north of Great Slave Lake, and twists and turns its way northwest across the Arctic barrens to Coronation Gulf on the Arctic Ocean 800 km to the north. It was to be a 30-day trip. Mike took his camera, of course.

From the minute the adventure began to the moment it ended, Mike, still just 22, was overcome by the Arctic. "It was so inspiring, so overwhelming. I felt such a sense of discovery and absolute elation in the landscape and the wildlife. My emotions were intense; my whole being vibrated. I felt a spine-tingling exhilaration of loving the land.

In the city, people are so bludgeoned with stimuli like lights and signs that they lose their natural sense of wonder.
– Mike Beedell

"There was a sense of history there, too. I had the journals of the British explorer, Sir John Franklin, who navigated the river in 1820, and Samuel Hearn's journals from the late 1700s. Along the route we camped at the very fireplace where Franklin had camped. I had a fantastic feeling of getting to know my country better. An absolute thrill overcame me."

That thrill never left Mike's mind, or his heart. The Arctic remains his magnetic north. It has touched his core.

"I kept asking myself: is this real? Is this happening to me? I was visually and physically inspired. I experienced a feeling of sensory overload, a euphoria like I had never felt before. My senses were totally exhausted from taking in so much.

"One day, we went fishing. Your lure would hit the water and you'd have an 8 to 10-pound char. It wasn't whether you were going to catch a fish – that was a given – it was, how big was it going to be?"

One of Mike's most memorable moments in the North took place on the side of a cliff during that life-changing trip. He had scrambled up in search of gyrfalcons. Suddenly, one landed next to him. Completely inexperienced with humans, the bird had intuitively trusted this new two-legged creature. Mike's heart began beating furiously. The falcon had a ptarmigan in its talons.

"I had my camera in my hand and I thought, 'Holy shit. Should I move?'" Slowly, he sat down. For the next four hours the two went about their business. Mike shot his pictures while the bird had its supper. Slowly, Mike inched his lens closer.

"By the end of the experience, we were just three feet away from each other, looking right into one another's eyes. The gyrfalcon's eyes were a beautiful coal-black. We seemed to share a mutual fascination. He had absolutely no fear of me."

After the bird had eaten, it fell asleep right beside Mike. If he'd wanted to, he probably could have reached out and stroked it. It was an association not unlike the one he'd had with his praying mantis as a boy. "There was an unbelievable feeling of trust; no fear was transmitted between us. It was total acceptance."

Mike's life, indeed Mike himself, was never the same after that. He returned from the North with his first true sense of direction. At last he knew what he wanted to do in life and where he wanted to do it.

163

"I remember thinking: I've got to find a way to come back here all the time." It did not take long before Mike discovered how. When he got home, he put together a slide show of his adventure. After the show, he sold prints of his slides to help pay his way through university. Eventually, he got together enough images for exhibits in Toronto and Ottawa. During one of these, an official from the Canadian Parks Service happened to pass through. He gave Mike his first professional assignment in the Arctic. All of a sudden, Mike was being paid to pursue his greatest love. His career was launched.

"I spent 1978 discovering my blossoming talent. When I came back, I was absolutely overjoyed with the images I had. I hadn't believed I could take pictures like that. A lot of my most favourite photographs, even after an intense decade of photographing, are some of my first images taken on my very first trip North. With the magic of the light and the colours, a new attunement to the land evolved in me. I felt more vibrant and excited. I felt a reverence for the North."

Mike's northern discovery was followed by years of low pay and hard work. His love of photography, adventure and the Arctic pushed him on. He had to go on so he could return.

"He always, in his own way, desired perfection," says his father. "In his adventures, he had to ensure it was done right."

Two years later Mike accepted another major photographic challenge: a climb of Mt. Logan, the highest mountain in Canada. Mt. Logan is in the Yukon and has an elevation of 6,050 metres. To go there, he had to miss one of the university courses required for graduation. This did not greatly disturb him. Degrees or labels do not mean much to him. In his view, it's not what you do, but how you do it. What counts is the integrity with which you approach a task.

"I don't do any of my journeys for fame and fortune, although I've got mixed up with individuals whose only purpose is to sensationalize their endeavours and make them far more than what they are in order to build a false image of themselves. I quite detest that because I think people who get like that must be very desperate. They begin to stomp on other people and lose their sense of morality. For me, it's the joy of the experience and the joy of sharing. The priceless jewels of deep experience are lost too often to man's thirst for fame and fortune."

Mike adheres to the philosophy of British writer Miles Clark. In Clark's view: "The acid test of a true adventurer, if presented with certain anonymity, is whether each of us would still have made the journey beyond that last blue mountain."

"Mike does not want to set the world on fire," his father says. "Money is incidental to him. If he wants to achieve, he'll take everyone he knows with him. He enjoys recognition, but he doesn't trample on others to achieve it."

Mike's climb to the top, not just of Mt. Logan, but to the upper echelons of the outdoor photographic world, was anything but easy. In summer 1981, he almost died while on a solo trip to Hudson Bay. Twenty-four kilometres from the nearest town, he came down with acute appendicitis. He managed to stagger back through the bush to a hospital with a 27-kg pack. It took him two days. When he finally arrived, he was bent double in pain. Because of inadequate medical facilities, he was flown out by air ambulance and was operated on just hours before the organ would have burst.

165

This was not an isolated incident. Mike has had more than his share of close calls, all of which lead him to believe that he's here because of some larger plan. "I believe in good fortune, or karma," he says. "I don't know where it comes from and I don't know if someone is overseeing me. One day, it may run out, but up to now..."

Mike is not religious in the formal sense. If there is spirituality in his life, it comes from the land he loves. "I feel an incredible spiritual growth from a lot of things I do. I consider the wilderness landscape as a place where I get profound spiritual feelings. I don't go to church often, and I wouldn't go to one for spiritual guidance. I find great spiritual fulfillment in the places where I do my work."

"Here," Qitdlarssuaq expedition member Paul Apak declared after taking a huge bite of steaming seal brain. "Try some."

Mike felt his mouth go dry. The organ was still pulsing with blood, fresh from the body of its dead host. It wasn't exactly what he had in mind for a celebration. But not wanting to upset his Inuit companions, he accepted it with hesitation. "I felt queasy, but once you throw away the cultural hang-ups, you wouldn't believe what you can eat. Actually, it was pretty good."

The team deserved a celebration. After being stopped by open water from traversing over the ice to Greenland, they'd been forced to backtrack inland through a glacial minefield of 60-metre-deep crevasses. For days they'd lived on the edge, losing dogs down fissures and not knowing whether their next step would be into empty space.

Painstakingly, they'd got through. All the while, they'd had an unsettling feeling that someone was watching. Qitdlarssuaq, they knew, was buried someplace nearby. As they edged nearer to their final destination, it seemed like things were getting more and more difficult.

At last, they'd made contact with the Greenlanders, another pair of Qit's descendants. Shortly thereafter, they were joined by two more of his descendants, Miunge and Inaluk, a husband and wife team. After successfully bridging the gap between Ellesmere Island and Greenland, Mike and his companions could now sense the finish.

Miunge and Mike hit it off right away. Within an hour, Mike had him out on skis. In return, Miunge taught Mike how to hunt seals.

"I liked him immediately because he exuded fun and a positive attitude," Mike recalls. "He was obviously very talented. He had a superb dog team and he was very keen to learn to ski."

Despite a significant communication gap, Mike and Miunge lit up together like a couple of sparklers. Each fed off the other's energy, and before long they were cackling with laughter. There was an unspoken understanding between them, like they had known each other for a long time.

That evening was the highlight of the Qit journey for Mike. After deciding to tent it rather than build an igloo, all nine people circulated from abode to abode, swapping stories and telling tales in Inuktitut (the language of the Inuit). Paul Apak and Theo Ikummaq, two of the three Canadian Inuit, translated while Mike and Renee listened attentively. Everyone took pictures. It was a memorable night.

As the evening wore on, Miunge and Mike continued to develop their friendship. Miunge tried to teach him how to use his whip, but Mike was useless. He succeeded only in wrapping it around his head, instead of the target six metres away. They were like a couple of kids at a two-person show-and-tell. The performance went on for hours. In the still of the midnight sun landscape, peal after peal of laughter echoed over the frozen land.

By the next morning, however, the scene had changed. Miunge had fallen ill during the night and was complaining of a bad stomach ache. Mike gave him some Gravol, but he didn't get any better. After a while, he was unable to drive his sled. In a matter of hours, his condition deteriorated to stomach cramps and from there to severe abdominal pain.

In a desperate attempt to give him some comfort, the party stopped and put up the tents. They radioed out to try to get his medical history. It revealed that he had once had a twisted bowel.

167

Mike became very concerned.

"The pain got so bad that he began to scream and scream. We gave him the most powerful pain killers we had, but he got nauseous and just threw them up."

Mike spent eight hours bent over his new friend, holding his hands. He tried to help Inaluk, Miunge's wife, to comfort him, too.

"He appreciated it, I know. Between spasms he'd smile at me and ask questions, then thank me with his hands."

Inside, Mike was in emotional agony. He felt powerless to do anything. At one point, he had to leave the hunter's bedside for a rest, but Miunge leapt up and tried to grab his gun.

"The pain was so bad, he tried to blow his head off."

In desperation, the team contacted health officials by radio, but there was little they could do. A rescue helicopter was requested, but was grounded because of bad weather. No one knew when it might arrive. There were no injectable pain killers and every time they tried to put oral ones into him, he would vomit.

"At one point, he motioned to me that he was going to heaven. I didn't believe him. Then, with his Bible in his hand, he thanked me in his language, held my hands and called my name."

Mike couldn't take it any longer. He went outside. The Arctic seemed unusually cold that day. He felt the cold not just on his face, but in his guts. At the point of tears, he hung his head and said a little prayer.

Then the call came: "Mike! Hurry! He's stopped breathing!"

Before Mike could enter, Renee stopped him. "It's too late Mike. He's gone."

Mike refused to believe it. Not Miunge. He had been so alive only yesterday, so full of life and joy. It couldn't be. It just couldn't be. He pushed past Renee and burst into the tent. Mike began artificial respiration and cardiopulmonary resuscitation. He began to push madly on Miunge's chest and as he did, he felt one of the man's ribs crack.

Mike yelled to Renee to come in and help with CPR. They spelled each other off. Then the end came. "We kept going and going, but I felt the warmth just dissipating out of him...

"It was a terrible feeling knowing that he was really gone and I was only breathing air into a dead man. It was a profoundly terrible experience to desperately try to keep him alive. But there was no way; he was gone. I remember closing his eyes; he was staring a dead stare up into mine."

Everybody has hidden qualities. Many never discover them because they're too wrapped up in their security blankets. They stifle the best qualities within themselves. Make the necessary preparations, then throw away your security blanket.
– Mike Beedell

169

Mike can still see those haunting eyes. As he tells the story, his own eyes look dead, like he's looking right through you. Even his voice is lifeless.

After holding Inaluk's hand for a while, Mike went out of the tent and collapsed in the snow, sobbing uncontrollably. He tried to wash his mouth out with snow, but it was futile. He couldn't seem to get the foul taste of death out of it. It stayed with him for days.

"I wished I could have done more, but I did what I could. We had taken all the steps we possibly could. He was such a vibrant individual just a day and a half earlier."

The Greenlanders took some of their dead friend's belongings from his bedside and prepared a small funeral

Working as a team, you can overcome unbelievable odds and achieve things that others believe to be impossible.
– Mike Beedell

pyre. They set his boots and some of his other personal things on fire out on the sea ice. The body stayed in the tent waiting for the chopper. It finally arrived, four hours too late.

"His wife gave me the dog whip and told me that his last wish before he died was that I should have it. It was one of his most prized possessions."

An autopsy was performed but, mysteriously, it revealed nothing. No cause of death could be determined. The local talk was that Mike's team had been too close to Qit and his journey, and that Miunge's death was a retaliation. Qit had died on the same sea ice on which Miunge's personal effects had been

burned and in almost the same place a century before. He, too, had died of terrible abdominal pain.

Mike struggled to come to grips with the whole thing. This was supposed to be an adventure, he thought, not some kind of hex.

"I accept it as a very odd situation," he says quietly, as his voice drifts off. "I've never come to any conclusions."

"The one thing I really respected about Miunge and Inaluk was that they knew they were completely responsible for their own lives. They carried no radios, nothing, just their dogs and their abilities. They were totally independent human beings with no need for security blankets."

Mike still gets letters from Miunge's wife, and he writes back. They have formed a close friendship.

"It was very sad, and the circumstances were quite unusual," says Renee. "I'm not a superstitious person, but the circumstances behind this are enough to turn you into one. It was almost as if Qit's spirit was saying, 'Well, you've come this far, but if you think you are going farther, I'm going to make it rough for you.'"

For Renee, Mike's behaviour served to affirm what he already knew about his friend. "That incident pointed out the high degree of sensitivity Mike has to the sufferings of others."

The end of the expedition, as is so often the case, was a little sad, especially for Mike. It was simply the last step in a series of steps that had begun months earlier. There was elation and joy throughout the journey, but there was also the realization that the Qitdlarssuaq expedition really was finished. It was a bittersweet ending to a truly remarkable adventure.

As Mike and his companions finally pulled into Qaanaaq, Greenland, after groping like blind men for a day through the worst ground blizzard of the trip, they were met by the entire population of the town, some 500 people. As a small convoy of 20 dog teams rushed out to meet them, Mike felt a sudden surge of pride.

"We shook hands for a solid hour. Hundreds of people flowed to us over the ice and all shook our hands, greeted us, welcomed us and congratulated us. It was a wonderful moment.

"I remember crying as I was driving the last few miles into town. I was on the sled by myself at this point and the others had gone ahead to meet the huge welcoming party and dog teams that had come out from the town. I guess it was the combination of relief, the achievement of our goal, the death of Miunge – all the things that had happened on the journey; I just sort of let go."

As the patting sound of the dogs' footsteps came back to him from ahead, Mike gazed for one last time over the magnificent Arctic wilderness. Despite the harrowing events of the previous three months, it seemed as it always

---

ACCEPT THE RISK IN LIFE

All of us are faced with risks on a daily basis. Every time we get into an automobile or step out onto the street to catch a bus, we assume risk. Life IS risk. Getting out of bed in the morning is a risk. Riding the subway is a risk. Taking out a loan is a risk.

To laugh is to risk appearing the fool.
To weep is to risk appearing sentimental.
To reach out for another is to risk involvement.
To expose feelings is to risk exposing our true selves.
To place your ideas, your dreams before the crowd is to risk loss.
To love is to risk not being loved in return.
To live is to risk dying.
To hope is to risk despair.
To try is to risk failure.
But risk we must, for the greatest hazard in life is to risk nothing.
The man, the woman, who risks nothing does nothing, has nothing, is nothing.
-Unknown

Our society discourages risk. It starts with parents cautioning their children from venturing too close to the top of the stairs. It is, on one hand, an instinctive parental reaction. But it forms the basis for North American society's "security syndrome." In kindergarten, students are taught not to play with matches. In elementary school, they are told not to venture too far from home and in high school, they are disciplined for staying out too late. All of these controls can be healthy, and often are. Yet they can also produce generations of adults who, as Mike Beedell says, are strangling in their "security blankets."

172

did: vast, cold and silent. Somewhere out there, he feared, Qit was watching. As the tears streamed down Mike's face, he knew Miunge was watching too.

The house Mike calls home is an enchanting Austrian-style chalet on the banks of the Gatineau River just north of Ottawa. From here he launches into untold adventures. Surprisingly, Mike is most at home in the south. "The Arctic is very much a part of my life, but there are so many other places that I enjoy and wish to explore in the future. Still, I like my home base to be here. Even though I might spend seven months a year in the Arctic, I was born in the Gatineau, in this landscape, and it's still very dear to me. No matter where else I may live, I will always consider this as home."

173

It is a cold, wet April morning in Quebec. As the rain drums a soothing staccato on the roof of Mike's home, the smell of freshly brewed ovaltine wafts out of his kitchen. With the woodstove blazing in the living room, he moves quietly, preparing a breakfast of muesli, unsweetened yogurt, pears and powdered skim milk.

Welcome to the personal world of Mike Beedell, a rustic place where wooden walls, antiques and a cozy, quiet comfort abound. Scattered throughout his newly purchased house are dozens of timeless and priceless Arctic artifacts, everything from carvings made from 500-year-old whalebone to a meathook fashioned from a caribou antler, even walrus teeth. Miunge's dog whip is propped against a desk on one side of the living room, while the multi-coloured bridal necklace of Inaluk hangs on the opposite wall. Neatly framed on another wall hangs Mike's favourite piece of prose:

We need the tonic of wildness, to wade sometimes in marshes where the bittern and the meadow-hen lurk, and hear the booming of the snipe; to smell the whispering sedge where only some wilder and more solitary fowl builds her nest, and the mink crawls with its belly close to the ground. At the same time that we are earnest to explore and learn all things, we require that all things be mysterious and unexplorable, that land and sea be infinitely wild, unsurveyed and unfathomed by us because unfathomable. We can never have enough of nature. We must be refreshed by the sight of inexhaustible vigor, vast and titanic features, the sea-coast with its wrecks, the wilderness with its living and its decaying trees, the thunder cloud, and the rain which lasts three weeks and produces freshets. We need to witness our own limits transgressed, and some life pasturing freely where we never wander.

From "In Wilderness Is the Preservation Of the World," in *Walden*, by Henry David Thoreau, 1854

Mike moves about his house in the smooth, unrushed fashion that is as much a part of his inner nature as it is his outer appearance. He seems almost becalmed, at peace. Unflustered by the plumbing problems that have left him temporarily without running water, shower or toilet facilities, he quietly sets about trying to fix the problem. Without a word, he heads down to the crawl space in the basement to have a look at the water pump.

"Initially, I was flustered by the trials of owning my own home and the amount of time consumed looking after it. Now I enjoy the process and take it in stride. I realize that I actually enjoy puttering around, like discovering how to run my own pump.

"I think it's in my nature to adapt to a situation and to maintain a sense of humour and acceptance, and not have unrealistic expectations. I'm a firm believer that if you can't maintain a sense of humour and a sense of play, and laugh-off a lot of the more severe situations, then you can't deal with the task at hand properly. Too much of your energy goes into cursing and swearing, into negativity, and not into concentrating on the positive things that you need or want to do."

Mike carries this same attitude into everything he does, regardless of whether it's something as insignificant as plumbing or as life-threatening as a bitter Arctic wind.

"Laughter can be such a great reliever of tension," he says, as he continues to tinker with the pump. "When I'm on the edge I feel the pulsing of adrenalin and, not so much a fear, but an incredible surge to beat the challenge. I just don't seem to feel the kind of fear that cuts my ability to react or perform. Usually, after dealing with a challenge, I almost break up laughing. I may whoop and yell and expel a lot of stress; sometimes I leap about and act a little crazy."

Mike flatly denies claims that the risks he takes are crazy. "I don't see what I do as being on the same level of risk that people on the outside may see it. For example, I consider driving on a major highway more risky than most wilderness endeavours because on the highway you have so little control over the loony-tunes coming at you from the other way. When I'm in wilderness, I feel more in control of the variables, and skilled enough to be able to know and read those variables.

"Having a perspective of what you're doing is important. I'm not a daredevil type. All my risks are calculated.

You always have to be a creative thinker, accept what happens and then deal with it. You should never let anger or frustration overtake your emotions to the point where you cannot funnel positive energy into a positive solution.
– Mike Beedell

175

Anybody who achieves at a high level in any endeavour has to take high, but calculated, risks.
– Mike Beedell

I plan quite meticulously and am prepared to deal with and accept total responsibility for my life. I have no death wish. I have the desire to live life to the fullest, to draw out of myself my greatest potential and share the rewarding experiences with others."

At the time of this writing, Mike had been a homeowner just six months. Until six weeks ago, he lived where he always did, either in a tent, in the back of his Volkswagen van, or at his mother's house where he has his office and slide library. The "nesting instinct" is a new adventure for Mike and one which has marked a significant change in the way he views his life.

"There's been a movement away from needing external motivation, discipline and recognition," says his brother Jeff. "In his teens, Mike very much needed peer support and he was very social. But as he moved through his 20s, his sense of self-confidence improved. Now he's beginning to hit a point where he needs some roots, a home and maybe a girlfriend."

"In the last few years I've realized that intimate relationships are very important to me," Mike says, after emerging from the basement and looking out on the forest of pine, birch and maple that graces his new property. "In the past I was striving to achieve a great deal, too much at times. Achievements are far more meaningful when they can be enjoyed and shared with a loved one."

That loved one is Jacquie Czernin. She is a former freelance announcer with the Canadian Broadcasting Corporation in the Arctic, and is now the host of her own radio show at an English language CBC station in Quebec. She first heard about Mike while covering the Qit expedition from Inuvik, at the Mackenzie River delta near the Beaufort Sea. After several interviews by phone, she found out he'd be speaking at the University of Ottawa. They met there.

"He was fun," she remembers of that first encounter. "He seemed to have time for everyone. He was introduced as crazy and fun-loving."

After Mike's presentation, Jacquie insisted she had to complete the interview that weekend. She and Mike went for a walk along a marshland on the Ottawa River. "He told me how ice formed on the river, explained all about beaver dams and interspersed the whole thing with a lot of jokes. I thought he was great. Then he stopped suddenly and said, 'Listen. Listen to the bird.'"

You've got to measure the wealth of your life by the depth and quality of your life experience.

– Mike Beedell

177

Jacquie was immediately intrigued. Together, they discovered a mutual love not just of the North, but for each other. On a climb in the mountains he impressed her with a bouquet of flowers on the 3,350-metre summit.

"He who loves, loves himself," she says. "Mike brings out something in you. He brings out play."

Since they met in 1987, Mike and Jacquie have formed a strong and unique long-distance relationship. While Jacquie continues to pursue her career ambitions as a broadcaster, Mike continues to jet up to the North for his annual travels. They get together whenever and wherever they can, usually when Mike comes home and makes the pilgrimage to Quebec, or Jacquie the trip to Ottawa.

"I'm not jealous when he's away," says the woman who has as much energy and vitality as Mike. "It's never so long that it becomes a loneliness. I think he's had problems in previous relationships with women who didn't give him independence."

Most importantly, success is your own state of happiness and satisfaction with what you've achieved and how you've helped others.
– Mike Beedell

Mike had a previous close relationship that lasted two years. When it was ended by his female partner, he was devastated. "I just lay in bed for weeks and experienced intense emotional pain and depression. I kept asking Why? There was some crying, but it was more retrospect. I had to choose between my passion for adventuring and the relationship. It's very stressful when you're away for months on end.

"It was a great growing period for me, but a painful one. I finally realized that I had to move on. I couldn't just sit there and feel sorry for myself; it was too damaging. I guess it's part of the price you pay when your life is so transient."

Mike must now make one of the most difficult decisions of his life: whether to continue to pursue his career in the North, or settle down, get married and have a family. It's not an easy decision for Mike. He is a man stuck between two worlds; not only between North and South, but between opposing emotions.

It is surprising that a man who makes life-and-death decisions in an instant cannot make one with less life-threatening consequences, but this is part of the enigma of Mike. He does feel fear, especially a fear of failure.

"I have had relationships that I wanted to go on and on that have ended. So that's why, I guess, I'm afraid of this commitment, in case it ends for me once more. I definitely have a problem with rejection."

With breakfast now over, Mike moves to the living room. Seated by a roaring fire, he clasps yet another cup of ovaltine, this one sweetened with honey.

"Many people might not consider me a success," he says

as he chomps on an almond. "Success has to be an internal feeling. Although many people call success some level of monetary status, I'm virtually penniless. I measure my success by the richness of my experiences."

You must pursue your passions and pursue them with a sense of urgency because we're all here for a very short time.
– Mike Beedell

If experience is the measuring-stick of Mike's wealth, he is a billionaire. At 23, he had completed his first photographic book, *The Magnetic North*. He became the youngest author/photographer Oxford University Press had ever published. His work has appeared in "National Geographic" and dozens of the world's most prestigious magazines. One of his photos alone generated 15,000 telephone inquiries over a six-month period about adventuring in the North.

179

"I feel I have a responsibility to show the environment to people as it should be used, because I want this landscape preserved. I want people to appreciate and respect it. If I can have people experience even a smidgen of what I have, maybe they'll do their damnedest to protect it."

Mike has led over 1,000 people on wilderness journeys to some of the most remote regions in the world and has toured Australia, Tasmania, New Zealand, Mexico, Alaska and the Bahamas. He has driven across Canada three times, and in 1985 drove from the southern tip of the Baja Peninsula in Mexico to Tuktoyaktuk on the Beaufort Sea, high in the Canadian Arctic. He has also been down the Colorado River. His goals include doing books on Gatineau Park, the Qitdlarssuaq Expedition and the Northwest Passage. Renee Wissink has planted the seed of a dream which would see the two circumnavigate the northern polar world by dogsled and kayak. That journey, Mike estimates, would take at least two years.

In order to achieve, the first thing one must have is a boundless spirit and a fortitude that never backs down. Then, you have to believe in yourself.
– Mike Beedell

Nestled comfortably in his Victorian chair, Mike is as down-to-earth and disarming as they come. As he begins to unravel the stories of a lifetime of adventure, his speech quickens and increases in volume and inflection. Ignited like the fire beside him, he is fueled not by wood, but by film and fun.

"I'm pursuing something that I love to do, that I passionately want to do. I have to work incredibly hard to do it. I have to work very hard at my play and play very hard at my work. But there's no distinction between my work and my play because I'm pursuing a lifestyle; I'm not pursuing work. I could never conceive of doing some of the drudgery and terrible jobs that some people, unfortunately, have to do."

In many ways, Mike Beedell is a man stuck between two worlds. He has the savvy to survive in life-threatening conditions, but is sometimes lacking in the subtleties required to survive in urban life. He openly admits that the only thing that allows him to be a businessman is a calculator. While the statement is probably more a reflection on his math skills than on his business acumen, it may not be far from the truth. He is frequently late and sometimes disorganized. "I often have difficulty making the transition back to a modern lifestyle down here in the south. I occupy my time wonderfully, but I keep track of it poorly. I have a problem with time."

"You can't sit down in the fall and ask him to plan his year around your advertising," says Mike's long-time friend and business associate, Wally Schaber of Ottawa's Trailhead outdoor store. "He's not unreliable, but he looks at every year like it's his last."

Mike's other shortcomings, Wally says, include procrastination, an inability to say no that often causes him to burn himself out, a lack of self-discipline in the area of writing, weak marketing abilities and the tendency to take too many chances – both personal and in business. "It is sometimes a naive innocence, but he's getting street-wise," Jacquie maintains.

In recent years, Mike has matured in the face of some major personal challenges. Just days after his triumphant completion of the Northwest Passage, his father fell three metres from the second floor of the summer home John was building in Quebec. He landed on a bare concrete slab and suffered severe brain damage.

"I remember the first time I saw him in hospital," Mike says, as once again the life goes out of his voice. "I was devastated; he looked like he was 80 years old. He was in a wheelchair and babbling incoherently; he had no idea what he was saying. He knew about three words and just kept repeating them.

181

"It really hit me, like a sledgehammer in the chest. At first I saw him from a distance. I heard him talking and thought, Oh my God. I had to walk away and get hold of my emotions. It was such a shock to see him that way because he was so transformed from when I'd said, 'See ya later' just a few months before."

Miraculously, the former Olympian has made a fantastic recovery. He can now talk smoothly and coherently and is even painting, a skill usually reserved for the well-coordinated.

In spite of his hardships and successes, to this day Mike remains compassionate and sincere. There is no facade to Mike Beedell. In a society in which so many are masked, he is open and genuine. Though he may at times wear his heart on his sleeve, he has never changed his shirt.

"I like his vulnerability," says Jacquie. "He's extremely honest. There's something about Mike that isn't put on. He's really a big little boy."

It is this enduring authenticity and unpretentiousness that are two of Mike's finest qualities. They demonstrate a solid self-understanding that is unaffected by the perceptions of others. He simply is who he is. He has little desire for notoriety, at least in the sense of fame. If anything, he would probably like to be known more for his antics than his artistry.

"I think he likes, in one sense, to hold the public eye," says Renee. "He wants notoriety in the infamous sense. He wants to be known for his unusual sense of humour."

In Mike's kitchen, taped alongside a list of environmentally friendly products, is the following list of some of the keys to success:

1. Find your own particular talent.
2. Be big.
3. Be honest.
4. Don't worry about your problems.
5. Live with enthusiasm.
6. Don't let your possessions possess you.
7. Don't cling to the past.
8. Look up to people when you can – down to no one.
9. Assume your full share of responsibilities in the world.
10. Pray consistently and confidently.

These just may be the only rules he's ever really wanted to follow in his life.

The dream of making the first non-motorized transit of the Northwest Passage had been the goal of hundreds of

Arctic adventurers for over 400 years. Every one of them failed. Many had died trying.

When the Passage was finally navigated in 1906 by Norwegian Roald Amundsen, he did it with the assistance of an engine. Jeff MacInnis and Mike Beedell had no engine, only the wind and their ambition.

The "Polar Passage" expedition had been Jeff's idea. It had grown from his desire to experience the world of the early explorers. He had been introduced to that world in 1983, when his father led an expedition to find the "Breadalbane," the world's most northern-known shipwreck. Shortly after returning from that venture, Jeff decided to develop "Polar Passage" as a business project at university. It had grown into his primary focus.

For two years Jeff had recruited 30 corporate sponsors, more than 100 interested individuals and raised $150,000. When he finally asked Mike to join him as the expedition's official photographer and sole crew member, there were only a few months remaining before his scheduled departure.

183

"My first impression of Jeff was that he was incredibly young," Mike recalls; "he was only 22 then. I thought he was very courageous to take on this challenge because he knew very little about wilderness travel in the Arctic and what it would demand of us. But there is great genius in courage. Jeff is a visionary and a meticulous planner who pursues excellence with a passion."

Jeff's idea was to sail through the 3,840-kilometre ice-blocked passage, hopefully in a single summer. As the Arctic summer lasted a scant six to 12 weeks, this was more than an ambitious undertaking. Many regarded it as impossible. All knew it would be dangerous.

The history books are filled with grim stories of the Northwest Passage. Sir John Franklin and his entire 129-

man crew vanished there in 1845, causing one of the biggest and longest manhunts in English naval history. "How, in heaven's name, could two huge ships and their entire crews vanish without a trace?" British naval officials had asked. "Surely to God there must be floating debris somewhere? They can't just disappear."

English officials seated in the comfort of their homeland had no concept of the malignant nature of the Passage. It was not uncommon for ships to proceed into it only to be imprisoned in ice, not for days or weeks, but for years. During these times, the only means of making progress was by cutting the 3 to 4 metre-thick ice and inching forward a metre at a time, a process that was physically exhausting and extremely treacherous.

184

The pot at the end of the frozen rainbow was supposed to be the riches of the Orient. In its day, the quest to be the first to get through the Passage was like the modern-day race to the moon. That race was motivated by the forces of greed, patriotism and ego, elements to which the Arctic is totally indifferent.

To add to the challenge, neither the ships nor the men of the time were equipped for the rigours of the far North. The final nail in the coffin was that someone had underestimated the distance from Europe to Cathay by 11,200 km.

The Northwest Passage is widely acknowledged as the most difficult maritime route in the world. While tumultuous Cape Horn could instantly smash ships into little pieces with its colossal waves and fierce winds, the four-metre-thick Arctic ice would slowly drag men to their knees in prolonged agony.

First the ice would lock-in their ships. Then, over time, it would either exhaust their food supply or cause them to fall prey to scurvy. Some resorted to cannibalism. As crews faced the demoralizing Arctic winters of continual darkness, temperatures of minus 50°C and winds of up to 130 km an hour, their ships would be slowly crushed by the ice and, ultimately, swallowed up by the frigid sea. With their only source of shelter and security destroyed, seamen would soon succumb to exposure.

News of the ravages of the Passage was slow to get back to England. There were no phones in those days and mail service was largely by word-of-mouth. If no "mouth" returned, no news came back. Before long, the bottom of the Arctic Ocean between Button Point on Baffin Bay in the east and Amundsen Gulf on the Beaufort Sea in the west became littered with the wrecks of dozens of ships.

This was the land Mike and Jeff were headed into: "the land that devours ships." It was a destroyer not just of ships, but of dreams.

185

Jeff had a dream. He decided that sailing a catamaran (they used a Hobie Cat) was the key to succeeding where everyone else had failed. It was fast even in light winds, small enough to be paddled in no wind and sturdy enough to be dragged over the ice should they get locked in.

So on July 20, 1986, the pair set out from the mouth of the Mackenzie River on the Beaufort Sea in the Arctic Ocean. It didn't take long before they realized what they were up against. Delayed, as their forerunners had been, by foul weather and jagged ice, they were forced to stop on August 29, when the Arctic winter slammed the door.

"You only got half-way," a TV reporter had said. "Do you feel you've failed?"

"Not at all," Mike replied. "We did our very best and we're looking forward to completing it next year. The ice dictated that we couldn't make it all the way this year. We're very pleased with the section that we did do."

"I was actually elated that we would have another year to explore all that new area," Mike recalls.

Mike Beedell is disinterested with subjective worldly measures of achievement. He does not wish to be the first, fastest, wealthiest or most powerful. Instead, he has an unending fascination with the process of reaching a goal. He never describes any of his adventures as trips or expeditions to somewhere. They are always journeys, with no specific destination.

"To truly explore, I think you have to take your time and travel slowly and methodically; really open your eyes to what is around you. The end is an important point, but for me the integrity of the journey is what counts. With

KNOW WHAT IS IMPORTANT TO YOU

In our busy, crowded world, it is easy to lose touch with ourselves and our values. With so many possible roads to follow, it's sometimes impossible to decide in which direction to go. The choices can be overwhelming. This is when it is critical to know yourself and what is important to you, your values. What if you're unsure?

The method I recommend is to answer this question by asking yourself another question: If you had a whole day to do anything you wanted, what would it be?

Once you have an answer, figure out a way to do it. Better still, figure out a way to make a living at it every day. That way you'll be paid for what you love to do. And if you love what you're doing, you'll be successful at it.

The issue of how much money you can make in your chosen activity should not enter into your decision. Money may or may not be a healthy by-product of doing what you love. Even if you don't become a millionaire, you will be infinitely wealthier in terms of personal happiness. That's because you'll be in touch with what's important to you.

such a wonderful landscape, you have the responsibility to see, appreciate, experience and explore the unique character of the land. I am not interested in just tearing up a mountain to get to the summit."

It was this distinction between journeying and arriving that, from the start, made Mike and Jeff a curious combination. As a former national team downhill ski racer, Jeff's primary objective in taking up the challenge was to reach the goal in the fastest time possible. He did have a desire to experience the joy of discovery along the way, but it was not his primary motive. In his view, speed was safety. The dangers of sailing the Passage didn't afford the luxury of stopping to smell the roses.

Mike, on the other hand, wished to have an enriching experience by meeting Inuit families and sharing in their lifestyle. He wanted to feel the joy of the journey, to photograph and document the experience as much as possible. Together, the two men became a volatile version of the Arctic odd couple.

"I have the greatest respect for Mike," Jeff says. "We made an interesting team – the athlete and the artist. A tougher combination you couldn't have imagined. But the fact that we were different was not something awful. We came up with better decisions because of it."

With a crack, the only thing that separated them from an icy grave began to come apart. Electrified into action, Mike and Jeff heaved everything out of their rapidly sinking tent and stowed it onto their sailboat.

Outside, a severe storm had come out of the night, packing with it winds of close to 100 km per hour. Snow was being blown horizontally into their faces. There was thick fog. If there was one thing they didn't want now, it

You've got to aim for the horizon and never doubt that you'll make it.
– Mike Beedell

was to be forced outside into the elements.

They had no choice. The hockey-rink-sized pan of ice on which they had pitched their tiny shelter was breaking into pieces. With every passing minute, the piece of ice was being blown further and further out to sea. Out there, in the middle of the maelstrom, they knew there would be no hope. Their chances of rescue were nil 800 km north of the Arctic Circle in the heart of the Northwest Passage. The town of Resolute was 80 km to the north, but for all intents and purposes it might as well have been 800 km. In these conditions, there was no way a plane could even reach them, let alone land in the heaving pack ice.

188

Their only hope was to break camp and haul their 320-kg catamaran deeper into the pack. For Mike, there could have been no better training than the three-month Qit expedition he had completed just months before. Lean and strong from repeatedly hauling the heavy sled over sections the sled dogs had had no chance on by themselves, he was ready for the Passage.

Mike and Jeff pushed and pulled with everything they had. The wind tore through the boat's rigging, whistling with such intensity that both had to yell at the tops of their lungs just to make each other hear.

Well after midnight, after advancing a little over two kilometres, they were forced to stop in exhaustion. After hauling *Perception* up onto the largest pan of ice they could find, they put up the tent again and collapsed inside.

It was late August 1987. Now into their second summer of attempting to sail the Northwest Passage under wind power alone, Mike and Jeff again found themselves in the depths of an ice-choked hell. They slept fitfully that night. By 6:00 a.m. the wind had picked up. It got so strong they feared their boat would be blown right off their tiny island. Again they were being drawn out to sea.

Suddenly, the boat began to slide off the ice. They tried to hold it. If it went, they went.

Jeff and Mike scrambled to put on their survival suits, prepared the "sea seats" that would keep them afloat and upright if they had to take the plunge, and raised the antennas on their Emergency Locator Transmitters (ELT). In a frenzy, they got out some ice screws that had been brought to anchor the boat in an emergency. Mountaineers use them to anchor ropes to mountainsides.

The essence of achievement is to meet the challenge and do the best job possible. You will come out with a feeling that you have done your very best. That is success.
– Mike Beedell

189

The wind was now blowing up a terrific gale. As they turned the screws into the ice at a feverish rate, the boat periodically became airborne.

"I had to keep screwing the screws back into place because they'd get flushed out by the water," Mike recalls. "As Jeff steadied the boat, I'd have to stick my bare hands in the sea, which was just at the freezing point."

What made their situation even more tentative was the fog. It was so thick they had no idea where they were. Even if they could sail, they hadn't a clue in which direction to go. But just hanging on seemed senseless; they tried to raise sail. Instantly, the sheet began to tear. Their last option was gone. They couldn't sail and they couldn't stay. They were in the hands of fate. The seas began to build. In a matter of minutes, they swelled from 1.5 to 3.5 metres.

"I was thinking of scribbling down a message to my parents. 'Got to write a message down and get it in my waterproof sack,' I thought. I wanted to say: 'This is not a tragedy Mom and Dad. I was doing what I love to do best. This is the way I lived my life.'

Everyone has the ability to achieve great things – if they're willing to take the risks and that one step beyond.
– Mike Beedell

190

"Although things were looking very grim, I was planning for life and death. I started shooting photographs because I wanted to document it all. I wanted to make sure all the film was in a waterproof container so at least people would know what had happened right up to that point."

Jeff's mind was also racing. "The only thing I was focused on was how to stay alive: getting some food into us, directing the boat into the wind, watching our position on the ice."

They were on the absolute edge. In a moment, they'd be in the sea. Just then, a curious calm came over Mike. "I didn't see myself dying. I still thought we had great chances. I was completely petrified, but at the same time an incredible exhilaration came over me. It was an acute awareness, such a sharp-edged reality. It was a terrifying thrill."

Then, Mike's eye lit on a cliffscape through a break in the fog. It was land! "We hugged each other and screamed with glee. I just started laughing. I couldn't control myself. I just laughed and whooped." Incredibly, they were being blown toward shore. If their pan held together, they might make it.

Their celebration was short-lived. In an instant, they realized they were in even graver danger. "We started to hear a terrifying grinding sound as about four miles of heaving pack ice all around us began to pile up when the first pieces hit shore. I thought, 'Holy shit! We're going to be ground to a pulp.'"

Their ice pan was now the size of the boat – and getting smaller. As the massive forces of millions of tons of ice squeezed in around them, their pan could be crushed. If it was, they would be crushed with it.

Then a miracle happened. As the grinding, convulsing mass of ice moved closer to shore, it began to quell slightly. As it did, they saw their chance. "We pulled out the screws and put up a sail," Mike remembers. "We didn't care how bad it was blowing. We had nothing to lose."

When you take a calculated risk and commit yourself to it with all your soul, you begin to realize the great potential of the human spirit.
– Mike Beedell

Lying back over the wings of the boat, the two men sailed over the broken ice toward shore. In no time at all, they had travelled several kilometres. By mid-afternoon, after more hauling, they finally touched land. Struggling to hold back the tears, they dropped to their knees and kissed the ground. They were alive!

For the next 24 hours, they didn't move from that spot. They just put up the tent and lay there, completely spent. In their minds, they relived the drama over and over again, sometimes slipping off to sleep in mid-scene, only to awaken with a terrifying start believing they were just about to die.

191

Perversely, their ordeal wasn't over. When they awoke a day later, they realized that 16 km of jumbled, broken ice lay between them and open water. It took them days of hauling to reach it. When they eventually did, the boat was so badly riddled with holes from the endless dragging that it began to sink. As Mike bailed frantically, Jeff managed to sail to shore with just centimetres of freeboard to spare.

"I have a warped sense of humour when it comes to things like setbacks," Mike says. "I kind of laugh off the frustrations and say, 'We did our best today and we'll go for it tomorrow.'"

The next day there was another storm. It kept them tentbound for two more days. When they appeared bleary-eyed from their frozen enclave, they realized the obvious:

We have to be under heavy stress to grasp the real potential within us. We can't pull it out in everyday life.
– Mike Beedell

for the second year in a row the Arctic had won. Winter was upon them again. Although they had managed 1,600 hard-fought km through what is thought to be the worst section of the Passage, the brief summer was over.

Dejected, they radioed for pick-up. They would have to return again next year.

The Northwest Passage finally relented at 5:00 a.m. on Aug. 17, 1988, as the pair wearily sliced through the sea to a glorious dawn. Even until the last moment they were tested. Gusting winds threatened to knock them over a few times, but after 100 days of fine-tuning over three summers, Jeff's helmsmanship was superb. As they moved, the spray from the twin hulls of their craft made rainbows in the first rays of the day.

It was a picture-perfect finish, the kind sailors dream about. With the wind at their backs and the sun in their faces, Mike Beedell and Jeff MacInnis sailed out the eastern end of the Northwest Passage and into history. They had succeeded in doing what had never been done before. And they had done it together.

With sails full and spirits at an all-time high, they celebrated. Pulling up their Hobie Cat high and dry on understated Button Point, they walked into a lush green valley nearby. Mike knew of the site from personal explorations years earlier. In a centuries-old Thule ruin, they dropped their sleeping bags. The Thule were the forefathers of the Inuit, and master hunters of the bowhead whale. The two sailors were protected from the wind by sturdy, four-foot-high walls of rock and whalebone. All around them orange lichen crept silently over the stones. It had taken centuries to grow.

"It was very special to sleep on the platforms where generations of families had lived," Mike remembers. "I thought of them dreaming their dreams and pursuing their lives in the most demanding place on earth. Here we were within the confines of something they had created out of bone, stone and sod, so many centuries earlier."

It occurred to Jeff that they were in a place as old or older than the dream of sailing the Northwest Passage. But although they had endured tremendous hardship, Mike did not have an oversized sense of what they had done.

"To believe that we were facing scenarios like those of the early explorers is ludicrous. With all our modern amenities, we could not possibly have faced the hardships they did. We flew south every winter and radioed out every day. But we could get a taste – a feeling – of these earlier endeavours."

193

Comparisons aside, there was still magic in the moment. "I can remember the great look on Jeff's face and both of us smiling at each other, saying, 'We've done it.' I started snapping pictures of Jeff with the sunrise coming up. There was a great look of calm on his face."

At last the athlete had finished his race. The artist, as usual, wanted to paint the whole scene. Some things, it seemed, did not change.

Button Point marks the easternmost tip of Bylot Island, just north of Baffin Island where the Arctic Ocean meets the Atlantic. A 300-metre-high cliff rises sharply from the sea. Thousands of seabirds scour the food-rich waters nearby.

The point itself is a barren, windswept spot. That morning, however, it took on a different character. For Mike at least, it became home. That night he slept as soundly as he would have in his own bed.

The next day, his mother, Ann, arrived with an Inuit guide and film crew. "Mom had been instrumental in my success," Mike says. "She'd put up with all my travels and with me living in different parts of the country or in my van for months at a time. I always considered my home wherever she was. She helped with my business and slide library. It produced much of my income. Although she worried about my pursuits, she rarely forced her views on me. She somehow realized that I had to do it."

"Mike's a very focused person," Ann says. "Even as a child he could set a goal and achieve it, even though it often wasn't the goal we wanted. Still, he went his own way. I accepted the fact that that's what he wanted to do."

194

The thing that Mike wanted to do that morning was get his mother to the Thule site. They had to cross a creek to get there, but Ann didn't have proper footwear. So Mike picked her up, put her on his back and carried her across the stream. For so many years, he knew his parents had carried him, and now, for one moment, it was his turn. It was just a small return on their investment, but it meant so much to Ann.

"I went up north with the feeling that Mike would come back. When he climbed Mt. Logan, I was physically ill. But on Button Point, it was total happiness. I knew that this was a big thing in Michael's life. So I put some money aside each month. I wanted to see a part of what meant so much to him."

Mike took his mother around the Thule site, explaining in great detail what each bone was and how the house had been constructed. It was the kind of stuff parents dream about; one of those moments when all the nighttime feedings and diaper changes, and parent-teacher interviews paid off. And it happened because way back in that field behind their house, Ann and John had just let Mike be Mike.

The journey had been a personal passage for Mike. "I learned once more the incredible potential for the human spirit to endure all kinds of duress and still come out smiling and ready to take on greater achievements. All the horizons, the feeling of finishing and 'Wow, What we've accomplished!' If you looked at the whole picture at once and what was involved, it would completely exhaust you. But when you take it one step at a time, when you take one increment and work away at it, you can achieve great goals.

"I also learned a great deal of patience; new-found patience. It was the first time I had travelled with somebody who had very different views on life and very different ways of doing similar things. I learned new perspectives that gave me a more balanced outlook on how to pursue excellence. I learned a lot from Jeff's years of work to produce the journey. He worked incredibly hard to get things rolling long before I became involved. And he was absolutely tenacious in his pursuit.

"I also learned a lot about sharing – about sharing my knowledge and my experiences, and about how rewarding and mutually beneficial that sharing can be."

On that obscure piece of treeless gravel in the middle of nowhere, it all came down to sharing. When they had a quiet moment together, Mike took his mother aside and gave her a long, tender hug. Then he held her hand as they looked out on the Atlantic.

The joyous journeyer in Mike Beedell struck home after a brief whitewater canoeing outing one spring. Years after the "Polar Passage," we hauled our boat ashore after shooting some rapids in Ottawa, then we walked briskly back upstream.

There was something different about Mike just then. In the morning when we'd left his chalet, there'd been a change in his appearance. He seemed to transform when he put his outdoor clothes on: his face became narrower, his cheeks more drawn.

"I know I have a great deal to do in life while I'm here," he said. "I see my purpose in life as being one of celebrating the human spirit and learning about what we can achieve under very demanding situations."

More than his words, it was his eyes I most noticed. They became keen, catching every movement, shadow and scattering of light. His soaked head and face were so alive, his voice so vibrant. His cheeks glowed and his eyes sparkled. Energized by the power of nature, his spirit had instantly intensified. It was like putting a match to fireworks; everything lit up.

"I wish we could have done that all day," he proclaimed as a boyish grin spread across his face. "I suppose we could

UNDERSTAND YOUR VALUES

Commitment will be critical to our future. As the number and significance of obstacles and challenges increase, it will be necessary for us to possess a commensurate level of commitment. Without it, we will be overcome. With it, we will triumph.

True commitment goes beyond determination and tenacity, however. It is rooted in your values. Values are the foundation of commitment. Without them, no house of any strength can be built.

have stayed and played in the rapids, but I'd have preferred a full day's journey."

"I love the whimsical feeling of freedom," he said smiling. "The wanderlust is in me.

"The thing that's so special to me is the actual exploration, of going around the next bend, of seeing what's beyond. That, for me, is the greatest joy."

Just then Mike's Arctic achievements were whisked away. What replaced them was a true vision of the man – and the boy. He was an achiever to be sure, but it wasn't what he'd done that impressed you the most; it was who he was.

> *I was once, I declare, a Stone-Age man,*
> *And I roamed in the cool of a cave;*
> *I have known, I will swear, in a new life-span*
> *The fret and the sweat of a slave:*
> *For far over all that folks hold worth,*
> *There lives and there leaps in me*
> *A love of the lowly things of earth,*
> *And a passion to be free.*
> – Robert Service

197

Chapter 4:
THE TRIUMPH OF TEAMWORK

So closely interwoven have been our lives, our purposes and experiences that, separated, we have a feeling of incompleteness – united, such strength of self-assertion that no ordinary obstacles, differences, or dangers ever appear to us insurmountable.
– Elizabeth Cady Stanton

Profile on
Sharon Wood
of Canmore, Alberta

*First North American woman
to climb Mount Everest*

The Mission

I know that we reaped the benefit of those hard-earned lessons on the first attempt, and took them and used them to our advantage on this one. I think the core of people that came from the 1982 Canadian Mount Everest Expedition had a mission. We all had missions, but they had a real mission.
– Sharon Wood

Suddenly, Barry let out a muffled cry from under his oxygen mask. He pointed up. Crashing down towards them like so many bowling balls were rocks the size of breadboxes. There was no time to think – only to react.

Trapped in her hypoxia-induced inertia, Sharon Wood dropped to the ice-anchor at her feet. She had an immediate flashback to the year before when she had been ripped off her feet on the highest mountain in Peru. There, a small rock had shattered her shoulderblade in a second. She knew how much damage even the smallest rock could do, but here at 26,500 feet on the north face of the world's tallest mountain, she was powerless to do anything but pray.

Miraculously, the rocks went plummeting past.

Snapped from her sluggishness by a sudden surge of adrenalin, she became acutely lucid. Glancing around, things looked terrible. This May 19, 1986, the north face of Mount Everest was vicious. She, Barry Blanchard, Kevin

Doyle and Dwayne Congdon struggled against the weight of 30-kg packs. As the wind tore at them, they staggered with every step in the rarefied air. Like some mountain-made snow gun, the gale blasted snow crystals right through their zippers, driving cold to their cores. At times, Sharon would look up to see everyone face-down in the snow, cowering against the relentless force of the wind. It threatened to propel them into airborne oblivion.

"If this had been any other mountain, I would probably have turned back right there," Sharon recalls.

"It was like a statement from Everest: 'Commit or go home, but don't hesitate.'"

She did hesitate – they all did, if only for a moment. It seemed the whole day had been an exercise in extended agony. It had started at 9:00 a.m. in a ferocious gale and deteriorated as the day went on. Just minutes before, at 5:00 p.m., they had left the security of the three-mile-long fixed ropes. Now they were proceeding into the infamous Hornbein Couloir, a massive rock gash that slashes down the north face of Everest. Varying from one to nine metres in width, it was an eerie passage. The scattered remains of old tents and shredded scraps of rope from previous expeditions hung like crystallized cobwebs from the walls. Combined with these ominous spectres of broken dreams, the couloir could have been the highest junk yard on earth.

The temperature was minus 35° C. With near-hurricane-force winds deep-sixing the wind chill to minus 40° and 50° C, the atmosphere of the place grew even more treacherous and sinister.

The Hornbein serves as a huge funnel for snow and debris tumbling off the top of the mountain. Perched at a 45-degree angle, it is like a gauntlet thrown at the foot of climbers. It is also the gateway to the summit of

201

"Chomolungma" – the Tibetan name for Everest, meaning "Mother Goddess of the World."

The goddess was more demonic than benevolent that day. And while the oceanic view may have been spectacular from where they were, not one of the frozen four paid any attention to it. They were too preoccupied with hanging on.

Time was running out. The 13-member expedition had been battling the mountain for two months and was more than a week behind schedule. Within days, the summer monsoon would be upon them, if it wasn't already. At lower elevations, the monsoon would bring torrential rains. But at this altitude, that rain would turn to horrific snowfalls that would make safe climbing impossible. Add to that the fact that the climbing permit the Chinese government had granted the team would expire in about a week and things did indeed look bleak. If the climbers were to mount a summit bid, it was now or never. They literally and figuratively had their backs against a wall.

There was even more to it than time. An American team further out on the face had reached the same elevation as they had and was on a more direct line to the summit. They, too, had a female member on their team – Annie Whitehouse, from Albuquerque, New Mexico. She, along with her colleagues, was also hoping to make a summit bid. If she succeeded before Sharon, she would become the first North American woman to climb Everest.

After ferrying over three tons of equipment, food and supplies up and down the mountain an equivalent of almost 70 vertical km in oxygen-starved air, the team had established a camp at the base of the mountain's massive summit pyramid. But even at Camp 5 – at 7,775 m – they were still more than a vertical kilometre from the top, which scraped the sky at 8,848 m – almost nine kilometres above sea level.

Level of commitment equals level of performance. **– Sharon Wood**

By now, only four climbers were still well enough to keep pushing high on Everest. The rest had been forced to withdraw because of exhaustion and sickness. Drawn, frostbitten and with eyes devoid of any spark, they lay around as if they were dead. The west ridge route up Everest was proving why it had never been climbed in its entirety from the northern, Chinese side. And here they were trying to do it with precious little time, energy and human power left. It was a time for the extraordinary.

"Your concept of what is reasonable to do and what isn't reasonable to do in the mountains is significantly altered when you enter the realm of Mount Everest," says Sharon. "What you think is possible is pushed. That's the exciting part about it. You naturally start doing things beyond the realm of reasonable because you're in the grand arena; the place where peak performance counts. You do take risks. You do step out a bit more. To be successful, you have to try that much harder; you have to hang it out that much more and that's exactly what we did by entering that couloir. But once we did, we stepped over a significant threshold onto an entirely new level of commitment."

Sharon Wood had had serious doubts about leaving the fixed rope. In climbing, that 5.5-mm-thick piece of nylon is much more than a safety line. It is a type of physical and psychological lifeline to the security of the known world, an umbilical cord to reality. To come to the end of your rope in high altitude mountaineering is to take your first steps into the unknown. Every step is a precisely calculated risk. The higher you climb, the more delicate be-

203

comes the balance between your internal energies and the external demands of your environment. Here, there is no room for recklessness. There is only room for respect.

"You don't have the resources you have at sea level, either mentally or physically," says Sharon, "and what you do have you use very efficiently. You know the smallest mistake can have very serious consequences.

"The focus and presence is exhilarating. Everything you have flows into the next step – everything."

This was the world into which the four climbers were moving. They had traversed Everest's north wall to the base of the couloir at 8,080 m. But because of poor weather and the debilitating effects of altitude, even with the aid of artificial oxygen it had taken them six hours to travel just one kilometre. They were now in the area the Europeans call "The Death Zone" – the place where the air is so thin that the slightest mishap can have fatal consequences.

Suddenly, Dwayne, who had apparently not seen the rockfall, pulled up beside Barry and Sharon. "Well, what are we waiting for?" he declared in an uncharacteristically aggressive tone. "Let's go."

Barry, Sharon and Kevin looked at each other in disbelief. Dwayne was usually a quiet, habitually shy man who was forever cautious.

"I didn't see it as horrendous and I wasn't reckless," Dwayne says. "I felt, 'Ya, we can go up here.'

"Maybe I wasn't in touch with what was happening. I don't know where the confidence I had came from, but it was there. At the same time, there was a lot of power in the back of my head to really push it, to see it through. Whether or not that was just raw ambition or a combination of that and knowing where I had been before, I didn't know, but I did know it was going to take something extra."

Dwayne's goal, along with his three companions, was to erect one last tent part way up the couloir. It would become Camp 6 and from it, Sharon and he could go for the top. Without it, the team would be defeated.

Barry cranked the flow on his oxygen set up to four litres a minute and felt rejuvenated. Like the rest, he had been going extremely hard all day and was very, very tired. He knew that he had become a Sherpa for Dwayne and Sharon. He didn't like it, but he accepted it.

"You know before you start the expedition that there's a chance you're going to end up being in that role. But I just felt good that we were finally going to make an attempt at the summit. I was still very committed to the trip. It was exciting to see it finally happening."

Somehow, they dug out a tent platform a short way up the couloir. Kevin was too weak to do anything but struggle with the challenge of anchoring his pack. At sea level, it probably would have taken him 10 seconds, but here, strung-out in the empty air, buffeted by the wind and exhausted from the day's battle, it took him 10 minutes. By now, it was 10 p.m. and darkness had fallen. After helping Sharon and Dwayne begin to put up the tent, Barry and Kevin turned their backs and left to go down to Camp 5.

But before they did, Barry turned to say one last thing: "I love you guys," he said through the ferocious howl of the wind. "Go for it. Make it and get back down safely."

With that, Kevin and Barry disappeared into the night.

As Dwayne watched the beams of their headlamps slowly vanish from sight, he felt a tingle go up his spine.

"If I had any feeling, it was that little quiver. There we were, just the two of us; a tinge of fear, a tinge of loneliness."

Exhausted, Sharon and Dwayne finally got to bed around midnight. But they did not sleep in the true sense, they simply slipped into a semi-conscious state they imagined to be a brief respite from their environment.

Unknown to them, the door to the summit of Everest was slowly opening in the darkness above them. But to pass through it and return alive would take an effort they could not have imagined.

Struggling under the heavy weight of her extra load, "Woody" makes her way slowly up the trail. "Now I know what it's like to be out of shape," she quips. "I'm trying to keep my heart rate under 120."

It seems a startling statement to come from such an experienced high-altitude mountaineer, but it is true.

Three years after Everest, Sharon Wood, 32, is married and six and a half months pregnant. This day she is plodding her way up a hiking trail above her home in Canmore, Alberta, methodically placing one foot in front of the other the way she had so many times while attacking windblown snowslopes. She used to run on this same trail to train for Everest. As the glorious summer sun filters

---

STAND OUT WITH ENTHUSIASM

Enthusiasm is energy. And it can be tapped. If everyone else is dragging themselves through the day, an injection of enthusiasm can work wonders. If at first it is rebuffed, persevere. Those who are genuinely enthusiastic are genuinely valued in any organization, in any situation. If you want to be valued, be of value.

It is sometimes hard to be youthfully enthusiastic in our everyday life. Traffic jams, foul weather and irritable co-workers can make it extremely difficult. Yet those who are enthusiastic stand out immediately. And, as with great leaders, there is a gravitation to their enthusiastic energy.

through the pines, she forces out a smile and pretends she isn't feeling the effects of 14 extra kg.

Carrying extra weight is nothing new to her, except that usually she can take it off in a few seconds by removing her pack. Now, however, at 75 kg and gaining at a rate of about half a kilo every two weeks, this is a climb of a different sort. Accustomed to being in superb shape with a resting heart rate of just 38 or 39 (an average person's is usually about 70), she forces her 5-foot, 10-inch frame up the slope as the sweat begins to bead on her forehead.

Halfway up the trail, she pauses for a sip from a cool mountain stream. As she squats, knees apart and belly bulging over her feet, I have to hold her on the shoulder to keep her from losing her balance and plunging face-first into the icy water.

207

"It's like having Christmas dinner every day," remarks her husband of one year, Chris Stethem. "Except you can't work it off. You have to wait."

Sharon has been waiting three years for life to get back into balance after Everest. The delay has been an almost constant ordeal for her, and since her return she has been forced to come to grips with attention and acclaim she could not have predicted.

"It's been a long, hard struggle for me to actually interpret the experience of what Everest was, what Everest is, in myself, because other people were so busy interpreting it for me," says the climber with the quiet composure. "I had this hang-up with the media, with people who wanted to provide other answers before I was ready. It's been a helluva struggle."

In retrospect, Sharon's situation is somewhat ironic. Her whole life, this private, independent and staunch individualist spent much of her time trying to climb away

Success is just a launching pad for the next challenge.
– Sharon Wood

from mainstream society. Now, all of a sudden, she is thrust right into it by her own achievements.

"It has been difficult for her," says Sharon's best friend, Marni Virtue. "It was lonely. She dealt with that loneliness by finding something that was important to her – public speaking, family and home."

Sharon Wood is an enigma. She is a dramatic contrast between sensitivity and strength – quiet but assertive, gentle but tough. Her unobtrusive, polite disposition is coupled with a fierce desire to escape complacency, unlock limits and discover her true potential. She is like a sleeping tigress lounging in the shade; at first glance she seems pretty docile. But wave a challenge in front of her and she awakes.

Today, Sharon makes dozens of professional public speaking presentations each year. Together with her husband and their soon-to-be family, these three things have become the new focal points in her life after Everest. But it has been a long, hard road to the realization that there were other equally exciting parts of her life worth exploring besides her upper limits at the top of the world.

"People come up to me after my talks and say, 'Jeez, what's next? Now that you've climbed the highest mountain in the world, what is there left to do?'

"It turns something in me every time I hear that because they don't understand that more than anything the biggest conquest for me is having accepted how to take all those lessons I've learned through my climbing and put them to use in other endeavours. The bottom line is reaping that satisfaction inside myself."

For some, the pressures of constant media attention, never-ending requests for speaking engagements and lack

208

of privacy might have been too much. For Sharon, they haven't been. She has endured them, learned from them, but not embraced them. She remains to this day as humble, soft-spoken and driven as ever. It's just that she's shifted her focus. "I have one friend in particular who accuses me of selling out," she says, as her eyes reveal uneasiness. "He says, 'Your best days are over. You've done it, you're finished, you're not going back.' He just doesn't understand.

"Part of my identity used to hinge on what I did in the mountains. I don't feel like I'm confined or chained to that identity anymore. I don't need to be 'Sharon Wood, The Climber.' I don't need to be 'Sharon Wood, The Anything,' and that's the greatest and most fulfilling thing I derived from the Everest experience. I need to be fulfilled within myself; I need to be satisfied with what I'm doing. I need to be happy, and I need to feel I'm doing things for other people."

I'm not just a climber. The most important things to me are affecting other people positively, helping other people become confident and helping people see life as being more exciting and more of an adventure than it may appear sometimes. And to be a good parent. Success is contentment. **– Sharon Wood**

209

In spite of claims to the contrary, Sharon Wood is still climbing. Today we are on our way to a rock climb at the bottom of spectacular Chinaman Peak. It is July 2, the day after Canada Day, the nation's birthday. As thousands of vacationers pour into the Rockies, there is a festive atmosphere.

The forest is alive with families and small children playing by the spring – and glacier-fed lakes of the area. As Sharon and Chris gradually climb higher, the view of the Rockies becomes breathtaking. It takes Chris back to a special moment he shared with Sharon on a summit in Peru just a year earlier.

"When we sat up on top of the peak, it was fabulous. It was like sitting in our living room with a superb view. It wasn't euphoric, it was peaceful – just the two of us. It's unusual in a relationship to share that. It's often one person or the other."

From the very beginning, Chris and Sharon have enjoyed a special kinship. He is an internationally known natural hazards consultant who specializes in snow avalanche protection. They met at an avalanche course he was conducting in the resort town of Whistler, British Columbia, in the late '70s. They share a love not just for each other, but for the mountains.

"When I first met her, I thought she was very independent, athletic and strong-willed," he says. "But I see the sensitive side to her, too. That's a pleasant surprise to many people. They expect this hulk from Wrestlemania. Actu-

---

SUCCESS IS WHAT YOU SAY IT IS!

Society has established visible indicators of success. These include material security and wealth, fame and power. None of our adventure achievers use these scales. They value personal contentment, satisfaction in themselves, integrity, happiness and independence more than anything. More important for them is the satisfaction and deep sense of self worth they acquire from their achievements. They have little need to prove anything to anybody because they have proved it to themselves. They are, as psychologists say, "self-actualized."

The "adventure attitude" challenges us to re-think our conventional standards of success. It isn't, at least to the people you've read about in this book, an external, objective condition. It's an internal, subjective reality. But it is still measurable: by how we feel inside ourselves. Sharon Wood says: "Success is contentment."

ally, she would rather agonize over a field mouse than lionize a tiger who set the speed record."

Woody is not setting a speed record this afternoon. Sporting a light green sweatshirt, turquoise-coloured nylon track pants and Nikes, she blends in beautifully with the tourists and, except for the pack instead of a camera, might have pulled up in a motorhome on her way to nearby Banff.

At the base of a vertical and slightly overhanging wall of limestone, Chris and Sharon come to a stop. Suddenly, not more than 3 m away, a solitary climber is lowering himself by a rope, descending like a spider on a thread. He alights without a sound on the moss-covered ground at the bottom of the cliff.

"Howdy!" declares none other than Barry Blanchard, fresh down from a trip to the top of yet another rock wall. "How ya doin' Woody?"

Sharon's face lights up. It is a meeting of old friends.

"How ya gonna climb this?" Barry asks, peering incredulously at Sharon's round figure. "You have to hug the rock, but shaped the way you are..."

"No problem!" Sharon counters brightly, looking at the 20-m wall as if it were mere child's play. "I've changed my style. I climb like a short person."

I don't know what that means, but I'm about to find out.

Donning a full-body harness, she ties into one end of the rope as Chris ties into the other. He proceeds to move slowly up the face, anchoring the rope as he climbs. It is Sharon's job to stop his fall should he come off.

I watch with hesitation, trying to visualize the kind of stress such an event might put on her harness and body. I am no obstetrician and the thought of her going into premature labour does nothing for my confidence. I won-

211

Childbirth is the ultimate physical challenge. It's so underrated.
– Sharon Wood

der if there is a doctor within earshot.

"I really like Sharon a lot," Barry had said to me once. "I guess I like the delicate side to her. She's very kind and quite gentle, although a lot of the time she's a very motivated and driven person. Once you get past her armour, I like the sensitivity in her. I think she'll make a great mother."

"Men, people, tend to stand up and recognize things that women are doing in the physical realm, even if it's not done in the same way as men," she says, as a breeze blows back her straight, shoulder-length hair. "To actually find my own personal role – not the role that is expected of me, not the new role of supermom or superwoman that is being pushed on me – is a very big challenge. I have to find a balance, somehow find myself in it, in spite of all the conditioning, the expectations."

In no time, Chris reaches the top and Sharon slowly lowers him on the rope. Now, it is her turn.

"I want to raise my child as a free spirit and I want to help that kid, as much as possible, find its place," she says, as she checks her harness two and three times to ensure everything is in place. "I hope it's not high-altitude climbing though, because I know how lucky I've been. I know that to become a successful high-altitude climber, you have to learn through trial and error, and I've just come out on top."

Just as she is about to start for the top of this, yet another rock face, an unsuspecting hiker happens by. Staring in disbelief at what she sees, she inquires embarrassedly of Sharon: "Are you PREGNANT?"

"Yes, I am," Sharon replies matter-of-factly, then, without hesitation, turns immediately to her husband and says:

"Now, Chris, keep a snug rope. I don't want to fall very far in this harness, if I can help it."

Women have some wonderful strengths that we can tap into if we would just quit trying to be like men.
– Sharon Wood

The climb Sharon is proposing to do is rated at a difficulty of 5.10, an expert climb under the best conditions. But she is six and a half months pregnant and carrying 14 extra kilos; I shudder at the thought.

Slowly Woody starts up.

"Sharon went climbing on our wedding day," declares Chris, as he watches her intently. "She made me promise that I wouldn't be late, drink or smoke.

"So I'm pacing back and forth drinking 7-Up, and half an hour later she shows up with Scotch on her breath. Apparently she had to climb through the third-storey window of her sister's home in Vancouver so she could get started on getting herself ready for the wedding. Then, I guess, they decided to celebrate a little early."

Within minutes, Sharon flashes up the route. As she reaches the most difficult section, the one where Chris had plastered his abdomen against the limestone, Sharon simply turns her belly sideways and scampers up the route.

The words of 1982 Everest summiteer, Pat Morrow, echo in my mind: "As a climber, Sharon's one of the best I've ever seen and ever climbed with. She's unbelievable, really smooth, really safety-conscious. It's her trade."

It may have been her only trade at one time, but it is less so now. Time, experience and Everest have given Sharon a whole new perspective on climbing, success and achievement.

"I read this fascinating piece of fiction by Norman Mailer once, in which a mentor told his understudy that a man who masters competency in climbing is the master of

213

I believe that we're all climbing our own mountains, that every striving individual or organization is climbing its own mountains in pursuit of its own goals.
– Sharon Wood

214

his own will," she says. "He went on to say that in climbing there is a danger of becoming addicted, addicted to success, to doing something just a little harder. If you fail, it drives you on even harder; if you succeed, it's not quite enough. And it all ends up with the same result, so you just have to keep going and going and going. I almost fell into that trap myself.

"I don't have a need to work as hard now as I did then to look over the edge. I have different priorities now, but I did get a good look over that edge."

Today, Sharon has moved onto other mountains, one of which has been her marriage. As Chris gently lowers her down, the strength of their relationship becomes apparent. There is a tremendous mutual caring there, a deep love which has established itself over a decade of knowing each other.

"Relationships are a struggle," Sharon admits. "There are distractions, such as work, who vacuums or washes the floor, who takes the lead in initiating a discussion. They are dumb, small things; they're all distractions. But when you're climbing a mountain, it's quite simple; it's very tangible, it's visible."

An invisible asset within their marriage is that Chris is diabetic. Although this might seem like a disadvantage to most people, it isn't to Sharon.

"The diabetes turned Chris into a fighter," she says, "and that's what attracted me to him. He is very alive and strong."

"I remember once doing an ice climb with her and being so exhausted and weak because of my condition that I thought I might die," Chris recalls. "I felt like I was going to throw up, but – in this very assured tone – all she said was, 'You'll be okay in a few minutes.' And I was. She has a well-developed sense of purpose, but she doesn't step on people."

Sharon's friend, Marni Virtue, agrees.

"She brings out the best in me. She makes me feel good and she does it in a way that doesn't make her look better. She makes me feel like I'm climbing my own Everest. She allows people their own power."

One of the keys to Sharon's ability to motivate others is a strong sense of her own individuality. Friends and acquaintances say she knows and follows her own heart with passionate conviction. She is able to inspire others to loftier goals because she continues to aspire to them herself.

215

"I'm not sitting back on my laurels," she says. "I'm working very hard on some other things. They're more difficult to recognize because they're not as tangible and they're underrated. Having a child is a highly underrated challenge."

Sharon's drive extends into and beyond motherhood. She has applied it to her public speaking and in her marriage. Recently, she used it to write a magazine article about her Everest experience, for which she won a western Canadian magazine award.

"I don't know what it is about Sharon," Marni says. "She just won't settle for second best."

As a child growing up in Halifax, and later in Vancouver, Sharon Wood appeared to be very much one of the crowd. It wasn't long, however, before others discovered she was different.

In order to make a difference, we have to be willing to leave our comfort zones. In doing so, we start to struggle. It's in the struggle that we're given the opportunity to tap our reserves. This is when we see our personal best – in the struggle.
– Sharon Wood

216

"I hated school because I couldn't conform. I couldn't do what they wanted me to do," she says bluntly. "I just didn't have the same mind as the other kids, it seemed. I was supposed to do all my writing inside the margins, and I never could figure out the rules, so I always got slapped around. I thought you could write anywhere on the paper as long as you got your message across. I didn't do it right, so I would get rapped and slapped. The strap and the ruler were really popular items in the province of Nova Scotia at that time."

Sharon lived in Halifax until she was 7. The youngest of four children, she spent many a day hiking with her father in the woods of eastern Canada. Stan Wood was a pilot on an aircraft carrier in the Canadian Navy and Air Force. It was his job to land his propeller-driven plane on the swaying deck of the ship in full seas. Later in life he would turn his aviation skills to crop-dusting, fire-bombing and bush flying – equally dangerous vocations. It was from her father that Sharon had her first introduction to risk-taking.

In 1964, Stan was stationed in Vancouver, so the whole family moved west. It was here that Sharon's problems at school became more acute.

In Vancouver, Sharon was surrounded by houses on all sides. She felt trapped, lost in the groundswell of buildings, paved streets and people. She was terribly insecure. Her school was crowded and impersonal, and her teachers were simply too overworked to be able to provide individual attention.

"I felt like one of 2,000 very average kids being squeezed through the same hole. I couldn't accept being an average kid. I wanted to make a difference."

Adventure isn't an experience. It's an attitude that goes with an experience.
– Sharon Wood

Sharon discovered that she was different, but not in the way she had wanted. Skinny, flat-chested and something of an "ugly duckling," her friends teased her about boys and bras. She responded by becoming something of a loner. She played lead flute in the band and did a lot of drawing.

"My father would say the most important thing is to be an individual and know you're an individual before you are anybody else. I think he really encouraged me to think for myself and he realized that I was a free thinker, or a different thinker.

"My mom gave me a lot of positive reinforcement for doing anything, whether I was cutting pictures out of magazines or scribbling something on the walls.

"At school, that creativity was seriously quelled because I was forced to do or draw what I was told. I wasn't allowed to work with a medium I was good at working with. I had to do it their way. So I always felt very confined.

"When I'm with kids now, I encourage them to be and to think as freely as possible and to do things out of the ordinary. Like if we're walking down the street, it's okay to walk on top of the fence instead of on the sidewalk, or to step on the cracks instead of inside the squares."

One of Sharon's earliest explorations into adventure came on her bicycle at age 12. She used to ride it to her grandparents' home every weekend through downtown Vancouver, a distance of over 32 km that she usually did alone.

217

"I remember deliberately, methodically teaching myself how to ride. I started experimenting with speed thresholds and how fast I could turn when I was going really fast. I lived on a hill. At the bottom of the hill there was a sharp turn. I would try to go around it going faster and faster, each time letting go of the brakes a little sooner, a little sooner."

One day this almost led to a serious accident. While she poured over the handlebars like some downhill ski racer hell-bent for the bottom, a car suddenly stopped at the corner. Struggling to hold her line, she gripped the handlebars as if she would crush them. With everything she had, she leaned into the turn and with the front wheel jumping along the pavement, miraculously escaped within an inch of her life.

It was an incident that might have terrified the average child. But she was far from average. Throughout her life, even from an early age, she had the ability to maximize the learning from every situation, whether negative or positive, and use it to her advantage.

"What I remember most was going back to my house afterwards and disciplining myself. I wrote hundreds of times in a book something about the importance of thinking before you act."

Because Sharon did not fit in at school, drugs and delinquency became a temporary method of being accepted by her peers.

"I was very good at pushing the limit in anything I did. I could take more drugs and stay out later than some of the other students. And I became an experienced shoplifter. There was good adventure in that – really good adventure.

"I started making money on the side by taking pants. I was skinny, so I could wear one or two pairs of jeans inside a big pair of pants. I would sell them at school. I became a juvenile delinquent."

Then came the turning point. At 15, Sharon overdosed on LSD. She wandered the streets of Vancouver experiencing vivid hallucinations that left her weak, terrified and alone. Oddly enough, it was here that she began to turn toward Everest.

"It was a terrifying experience, which I believe affects my life right through to today," she says, as the wrinkles on her high forehead show the pain. "I never want to get that low again. It makes me strive for high quality, positive experiences, and to make life as good as I can because I've seen how ugly it can get."

All of a sudden it seemed like Sharon's life was coming apart. About the same time as her overdose, she got caught shoplifting. She had a huge shopping bag full of stolen goods.

We can't just drift through life and let the current carry us. There are demanding situations where you have to start paddling a little bit harder to alter your course, your speed, or your direction. Ultimately, we ARE in control. **– Sharon Wood**

219

Confined for a few hours in a detention cell until her harried and confused mother, Peggy, could come and get her, Sharon's life came into sharp focus when she heard the cell door slam shut behind her. All of a sudden, the free spirit was caged.

"The bars really brought it all home. I was only in there for a matter of hours, but it might just as well have been years for me. It was then and over the weeks that followed that I realized I was going to have to take responsibility for my own actions, that I could affect what experiences I was going to have. I had to take responsibility for my own life. It was a huge revelation. It's like I'm the writer, the director, and the actor in my own play."

> *It's too easy just to react to situations in your life, instead of creating them.*
> – Sharon Wood

It was from this realization that Sharon began to shed her despair and grow. Her mother was by her side the entire way, offering love, support and encouragement wherever she could.

"I wasn't getting enough of what I needed," Sharon recalls. "I didn't know what I needed at the time, but now I do. It was adventure."

Sharon was never charged with shoplifting, but she learned from the experience. Aside from the realization that she was responsible for what happened to her and that she could influence the direction of her life, she learned something more: that school was not the place for her at that moment.

220

She put her formal education aside and got her first job as an A&W carhop, then as a waitress in a pancake house. Finally, her thirst for adventure could contain itself no longer and she left home to go to Jasper, Alberta. She had already developed a close kinship to the mountains and the outdoors through her father. It was there that she experienced peace more than anywhere else. Following her instincts, she stepped into the unknown. It was a decision that would affect her for the rest of her life.

She quickly got a job as a tour conductor on world-famous Maligne Lake. A short while later, at 17, she and several of her friends hired a mountain guide to teach them rock-climbing. She had finally found what she'd been looking for.

"It was immediately there for me," she recalls of that moment of exhilarating realization. "It was incredibly adventurous and very stimulating mentally and physically. It only became more so for me as time went on."

Sharon became fascinated with the mental and physical gymnastics that rock-climbing demanded. It stirred something in her, forced her to reach higher and deeper than she ever had before. The higher and harder she climbed, the stronger her sense of self-worth, self-confidence and personal strength became. Then it all began to come together one day in 1974, when she met Laurie Skreslet at Outward Bound.

"I remember him being very approachable and friendly. From the first day, he made me feel special. He had that unique ability. He would pick something from a person and highlight it."

From rock-climbing, Sharon branched out to ice-climbing. It was here that she came to another important realization.

"I discovered it wasn't a matter of physical strength, but a matter of psychological strength. The contest lay within my own mind to penetrate those barriers of self-imposed limitations and get through to the good stuff – the stuff called potential, 90 percent of which we rarely use."

So began the next step in the natural progression: mountaineering.

In 1977, with no high-altitude experience whatsoever, Sharon was part of the first all-women team to climb Canada's highest mountain, 6,050 m Mount Logan, in the Yukon. From there, she moved on to the highest mountain in North America, Mt. McKinley (6,194 m), in Alaska, then to the Andes and the Himalayas. It was here that she began to lay the real groundwork for Everest.

On Mt. Makalu, in Nepal, she was stopped 915 m from the top. "It was definitely a most valuable lesson, although it was a failure. I'm convinced that it won my success on

221

Everest because I learned the value in failing. It made me decide that the next time, I wanted it so badly that I'd be willing to step further out of my comfort zone. It made me want the top."

She got it. Together with a partner, she climbed the sheer 3,050-m south face of Mt. Aconcagua in Argentina, a short while later. At 6,960 m, it's the highest mountain in all the Americas.

"I'd never been out so long or felt so committed to a wall like that one. There was no one else around. If we got in trouble, that was it. And I had never been subjected for such a long time to hazards like the icefalls that were above

LEARN THE LESSONS FROM EXPERIENCE

Failures can also be viewed in much the same way that obstacles can be seen as opportunities."Failure is delay, not defeat," said William Arthur Ward.

Sharon Wood used her unsuccessful attempt on Mt. Makalu as a springboard to the top of the world. Over and over again, those with the "adventure attitude" return to places of previous failures. They do so not only out of sheer persistence, but because they are slowly gathering knowledge that they know will eventually lead to success. For them, failure is used as a foundation for future success.

"The only failure in life is when we fail to learn the lessons from our experiences," John Amatt maintains. It is this ability to turn negatives into positives, obstacles into opportunities and failures into successes that, more than anything, will help us to succeed in the twenty-first century.

Experience is not what happens to you. Experience is what you do with what happens to you.
-Aldous Huxley

us all the time. That I could survive that kind of pressure and still perform was something fantastic."

Then, the final test – a 1,830-m unclimbed face on Mt. Huascaran Sur, the highest mountain in Peru. It was here that her shoulder was broken by a rockfall just days from the summit.

"I was torn off my feet and had a searing pain in my shoulder. I thought, 'Well, this isn't as hard as it could get on Everest.'"

It was now 1985, a year before Everest. She sensed this would be the final training ground.

Unaware that her shoulder was broken, Sharon persevered all the way to the summit. It took six more days. At times, she could not lift her arm more than a few centimetres, so she used her other arm instead. It wasn't until she finally returned to Canada two weeks later than she learned her scapula was broken.

223

"Finally, I had the perfect example of my potential. It was then that I realized that I could do way, way more than I thought I could."

She told a newspaper reporter: "I took a significant chunk of that experience and applied it to Mount Everest. I found that as long as I held together mentally, I could do it. I had significant pain, but it was the kind of pain I could transcend. It was fascinating to me. I could survive."

At last the mettle was ready. Once a lost, confused and frightened young girl who never seemed to fit in, Sharon, now 28, had truly found herself. Twenty-four thousand kilometres away and high above the clouds, the biggest challenge of all stood waiting.

It was time to go to Everest.

April 15, 1986: mid-way up the 1,200-metre ice spur that led up to the west ridge traverse, the wind was blowing

The way I perceive my environment is the only thing that makes me different – nothing else.
– Sharon Wood

hard. It was not a time for stubborn action, but for careful thought. To try to overpower the wind would be foolish.

Sharon was with "Big Jim" Elzinga, the expedition's unyielding leader. At 6-foot, 5-inches tall and 95 kg, he was a veritable pillar of strength and determination. Part of his training for Everest had been to run the stairs of Toronto's CN Tower eight times in succession, four or five times a week. At 550 m high, it is still one of the world's tallest free-standing structures and consists of a gruelling 2,570 steps. Each ascent of the tower took Jim just 12 minutes.

224

"At one point, the wind picked him off the ground and blew him back down the rope. He looked up at me as if to say, 'Are you going to go on today?'

"What I did that day was learn how to deal with it. I looked at the wind as being just another test. If I could pass this test, I'd be better able to deal with the hardships ahead of me because I knew they were only going to get worse.

"I learned to listen for when the gusts were coming and I would lie down. I simply treated it like something that was just there, that there was nothing you could do about it.

"It's a matter of not trying to alter your physical environment, because we're quite limited in how much we can change that. Instead, you alter the psychological environment, your perception of the situation."

May 10, 1986: A half dozen of the expedition members huddled together in the canvas-covered hole in the snow known as Camp 2, at the foot of the spur at 6,100 m. Sharon sat quietly as Jim went over his suggested selection of summit teams. Struck with a severe case of laryngitis early in the expedition, his voice had been hoarse and raspy for weeks. The team had dubbed him "Lizard" because of it.

"I think Sharon and Dwayne should go first," he said in a barely audible tone over the ever-present wail of the wind outside.

Sharon was defiant. She protested, maintaining that the decision did not make good logistical sense. She had been climbing for weeks with her long-time friend, Albi Sole. They had established a strong and effective working relationship.

Besides, Barry Blanchard and Dwayne had been working well as a team. They had also just finished a period of rest and were better prepared physically and psychologically for the trials of a summit bid. She insisted Barry and Dwayne go first. The meeting ended, but the discussion did not.

Sharon's friend and mentor, Laurie Skreslet, seemed disturbed by Sharon's decision. He saw this as a key moment in the development of her future. He knew that the Americans were preparing to make a summit bid and a battle began inside his warrior soul.

Laurie had first met Sharon when she was still a teenager. He had been her instructor at her very first Outward Bound course in Keremeos, British Columbia, in 1974. She was 18 at the time. "All the instructors recognized something in Sharon," Laurie says. "She had resolve. She had focus. And she had a hunger; it was a hunger to learn more. God, it inspired you."

"It just felt that I was there on Everest to help Sharon, to look out for her and make sure she got up to the top. So when her back was turned and it was discussed who would be the first summit teams, I thought, 'You can't let the

As Canadians, we are a new breed. We have a tremendous amount of potential, but we keep missing it because we are too busy trying to be like others.
– Sharon Wood

226

Americans be first. We can't let them beat us!'

"Why? Because it meant something for us as Canadians. We were not going to let an American woman get to the summit first. We were going to show them. And if it isn't clear now, it'll be clear years later."

Jim took Sharon aside. In his raspy, yet forceful way, he put the scenario to Sharon. She recalled: "I can remember him saying something like, 'Sharon, what's the difference between a Canadian and an American?'"

"I don't know. What do you mean?"

"Canadians always seem content with second place. Do you want it or not?"

"Of course I want it."

Jim was overjoyed. Laurie was relieved.

"It was okay when she said no at first to being on the first summit team," Laurie said. "That's understandable, because she's got this self-deprecation. She tries to be polite in everything; until you tell her it's okay to take the sword out of the scabbard. Because once she takes it out, that's it. That's what she focuses on and nothing is going to deter her from it. It's like watching a cybernetic torpedo lock onto a target. She just keeps re-correcting herself and going for it."

"I remember Laurie saying stuff like, 'Ya Sharon, when you're up on top for photos, make sure that you show your left profile instead of your right. Your left profile will look so much better in *Chatelaine*.' He helped bolster my confidence."

From Laurie's point of view, the rationale was simple. "I felt that maybe, just maybe, she needed encouragement.

There have been times in my life when it was nice to know there was somebody who believed in me."

Fantasies aside, Sharon was far from standing on the summit yet and she knew it. In fact, she wasn't even on the first summit team. It was time to go to Barry and ask him if he'd trade places.

Fortunately, he owed her a big favour. Before the expedition, she had taken over his duties as food-packing coordinator for two weeks so Barry could go on his honeymoon. "That's a lot, so the tables were turned on Everest," Barry says. "On my value-exchange system, this was my opportunity to repay that favour."

It's how I deal with challenge that makes the critical difference – I can let it control me, or I can control it. **– Sharon Wood**

227

It was this unselfish gesture, coupled with Laurie's lobbying in the background, that helped put Sharon in the right place at the right time. In return for this overwhelming vote of support, she went back to work high on the mountain to push the route higher. The weather had been horrid for days. There were heavy snow accumulations at the higher elevations. Without some kind of special effort on everyone's part, the door to the summit would remain closed to all, including her.

In spite of the terrible weather, she continued. It was as if someone had lit a spark inside her.

"I didn't see myself on top of Everest, but I did see myself doing something that no other North American woman had done. I dreamed of doing something great. I imagined how good it would feel."

For the moment, she only could imagine it. But the vision was made more tangible when, a few days later, the Americans announced they were turning back because of extremely hazardous avalanche conditions on their route. If the Canadians could avoid an accident, if the weather improved, if enough of the team stayed healthy and they were careful...

May 15, 1986: Dwayne, Jim and Sharon walked along the Rongbuk glacier towards Camp 2. In less than a week, if all went well, Sharon would become the first North American woman to reach the top of the world.

That day, as Jim lumbered over the rock moraine, he had his mind's eye on something else. He was thinking about the 1982 expedition, the lives it had taken, and how much he didn't want that to happen again. He took Dwayne and Sharon aside.

ENJOY THE JOURNEY

Adventure achievers don't adventure just to reach a summit, cross a finish line, or make it to a goal. They are there because they have a genuine love for the unknown, whether it takes the form of the sea, the mountains, the Arctic, or simply a long and winding country road. That is why they get involved in adventure and that is why they stay involved. Their primary motivation is not to arrive, but to travel. Success to them is not a destination, but a journey.

"It is the process of getting to a goal that really turns me on, rather than reaching the goal itself," Sharon Wood says.

This dichotomy of travelling and arriving is critical to success – and happiness.

"Reaching the summit is not the significant thing, because you learn nothing on the top," says John Amatt. "It is during the journey that the learning takes place. The important thing is to digest the experience, to learn what it was that got you there. Then you call apply this new knowledge to the future."

"You know," he said in his husky voice, "I just want to make sure that you treat this mountain like any other mountain you'd be climbing. You don't want to die for it. You don't want to push past the line of what you think is safe and what isn't. You don't want to lose it."

"I really respected Jim," Sharon recalls. "I completely and wholly accepted him as being the almighty leader. You're so tired and there's so much work to do, you look forward to someone else caring about the big picture. All I want to handle is my little world; I just want to think about what load I'm carrying that day and what I have to do. Jim had his eye on everything."

Two days later, after they had left Jim at Camp 2 and were en route to Camp 4 at the top of the spur, Jim's "Everest as any other mountain" theory would be severely tested.

The weather was terrible. Small avalanches were pouring down the route and, together with the wind, the snow crystals were nearly piercing their skin. It was like putting your face into the nozzle of a sandblaster. It ripped into your pores and eyes, causing a searing pain.

Sharon, Dwayne, Barry, Kevin Doyle and James Blench could hardly stand up in the driving wind. The temperature was well below freezing and the visibility was next to zero. The conditions were extreme.

Sharon decided to act on Jim's philosophy and proposed they come back another day. To her mind, they were wasting valuable time, energy and oxygen trying to persevere in a no-win situation.

Kevin didn't see it that way. Described as one of the most talented high-altitude climbers in Canada, he had scaled the entire north face of the Matterhorn in Switzerland in just six hours – alone. Over the years, this and many other extreme ascents had earned him a reputation for having a single-minded desire to "summit" regardless of the obstacles.

The decision to retreat or continue caused an instant clash of wills between Sharon and Kevin.

"I'm going down," she hollered through the deafening roar of the wind. "Jim said we should treat this mountain just like any other mountain."

Kevin's stare burned. "To hell it's like any other mountain. This is God damn Mount Everest and I'm going on!"

They did – together – stumbling, groping, and stumbling again – over and over – reaching inside for that elusive ingredient that separates the potential for success from the reality of failure. Somehow, they made it to Camp 4.

James Blench didn't stagger in until hours later. Coated from head to foot in ice, he looked like a walking icicle. His speech was slow and garbled, his skin ashen, and his lips and fingernails were a deep blue. These were sure signs of hypothermia, a condition in which the temperature of the body's critical internal core begins to drop. If it falls more than just a few degrees, death can be close at hand.

"He was in terrible shape, terrible, terrible shape and he seemed so helpless," says Sharon. "He was extremely hypothermic, and he had a horrible cough. He'd cough so hard he'd throw up. God, I couldn't believe the pain and discomfort he'd transcended to get a load up to Camp 4."

Conditions in camp were grim. It was an open snow cave with wind-blown snow constantly filling the door. Inside, everyone was spent and uncomfortable. Clothes, fuel canisters, sleeping bags and mitts were flung everywhere and the little flame on the stove used up any extra oxygen in the already thin air. This made them all hypoxic.

"In order to treat his hypothermia, we pulled James in and I cuddled with him all night," Sharon said. "To help him get warm again, we gave him hot water bottles. It was wonderful to look after your friend.

"James has always been a very people– and partner-oriented person. He isn't as selfish as some of us. I have a very selfish drive. While I'm a good team player, when I compare myself to James, there is no comparison. He just really wanted to see us make a success of it."

The night passed slowly. But at daybreak, they set out again. James could not make it. Exhausted, sick and wasted, he was forced to turn around. He had reached his summit.

The others continued through the wailing gale. It was Sharon's 29th birthday, but there was little cause for celebration. The wind along the exposed razor sharp ridge continued to be strong, at times clotheslining the climbers like sheets in the air. It was not until the late evening hours that they finally made it to Camp 5 at the base of the pyramid.

"I carried my birthday card from my Mom up there with me," says Sharon. "She'd written on the front: 'Do not open until May 18.'

"It was about midnight when I finally had the time to open it. It said some mushy thing. Mothers always read those words printed inside the card and for once, I did too."

The rest of the team members sang "Happy Birthday" to her over their walkie-talkies. It must have been the highest birthday party on earth.

After this brief celebration, Sharon's spirit took a nosedive. While rooting around the camp for supplies in the dark, she discovered that she could only find five gas canisters. She knew they needed more.

At high altitudes, there is a strong correlation between gas canisters and an individual's strength. Gas canisters fire the stove which melts the water. Adequate water is essential. Climbers must replace up to six litres of liquid that the body loses daily in the very dry air. With insufficient gas canisters, the ability to melt water is restricted and, at a high altitude, liquid intake is the number one determinant of physiological performance. In short, a few extra gas canisters can mean the difference between success and failure – even life and death.

Sharon knew this. Exhausted by the exertion, altitude and lack of sleep over the previous two months, she had reached the end of her tether. In a moment of hypoxia-induced hysterics, she decided she just HAD to have more gas canisters.

Grabbing the radio, she launched into a vicious tirade.

"I was clutching that radio as if it had been life itself. I was not going to let anyone else use it. I had finally broken."

One by one, the expedition members tried in vain to placate her – first Jim, then Laurie, Dave McNab, Barry, and the rest. Finally, Dan Griffith tried. He was a quiet, shoot-from-the-hip sort of man, known for his ability to keep cool under pressure. With his experience as the father of three young children, he seemed like the only member of the team up to the challenge.

"Okay Sharon, count your cartridges," he said slowly.

"I've already counted my cartridges!" came back the roar from the agitated tigress.

"Just count them one more time, Sharon."

She did. She discovered that in fact she had six.

"I see," said Dan. "Now if you use one tonight and two tomorrow, you'll probably have enough, won't you? You won't want to carry much more weight anyway, will you?"

That ended it. The tigress went to bed and Dan, in his own calm, methodical way, had sung her to sleep.

Perched in their tiny tent on the massive north face of Everest, Dwayne and Sharon awoke on the morning of May 20, 1986, already tired, alone and afraid. They could hear the wind whipping around the tent, as usual. As their eyes slowly opened, they realized they were both covered with snow.

During the night, the force of the wind had blown the tiny particles right through their single-walled tent, burying them in a thin layer. It was 5:00 a.m. They called the team on the radio.

The news was not good. The summit of the mountain, still more than 600 m above them, was capped in a malevolent-looking feature known as a lenticular cloud. This was a clear sign of extremely strong winds on top which could make a summit attempt impossible.

"But we didn't have any choice, really," says Sharon. "We knew we would never get there again. We thought we might as well make the right movements and pretend that we were going. So, we got ready."

It took a long time. Even with the aid of oxygen, they were both a bit groggy. Four hours later, at 9:00 a.m., they finally stepped out of the tent. That was when their problems really began.

In mountaineering, speed can often be translated into safety. If you start late, your chances of being forced to come down in the dark are high. That takes more time, and time is often a luxury you don't have. With just 10 hours of oxygen in their tanks, both Sharon and Dwayne knew their late start could mean disaster.

233

Sharon had serious concerns about it. "I visualized that over and over in my head, more subconsciously than consciously. I was terrified of that situation. I couldn't imagine a more frightening experience than coming down an 8,000-m peak in the dark, out of gas, out of energy."

"Our perception of reality is frequently much worse than reality itself. I'm always better – always – at imagining the doom and gloom and the unsuccessful steps before I imagine the successful outcome. So, I have to counter that. And the way I counter it is through rational thought, instead of just an emotional reaction. If I were just to react all the time, I would never take risks. But to take action is a counter-reaction."

As she stepped out of the tent into the frigid blast, she tried to remove the unsettling possibilities from her mind. She and Dwayne were here now, and they were going to try.

Sharon was wearing almost every piece of clothing she had brought with her, all six layers. They started with thick

PERFORM UNDER PRESSURE

When the chips are down and the gauntlet thrown, those with the "adventure attitude" don't just rally, they attack. For many of them, it is the times of testing that are as much the adventure as the exploration. The mountaineers have a chance to challenge not only the mountain, but the mountain environment. More importantly, however, is that it gives them a chance to challenge themselves. "We do not conquer mountains, nor tame the elements," says Sharon Wood. "The true conquest lies in penetrating those barriers of self-imposed limitations within our minds."

It is an achiever's ability to perform under pressure that is the acid test of their attitudes and abilities.

longjohns from top to toe, then a synthetic fur suit, a down suit, a double-layered wind suit, plastic boots and crampons. She felt like she was moving in a space suit, except that with every movement she was reminded that they were not in a weightless environment. Her one consolation was her $30 battery-operated pair of electric socks. She'd bought them at an outdoor store in Calgary before leaving for the trip. Powered by one D-cell battery per sock, they were to prove to be one of the best investments she'd made in her life.

Dwayne got started about 30 minutes before her. He, too, was conscious of the time. "The feeling I had at this point was that Sharon wasn't that keen," recalls Dwayne. "She was quite uncertain. But I felt a lot of confidence; I felt really aggressive about the situation. So I just went."

When Sharon finally caught up to Dwayne, they'd reached the narrowest part of the couloir, where it constricts to one body-width. It was like being at the mouth of a huge hourglass. Rocks were falling sporadically through the gap. If either climber chose the wrong moment to enter the couloir, they could be seriously injured or killed.

But the time they spent there channelled more than rocks. It channelled fear, especially in Sharon. "As we started up, it seemed impossible. I couldn't get enough oxygen and the wind was so strong it was blasting rocks from above. Dwayne and I looked at each other and said, 'Well, we're too late. It's just too horrible. It's too windy and we're too burned out. The most we can hope to do

It was the climbing above Camp 6 on that last day that was most daunting to me. I parallel it with childbirth now. The pregnancy and the after-effects aren't so bad; it's the actual last day that is the big unknown. It's the summit day.
– Sharon Wood

235

today is anchor some rope for a possible second assault team."

"I also knew the situation wasn't perfect," Dwayne says. "The skies had more or less cleared, but... You could hear the wind. It was just blasting above, really strong. I knew at the back of my mind that we didn't have much chance, but it was sheltered where we were. In my own mind, I felt we had to try and see what happened."

They did. Hugging the walls of the couloir to avoid the falling rocks, the two climbers slowly made their way onto an ice slope above. It was embedded with stones, a sure sign of sustained and prolonged rockfall. All it would take was a single stone and they knew their summit chances would vanish.

236

They tried not to think about it. The dread of the heinous cliff called "the Yellow Band" loomed over them. It had stopped numerous climbing parties in the past. Faced suddenly with the technical challenge of rock-climbing in such rarefied air, they had been forced to turn around and give up.

Sharon and Dwayne knew about that band of rock's reputation. They knew it could be their nemesis.

Suddenly, Jim's hoarse voice jumped out from the radio. "You gotta want it!"

Instantly the words echoed in Sharon's mind. They took her back three months to near the top of the CN Tower in Toronto where, just weeks before leaving for Everest, she had joined Jim on his daily masochistic workout on those 2,570 steps.

The day had been dismal. It was 7:30 a.m., cold and raining. Outside, the raindrops streamed down the windows of the stairwell. The clouds hung low over the city. About a third of the way from the top on their third assault, Sharon had heard Jim's footsteps pulling away from her above. Echoing down the upright corridor, they evaporated into nothingness below.

It was depressing. Graffiti and garbage were all around her. It was like climbing 550 m inside the world's biggest dumpster: dull and boring and sometimes repulsive. She loathed it.

All of a sudden, those inspirational words had come floating down the stairwell. "You gotta want it!"

Sharon was snapped back into the present by a gust of wind.

"It isn't strength, it isn't the conditions," she reminded herself. "It is desire. But that rock band was big! It was 150 feet high. It was the crux. If we could get through that, we could probably get to the top."

As they climbed towards it, they could see the tattered remains of ropes everywhere; the fading vestiges of past victories and failures. The difficulty was that you didn't know which line led to the top and which didn't.

237

Upon closer examination, the choice became more distinct.

There were two options: one obvious crack line, short, but difficult, or up to the right, a less direct approach which seemed to disappear into space offering no clear answer.

"It was very much like Rocky Mountain terrain," recalls Dwayne, "broken, but not really steep. It was classic mixed rock, snow and ice. It was easy for me to understand how people could take the wrong way."

It was an intuitive and instinctive decision borne from years of experience. They took the right way – the Rocky Mountain way.

Sharon took the lead.

"I got completely absorbed by the intense level of concentration that the climbing demanded, and the risk. You've got crampons on, you've got mitts on and every-

If you're totally committed to something, the discipline comes easy. When you're there – when you're all there...

– Sharon Wood

thing. It's taking up every ounce of your energy. No longer can you entertain any other doubts or sympathies towards yourself – anything. It's just climbing.

"It was like, 'Hey, wow, this is the Rockies. I've been here. I know how to do this kind of climbing. This is mixed climbing. This is what I like. This is what I live for. I love this kind of stuff.'

"And all of a sudden, there was a spark. I don't know, it was like a dance in a way – a mental and physical union of energy and direction."

The momentum of the climb's energy began to shift to Sharon. After Dwayne had given it the crucial kick-start, Sharon's motor was now running. They could hear the rest of the team on the radio, cheering and celebrating. Sharon and Dwayne had beaten the "Yellow Band."

Dwayne took over the lead above that. It was another steep snowfield, then an ice couloir, then another snowfield. It seemed to go on and on.

By 5:00 p.m., nine hours after setting out, they were still a quarter of the way from the top. They had only one hour of scheduled oxygen left.

For the next two hours, there was excited anticipation. Then, the tone of the voices on the radio gradually began to change from celebration to serious concern. Everyone knew that Sharon and Dwayne were experienced, skillful and cautious, but time was slowly catching up with them.

They didn't acknowledge their teammates' concerns. "We knew a bivouac (stopping to camp without a tent or sleeping bags) was impossible," says Sharon. "At best you come away with a few less fingers and toes; at worst you don't come away at all.

"But something uncanny was going on. At that point, Dwayne and I were so well synchronized in thought and concentration and decision and desire that we continued on. There was no verbal exchange. We just knew. We knew."

Their commitment became greater with every step. Time was running out, the day was running out and their oxygen was running out. But the weather was becoming comfortable. The sun had come around the north face and the winds had dropped. It was suddenly warmer, almost hospitable.

"The whole environment was such that it gave us confidence," says Dwayne. "It was a very strong feeling. Normally, we should have turned around at this point. There was still a long way to the top. I don't know where it came from, but I felt all this confidence. Maybe it was just the high altitude; you hear stories of people going for it and not coming back. But I thought we were fairly lucid. We really didn't discuss it much at all. We weren't talking that much. It took too much effort."

"Too much effort" was how Dan Griffith described what he had been going through while Sharon and Dwayne were struggling to the top. He was involved in a different but equally important drama unfolding lower down the mountain. At Camp 4 at the far end of the West Ridge, he and Laurie lay exhausted in their tent.

"It's amazing," Dan said. "You sit here in the tent and it's calm. You go up on the ridge, not 40 feet above, and it's blowing 70 miles an hour. The ropes pull you across the ground when you're in the middle of the loops."

Earlier, Dan had struggled to make it across the ridge to Camp 5 at the base of the summit pyramid. He had to get there to be in a position to back-up Sharon and Dwayne in the event of an emergency. Given their late start, lack of light and low oxygen, he knew that the success of his mission was critical to their safety.

The mountain had turned him back. The cold and the wind had forced him to return to Camp 4.

"I get the feeling I'm going to have to try it," Laurie said, his face registering the misery he was feeling.

"You go ahead," Dan said, as his inert eyes telegraphed like an automaton. "It's late for you to go, too."

VALUE THE STRUGGLE

240

People with the "adventure attitude" can endure physical discomforts that border on unimaginable. Throughout intense effort and extreme pain, they are able to hold fast to their dreams. While they are actually struggling, there is tremendous malaise. But if they are able to overcome that discomfort, they meet with invaluable rewards. The greater their struggle, the greater their reward.

"In order to make a difference, we have to be willing to leave our comfort zones," says Sharon Wood. "In doing so, we start to struggle and it's in the struggle that we're given the opportunity to tap our unutilized reserves. This is when we see our personal best – in the struggle. The conquest lies in penetrating those barriers of self-imposed limitations and getting through to that good stuff – the stuff called potential, 90 percent of which we rarely use."

Struggle is central to success. The trouble with struggle, of course, is that it often hurts. It can hurt physically, psychologically, spiritually, emotionally or financially. It's easier and a lot more comfortable just to avoid it. But no goal of significance is ever achieved without struggle. Those who endure will excel. Those who avoid it survive, but they fail. Struggle is the separator between the winners and the also-rans.

Dan knew that traversing the west ridge alone would take Laurie at least four hours. It was time they talked to Jim.

"Hi Jim, I'm back at 4," Dan said.

"You're back at 4?"

"Ya, the wind on the ridge is unbelievable. I was losing my fingers and toes so I dropped my load and came back."

There was a long pause. Then Jim spoke in a voice stiff with control: "Dan, you don't have to carry your load. But you've got to get yourself to 5."

Dan put down the radio. He knew what had to be done, but he was breathing hard just talking. Beside him, Laurie wasn't much better. He was sitting at the back of the tent, coughing and wheezing sporadically, fighting hard just to take in air.

241

It was a moment of tremendous personal struggle – the moment to dig deeper for the resolve to go higher; the moment that separates individuals from teams, the group achievement from the individual one.

Slowly, laboriously, Laurie spoke: "Okay Jim, don't worry. I'm leaving right now and I'll try to get over there. I'll hang around until they show up. I'll contact you when I arrive. Over."

Once again, Laurie was delivering on his personal adage "Once in your life, if you're lucky, you get to make manifest what you profess to believe." From the very beginning, his own personal hope had been that Sharon would make it.

"In my view, the '86 climb was a mission," he said. "The mission was to get Sharon to the summit."

The tone of Jim's voice changed suddenly. It became softer. "Okay Laurie, thanks. We've got to get somebody over there because they are going to need help."

Dan breathed a heavy sigh. It wasn't a question of his will. It was a matter of his survival. At that moment, he just didn't have enough to go on. "I feel shitty," he said dejectedly.

"Don't," Laurie replied. "Don't, not this close to the end. Let it go. God! I hope I can get over there."

Slowly, Laurie readied himself. "Well, if it's getting close to six o'clock," he said after a while, "I guess I better get outa here."

He left. Out on the ridge, he faced one of the biggest physical challenges of his climbing career. The wind was howling at 100 km an hour. The roar was deafening. It took everything he had just to move five or ten metres.

"It was like what you read in all the war stories about doing things for your buddies and they stay with you. There was no question; Sharon and Dwayne are up there and they need backup, so you go. It's not, 'I don't know if I can do it.' It's 'I am going.'"

Somehow, he made it. At 11:00 p.m., while Sharon and Dwayne were still above him, Camp 5 finally appeared. "When I got there, I was crawling on my hands and knees. The winds were howling. It was awful. The tent was buried. I had to dig it out, get in there, try to get water melted."

In the space of those hours, that single effort perhaps better than any other captured what Everest extracted from the individual. There was Dan's exhaustion, Jim's unwavering appeal for the goal and Laurie's unselfish commitment to the team. But more than that, amid the coughing and the puffing and the groans, you could see the indomitable strength of the human spirit, the agony of effort and the stuff of dreams. While the rest of the world would be transfixed on the glory of the summiteers, the contributions of the dozen or so others on the entire '86

242

team would go largely unnoticed, blown into obscurity with the wind.

But they were all there; all of them were going for the summit – fighting, striving and eventually triumphing together. That, perhaps as much as anything, was the strange but inexplicable strength and confidence Dwayne and Sharon felt. It came not only from inside, but from outside and, like a levitating force, helped carry them to the top.

Early the next morning, Dan also stumbled into Camp 5. After resting in Camp 4 until 2:30 a.m., he had summoned every ounce of energy and drive he could find to make the torturous traverse across the ridge. As the wind whipped swirls of snow around him, he zipped open the tent and collapsed inside. They were ready for Sharon and Dwayne.

We do not conquer mountains, nor tame the elements. The true conquest lies in penetrating the self-imposed barriers, those limitations within our own minds.
– Sharon Wood

243

The wind began to die down as the pair finally reached the summit ridge.

"From my perspective," Dwayne says, "it wasn't like, 'Here we are, we're going to the top of Mount Everest.' That wasn't what was in my mind at all. It was simply, 'Let's just do this job and get the hell out of here.'"

In a very uncharacteristic move, Sharon left her ice axe behind in the snow, thinking they were just minutes from the top and faced only rock climbing above. It was like a highly experienced parachutist exiting an aircraft without his reserve parachute – if something went wrong, there was no way of stopping your fall.

"That frightened me after I realized what I'd done," Sharon recalls. "I realized I hadn't been thinking very clearly."

Setting foot on the highest point on earth was not the climax. It was the process of getting there....
– Sharon Wood

Two hours later, after one false summit after another, they finally approached the top. Beaten by the wind and burdened with the weight of their fast-emptying oxygen bottles, they moved in slow motion. Time seemed to stop. But there was no emotion. They were numb.

At last, they arrived. At 9:00 p.m. on May 20, 1986, 12 long hours after setting out, they stood on the roof of the world. Below them, they could see clear to the horizon: the profile of nearby Mount Makalu, the entire west ridge of Everest and beyond that, the Himalayas.

Stumbling around exhausted, they managed an awkward embrace. "I think we sort of hugged," Dwayne remembers. "We were just too busy being there. It was simply a moment to catch our breath and rest our legs a bit."

"The sun was setting," says Sharon. "It was pretty unbelievable. I felt like I was walking on the moon, or in some kind of crazy dream.

"Setting foot on the highest point on earth was not the climax. It was the process of getting there; those moments of exhilaration when it was still happening a few hundred feet below the summit, where you're completely bewildered by the potential, the strength, the stuff that you never thought you had that just keeps issuing forth. You think you've reached the depths a long time ago and yet you're awed. You're wondering how much is really inside you and you're hoping there's going to be enough left to get you down."

Looking at the piece of ground beneath her feet, it all

seemed a little anticlimactic. It was just barren, windblown rock and snow; hard, hard snow packed like cement and scoured by the winds of time.

"It's a place where no man or woman belongs. You know you're just a visitor and you'd better make your stay as brief as possible."

In their moment of greatest glory, they knew they had never been in greater danger. Running out of gas, wondering whether their lives would disappear with the setting sun, they hurried to take their pictures and fly their flags. One banner was ripped like tissue from Sharon's hands. She watched it disappear into the icy expanse – the way she knew they would disappear if they didn't get down.

But as much as they tried to hurry, they could not. Every small movement took so long. Five minutes worth of work became 25.

Dwayne's girlfriend at the time, Colleen Campbell, recalls her mixed emotions at that moment. She had watched through a camera from Camp 1. "We were all saying, 'What the hell are they doing up there?' We could see the flag blow away and we wondered how long it took just to take a few pictures. 'Why don't they start moving down. They're running out of time.'"

Although she was powerless to stop it, Sharon's worst nightmare was becoming a reality. They were coming down in the dark, out of gas and out of energy. She did not know it then, but soon she would also be alone.

The summit of Mount Everest gives climbers little time to savour their achievement. It is not a place for jubilation, as so many imagine. Every ounce of energy is used just to stay alive there and, once on top, the only thought is how to get down. In a fitting display of the fleeting nature of

245

fame, no sooner do you arrive at the top of the mountain then you must return to the valley once more. No one stays on top for long.

Unlike the world below, however, here you do not fade quietly from the spotlight. If you linger too long, you are instantly removed from reality. No mountain, especially Everest, shows the slightest remorse; it executes with complete indifference.

"Thank God we're here," Dwayne thought to himself. "Now, let's get down."

They did.

Within minutes, the moon came up. It was a special, almost magical omen. Its white streaks of light reflected off the snow.

They enjoyed one saving grace: the weather was in their favour. The wind had died down, but continued at about 50 km an hour; the temperature was minus 30° C and the sky was clear. Thankfully, it did not appear that they would have to face the trauma of a serious storm.

Dwayne led the way down. His steady but ever-cautious steps gave Sharon confidence. There was something about Dwayne that communicated a feeling that he could survive almost anything in the mountains. Pat Morrow had once said: "Dwayne's really as close to a Sherpa as I can imagine, both in mentality and physical attributes. He's really strong and courageous, and he never complains even under the greatest stress."

"On a mountain, I'd trust my life to Dwayne," John Amatt had said.

Sharon took comfort in these statements. She knew she was with the best person for the job. If she wanted to go through a nightmare with anyone, it would be with Dwayne.

They were both extremely tired. It would have been so easy to collapse into the snow. Dwayne had seen the ghastly form of a dead Czechoslovakian climber frozen into the mountain high on Makalu the year before. In his mind's eye, he replayed that horrifying vision over and over in his head, trying to use fear as a motivator.

Sharon felt like she had a revolver pointed at the back of her head. It wasn't Russian roulette, the way it had been in the couloir on the way up. It was choice. They had to choose their steps carefully. Mistakes would not be tolerated.

"You had to be determined to get to Camp 6. You knew it was a matter of survival. You had to get there. You didn't bother entertaining the consequences if you didn't. All your energy now went into the next step ahead of you."

247

Miraculously, the oxygen was still flowing. Where it was coming from they didn't know. Nor did they know they'd stopped sweating, a sure sign of the onset of dehydration. They hadn't had anything to drink for 13 hours. Slowly, the cards were stacking against them. Sharon wondered when the odds would catch up with them.

Then, they did.

About 150 m below the summit and just above the notorious Yellow Band, they got separated. To this day, neither one of them knows how exactly. It just happened – slowly, imperceptibly.

At 8,690 m, Sharon waited 30 minutes for Dwayne to appear. She began to lose the feeling in her fingers and toes. Powerless to do anything but stand there, spent and semi-conscious, she nodded-off against the rock.

She awoke with a start. Her nightmare was real. It was dark, she was on Mount Everest, her oxygen was running out and now she was alone. The tigress inside her sprang to attention. It acted instinctively.

"I have a hard time describing it and people don't understand my decision," she says, as her fingers touch her temples and her eyes stare into space. "People don't understand it. I deserted my climbing partner at 28,000 feet. How could I desert my climbing partner? They don't understand.

"No one, not anyone, whoever they are, can make a judgment on the decision I made at that moment, on that night, in that particular place.

"People think they can, and they think it's morally wrong, or right, or whatever, but even I can't say. Even I can't judge it now. A decision was made. That's all."

She started down.

"Even though the lights of their headlamps were separated, I remember automatically assuming that the second one was Dwayne," recalls Colleen, who, along with the entire American team had been cheering Sharon and Dwayne on all day. "It was just intuition. But the lights kept moving."

The reality for Dwayne and Sharon was becoming apparent: they were in trouble. Sharon moved over the Yellow Band into the narrow couloir. All the while she struggled to keep panic at bay. If she panicked, she knew it was over. She tried to use the fear to keep her motivated.

Then another crisis: where was the tent? Had she climbed past it? If she had, she'd have to go all the way down to Camp 5, and in her state, she knew she wouldn't make it. She certainly didn't have anything left to climb up again. Where was the tent? God, where was it? She began to ask herself if she'd lost her mind.

A moment later, by the light of her headlamp, she caught the reflection of an old oxygen tank. Just a few feet away was the tent. As she entered its snow-filled interior, she discovered it was also cold and empty – the way she felt inside.

She fumbled with the stove. Everything seemed to take a herculean effort. Breathing was not only difficult, but painful. The lining on the back of her throat was swollen and sore.

In the darkened gloom of the tent, she tried to keep busy by melting snow. She wanted to be ready for Dwayne. Slowly, as her mind slowed down, the magnitude of the situation sunk in. She had broken the cardinal rule of mountaineering. She had left her partner alone. He could be in trouble.

The next 90 minutes were the longest of her life. We will never know the anguish she endured, the kind of psychological pain which makes physical pain seem so insignificant. For most of that time she can recall only that she continued to be blessed with total focus. Her next step was no longer to move forward, but to melt snow for water.

Eventually, there was relief. It came in the form of the sound of crampons in the snow outside the tent. Beleaguered, Dwayne finally crawled in.

His eyes were lifeless, his feet and hands numb. He moved like some kind of slow-motion marionette powered only by the invisible threads of his own wavering will.

His oxygen had run out above the Yellow Band. Suddenly starved of life-giving gas, he had had to rip off the oxygen mask that had threatened to suffocate him.

His fingers soon succumbed to minor frostbite. Forced to stop every few minutes just to get the circulation back into them, he had struggled to maintain his composure.

"I wanted to throw the empty oxygen bottle off because it was just dead weight, but I couldn't because Sharon was below me. I was even tempted to tie it on to some anchor

249

point somewhere, but I just couldn't find a place and I didn't have the fortitude to deal with that. I just didn't want to risk dropping it on Sharon. That would have been horrendous.

"Initially, I was quite concerned because I'd lost contact with Sharon. It came to a point where I was trying to catch up and I was rushing myself. Just forget about Sharon, I'd said to myself. Don't worry about it. Just slow down here and take it one step at a time.

"I caught myself and changed my whole outlook. Five minutes at a time was all I was climbing for. It was a pretty lonely existence. I only had a circle of light from my headlamp and that was it. In a way, that was good. I couldn't see the exposure below me. I just dealt with that little illuminated island of existence."

Another person might have panicked in the same situation. Another person might have died. But Dwayne's mettle had come through.

"I could have helped him if I'd waited," Sharon says. "This is the thing that kills me. I could have helped him. I agonize over that. Sometimes, I have nightmares about it."

But the horror show was far from over.

Because Dwayne couldn't move his fingers or toes, Sharon took his crampons and boots off for him and tried to warm up his hands and feet.

It was at this moment that something began to creep into the back of Dwayne's pounding brain. "We both knew we weren't over it yet. I didn't think everything was normal, but I didn't say anything. Something was wrong, I thought."

Sharon had made a pot of water and passed it to Dwayne. As he held it in his lap at one end of the tent, she reached over to light the stove again, but discovered the fuel canister was empty. After replacing it with a fresh one, she flicked the lighter.

Suddenly, the inside of the tent was engulfed in flame. It instantly removed all the hair from Sharon's face and sent the whole tent into spontaneous chaos. Dwayne tossed the pot of water and went for the door. Sharon jettisoned the flaming torch into the night air and scrambled to save herself.

But as soon as it had begun, it was over. The oxygen-starved air that threatened their existence also saved their lives. The flame was out in a second, but not before it had burned a skylight the size of a football in the roof of their tent.

As the two summiteers lay panting halfway out of the tent, a minute later, the stove reached the glacier below. They did not hear it land. It was too distant.

251

The reality of what had happened soon became apparent. There had been a leak between the fuel canister and the stove. In her fatigue, Sharon had been unable to make a proper seal.

"God, I wish I hadn't been so tired," Dwayne recalls. "There was a pretty unbelievable sigh of relief between the two of us."

They forgot about the water. They went to sleep instead – like two zombies clinging to the edge of the mountain, and to life.

The next morning they awoke with parched mouths. They were a couple of morning-after climbers with colossal hangovers. They felt nauseous and totally spent.

"God, it was painful," Dwayne remembers. "The hardest thing I've ever had to do was get ready to go down that morning. It would have been so easy just to stay there. I was just so tired, so dried out."

I think Canada's first step in 1982 was a significant one. It was a much maligned expedition, but without that first step, we wouldn't have done it in 1986. I believe that. We jumped off the shoulders of those guys.

– Sharon Wood

On his way down from the summit, Dwayne had found an antenna in the snow. He hadn't made the mental connection then, but he soon discovered that it belonged to their radio. They hadn't spoken with the team since before the summit. Below, everyone waited in anticipation for the news.

"Hello, Jim?" Sharon declared in a feeble voice. "We're coming down."

They got going at 9:00 a.m. – late again. It was difficult to move, let alone walk. Why couldn't they just stay and rest a while?

They both knew why not. Battling back the forces of fatigue once more, the punishment continued.

"I was surprised at how strong we were once we finally got going," Dwayne says. "It is totally amazing how much there is in our bodies. It's unbelievable. I'm sure prisoners of war will tell you the same thing."

As they retraced their steps, they eventually crossed through the fearful passage, arrived at the base of the couloir, and entered the real world once again. With those steps, Sharon became one of only five women in history to have reached the summit of Mount Everest and return alive.

And there, waiting for them with warm hugs and liquid, and even a video camera, was Laurie. He had come up from Camp 5 to meet them as they descended from Camp 6.

"It was like coming home," Sharon says as her eyes gloss over. "That was the summit for me. Laurie was quite sick at the time, very sick, and I was overwhelmed. I was quite teary when I first saw him, because I was overwhelmed by his commitment to us. He had been having a heck of a time acclimatizing, yet he came all the way across the face to meet us. It was part of the power, it was part of the answer to why we had been there, why we got there.

"Psychologically, I let go then. Up to that point I had been very task-oriented and very strong. But as soon as I saw Laurie, I let go of part of that."

"I KNEW she was going to make it," Laurie recalls. "There was no doubt in that at all. It all made sense; why we'd met at Outward Bound. There's something about Sharon and over the years, even though we've had our moments, there we were on Everest."

Together, the three climbers, the old summiteer and the two new ones, the mentor and his pupil, huddled together under a rock overhang. With hoods, black-lensed goggles, oxygen masks and bags, they looked like creatures from another world. But it was like coming back to Earth.

253

"The highlight of the whole climb wasn't making the summit," Dwayne says. "It was seeing Laurie again. I've never had a hug from Laurie before, but we hugged then. It was a pretty powerful moment. We didn't really say a lot, we just hugged, but we both knew.

"Laurie Skreslet is like a father to me. Laurie was there taking care of Sharon and me like we were his son and his daughter. Everything went well because Laurie was there thinking about us."

At 12:50 p.m., with legs like rubber, the little three-person regiment and its leader made its way back to Camp 5. There, Laurie and Dan filled the two triumphant climbers full of liquids and oxygen and kindness. By nightfall, Sharon and Dwayne were safely down the mountain.

The last one off the mountain was Laurie. Hiking down beside the glacier one evening, he could hear the sound of a big party in base camp. Wild whoops and singing echoed over the glacier through the cool air. Looking up toward Everest for one last time, he felt enormous pride in what the team had accomplished.

"Because Sharon got to the top it would mean that there were going to be a lot of women back in Canada and the United States who would have a role model to look up to in a world where more and more women are playing key roles in business and in making decisions about things that happen in our lives, in our future, in our country and in our communities. Sometimes women have been held back by fear and self-doubt because it used to be a "man's world." But all they need is that little extra lift from one of their own. That's the pivotal role Sharon's playing."

With that thought, Laurie's eyes turned back toward camp. In a few minutes, he too was celebrating.

It's not hard to put your finger on exactly what contributed to the Canadian success on Everest in 1986. It was hard work, courage, commitment and endurance. But in the end, it was something more.

It was not a solitary triumph. Although they were not physically there on top with Sharon and Dwayne, the entire team contributed to the achievement. The steps of the summiteers were made possible by the steps of a dozen others who stood beside them along the way, who cut a swath through the snow ahead of them, and whose spirit helped carry them to the top and back again safely.

In the end, it will be Sharon and Dwayne who will be remembered. But for those who were there, the reality is that they were not alone. It was a true team triumph; a stirring example of collective greatness.

The members of the 1986 Canadian Expedition to Mount Everest were (cities and towns current at the time of the expedition):

Barry Blanchard, Canmore, Alberta
James Blench, Canmore, Alberta
Dwayne Congdon, Canmore, Alberta
Kevin Doyle, Calgary, Alberta
Jim Elzinga, Toronto, Ontario
Jane Fearing, Banff, Alberta
Dan Griffith, Field, British Columbia
Dr. Bob Lee, Calgary, Alberta
Dave McNab, Canmore, Alberta
Chris Shank, Yellowknife, Northwest Territories
Laurie Skreslet, Calgary, Alberta
Albi Sole, Vancouver, British Columbia
Sharon Wood, Canmore, Alberta

255

Postscript:

On September 26, 1989, Sharon Wood gave birth to Robin, a healthy baby boy weighing 10 lbs. 2 oz. in Canmore, Alberta. During maximum labour, Sharon's highest heart rate was just 55 beats a minute.

Chapter 5:
THE EXCELLENCE IN ENDURANCE

He conquers twice who conquers himself in victory.
– Publilius Syrus

Profile on
Laurie Dexter
of Fort Smith, Northwest Territories

Member, Soviet/Canada
Polar Bridge Expedition
First expedition to ski from the USSR
to the North Pole and down to Canada

Ultra-Marathon Runner

The Marathoner

No matter how much I hurt, and how slow I may be going, I usually finish because finishing is what's important.
– Laurie Dexter

It began, as so many great achievements often do, in an obscure spot on the globe. In the twilight grey of an Arctic day, 13 tiny figures stood silently on the Siberian shoreline. Shouldering back-breaking 45-kg packs, which caused them to teeter precariously on their skis, they paused briefly on the threshold of a dream.

Ahead of them lay 1,800 km of ice – some of it solid, some of it paper-thin – all of it in constant motion. Not far from shore huge pressure ridges rose like miniature mountains in all manner of jagged shapes and sizes. Chunks of ice the size of houses were turned on end and shattered; razor-sharp edges laid bare against the minus 40° Celsius air.

This was the start of the Soviet/Canada Polar Bridge Expedition – nine Soviets and four Canadians thrown together to attempt what had never been done before: to ski from the Soviet Union to the North Pole and on to Canada, straight over the top of the world.

The expedition's primary goal was adventure. The trip

would also provide an opportunity to collect data on the effects of prolonged physical and psychological exposure to one of the most hostile environments on Earth. A secondary goal was to see whether the citizens of the world's two largest countries could work together toward a common goal.

One of those citizens was Laurie Dexter, an Anglican Church minister from Fort Smith, Northwest Territories (NWT). He first heard of the expedition when it was proposed for 1980. But because of the Canadian boycott of the Olympic Summer Games in Moscow that year, the Canadian government had forbidden the Soviets from skiing into Canada. Now, eight years later, the political climate had changed. It was decided that 1988 would be the year of "The Polar Bridge."

"We really don't know who first coined the title 'Polar Bridge'," says Laurie, "but for me it expressed a great deal of my aspirations. I really did believe that if we could work together through all our differences: political, linguistic, social, cultural and ideological, and overcome the problems those differences would likely create; if we could survive in close contact and remain friends in these incredibly harsh and dangerous conditions, that we would demonstrate something of value to our two nations and to the world. We must build bridges."

From the beginning, the foundations of the bridge were shaky. The night before the expedition was to depart from Cape Arktichesky – the northern-most point in what was then the USSR – there had been a heated debate. One of the Soviet members had been informed that after six years of personal effort, he had been cut from the team. In a rage, he had hurled a scientific instrument worth $12,000 against a wall and threatened to scuttle the whole expedition.

Laurie had stepped into the middle of the skirmish. He tried to mediate a solution, but in the end, succeeded only in exhausting himself. When the expedition's leader, Dmitri Shparo, hid the affair from the public, Laurie started the journey with a foul taste in his mouth.

"We were physically and emotionally exhausted, and felt totally let down by our leader. By the time we got on the ice I had plummeted from an idealistic high to the lowest depths of disillusionment."

There were other factors that entered into Laurie's personal situation which made the team's departure from land especially difficult. Besides the obvious anxiety of leaving the security and comforts of civilization for three months of unknown hardships on the Arctic ice, there was the nagging realization that his father, Bill, would likely die before Laurie reached land again. Coincidentally, their day of departure was Bill's 80th birthday.

On top of this, Laurie was still recovering from a nagging groin injury acquired on his last 100-km "ultra-marathon" run. Not wishing to appear that he was looking for sympathy, he told only the Canadian doctor, Max Buxton, of his ailment.

All of these challenges set the stage for a less than confident beginning for Laurie. As the last of some 100 journalists and supporters finally roared off in helicopters, 13 men with a mission finally realized the enormity of what lay ahead. With their ticket to Siberia now punched, there was only one way home – the long way.

It was March 3, 1988. They were 1,000 km from the North Pole. After 10 seconds of silence, they all yelled "Demoy! Demoy!" meaning "towards home, towards home," in Russian. Then, at 2:30 p.m., they began one of the most unique polar odysseys ever recorded.

Within minutes of taking their first tentative steps onto the ice, the falling began. First, one man tumbled sideways as his huge load got away from him. Another followed soon after, as he fell face-first into the snow. In all, there were dozens of awkward stumbles as Laurie and his companions struggled for balance.

For three hours, Laurie and the others inched their way toward the horizon, then finally made camp by the light of an eerie full moon. Before turning in, Laurie took one last look at his skis. He had marked each one with a crucifix at the tip. Below that, he'd added the names of his wife, Sheena, on one, and those of their two children, Andrew and Alison, on the other. He said a little prayer for them, and for his father and mother in Scotland. Already, he had to admit, he was looking forward to the end.

The essence of adventure is being willing to step out into an experience that you don't totally understand or know. The essence of achievement is exploring that unknown.
– Laurie Dexter

261

The first day on the ice had not been the most difficult one on the expedition so far. That day had come a month earlier when Laurie had said goodbye to his family at their home in Fort Smith, just north of the Alberta border.

February 4, 1988 had been a beautiful, crisp winter's day. The temperature had hovered around minus 12°C. As Laurie had hurried around making last minute preparations for departure, he had called Sheena, Andrew and Alison together in the living room.

"We talked about my hopes for our children as they grew up, in case I did not return," Laurie recalls. "The essence of what I said was that I didn't really care how much they succeeded financially, or how much they succeeded in terms of what most people would consider

The greater the risk, the greater the reward.
– Laurie Dexter

important in their jobs, in sports, or in public acclaim. Most of all, I wanted them both to grow up to be a man and woman of God. I wanted them to have a clear Christian commitment.

"We talked a lot, we prayed together and we hugged each other over and over again. I said, 'This is our goodbye. The airport is public. We won't hide our emotions there, but we won't go through this.'

"I felt a sense of fulfillment in that living room. If everything went well on the expedition, that departure would become relatively insignificant. But if something did happen to me, it would be something they would never forget and it would help to hold them steady throughout their lives. Inside, it was tearing us all apart. The incredible gut-wrenching emotional upheaval of that is something that's hard to describe."

"I thought about the fact that he might not come back," Andrew remembers, "but not a lot. He's small and he doesn't appear strong, but he's a lot tougher than he looks. He can stand the cold and he can put himself through pain."

In addition to the personal difficulties of Laurie's departure, he also faced professional challenges. While Laurie's 200– to 300-member congregation gave him unending support and encouragement, a number of people outside his own parish did not. They maintained it was irresponsible and selfish of him as a minister to leave his congregation for the four months the expedition would require. Laurie's reply was direct:

"While I feel called to a parish ministry, I do not believe in being a one-man Christian Rambo. I'm not the one who has to do everything and be everything and shoot everybody up sort of guy. The Church must exist by its own people, its own members. I'm merely a facilitator, a catalyst, and so I believe for the sake of the church that I have to have the freedom to branch out. I also feel that the Christian Church in general does a wonderful job of nurturing its own people, but in many cases does a very poor job of reaching out beyond the confines of its own world." While he was away, lay members of the congregation took over Laurie's duties.

"The foremost reason for my involvement in Polar Bridge was spiritual. The second reason was the international political implication. The third reason was the physical challenge."

The first two weeks of Laurie's Polar Bridge trek were agonizing. He was struck by a debilitating series of painful injuries. Before long, he was in serious trouble.

263

Within 48 hours of leaving Siberia, he had frostbite on all his fingertips. They blistered badly, then broke open, exposing super-sensitive bare flesh. In no time, his fingers began to ooze pus. The pain was excruciating. Every movement hurt, including grasping ski poles.

Shortly after, he got major foot blisters, one of which covered almost half of the bottom of his left foot. After that, he pulled a muscle in his right shin during a fall.

All of this, combined with the extreme cold, made it impossible for him to sleep properly. His feet, legs and hands throbbed. His groin produced periodic, stabbing pain. While the rest of the team members experienced most of these ailments at various times, for some reason Laurie was struck by them all at once. Accustomed, as a runner, to being one of the leaders, he was suddenly relegated to the rear of the line of skiers.

His other commitments to the expedition did not help his situation. In the evenings, while the rest of the members were sleeping, he was fulfilling his role as the English radio operator, relaying the team's position, reporting on the day's activities and sending and receiving messages. In a radio transmission 12 days after leaving Siberia, he described his ordeal:

"Extreme cold, rough ice, open water, heavy packs – these are the things everyone is aware of. They are real, but they are all inanimate. The real story of this expedition is blood, bone, sinew, muscles, pain, fear, living, breathing, being against an unseeming environment. Remember that each of us out here on the Arctic Ocean is made of the same tissue as all other people, and feel the same things. I know what it is to feel a surge of adrenalin when facing danger, and to sense a certain exhilaration of my heartbeat when struggling through a pressure ridge and listen with concern as the ice breaks apart with a grinding rumble only metres from the tent. We know fear just as everyone else, but we must use it to stimulate us into action rather than

264

ACT OUT OF COURAGE

Courage is not only the ability to risk your life, it is the ability to stand fast when everything else around you is falling apart, to remain calm when everyone else around you is losing their heads. In the simplest sense, it is getting up every day to make a better life for yourself, or starting a new job, or re-marrying, or moving to a new city.

If you are faced with a decision, no matter how small, ask yourself if you are acting out of courage or out of fear. If you are acting out of fear, the result will be predictable. If you are acting out of courage, success could be within your grasp.

allow it to paralyze us; we must use it to make us work together as a team rather than for selfish preservation.

"During these first two weeks I have had many problems and have been the weakest member of the team. I have travelled widely and been on many expeditions – mountaineering, kayaking, skiing – and know the Arctic well, but this expedition is made up of some of the toughest men I have ever known, in my case, a new kind of toughness. I am having to learn the toughness to acknowledge weakness and pain and to accept help with humility and gratitude.

"I have to be honest with myself. I know I have not contributed as much as I should have so far. I have had a series of problems – painful blisters on my feet, frozen fingertips and tendinitis in my shin. I reckon I've fallen more than any others on the team. Whenever I've been in trouble, Anatoli (Fedjakov) has always been there, but not by accident. He always skis just ahead of me or just behind, and on countless occasions has helped me up or done some small task to help me with the equipment. He and I speak almost nothing of each other's language, but here is an ideal example of what this expedition is all about. I would have had difficulty getting through these first two weeks if it had not been for the help of this man. As two nations we travel together, held together by a common bond of the need to survive. As we look at our world, if we are going to survive we must also recognize the need for a common bond. It is not enough to be tough in the sense of waving fists full of rockets at each other. We must be tough enough to reach out to others in need and perhaps we need to learn a new kind of toughness: the strength to acknowledge our national and personal weaknesses and to accept help with humility and compassion."

265

On top of the physical pains he had to endure, Laurie was faced with a legion of emotional stresses. He knew his father was slowly losing his battle with cancer. There was something of a tumour developing between some members of the expedition, as well. Two members were blatant and open in their expression of dislike for Laurie. One maintained that anyone who was a minister lacked direction in life and so went to the Church to find it. The other held that he was eager to see Laurie fail because of his

APPRECIATE THE STRENGTH IN DIVERSITY

The 1990s will be a decade of struggle for Canadians. As our efforts to redefine our national identity and political structure continue, the need to work together will become even more important. While differences between West and East, English and French, the haves and the have-nots may threaten to pull us apart, they can actually be used to hold us together, because it is precisely these differences that make up our national identity.

Canada is a country of diversity – not just linguistic and economic, but geographic, cultural, climatic and social. Unlike some nations whose essential character can be described with less difficulty because of their size, geography or cultural makeup, there is no stereotypical Canadian. While we have been wrestling for decades with our national identity, it's been staring us in the face. Our face is many faces – and places, customs, climates. The one thing we have in common is the potential to become a team.

Differences can be seen as positives or negatives. Since adventure achievers have the ability to turn negatives into positives, the differences which have threatened to divide us can easily be used to unite us – if they are approached with the right attitude. If we work together and build on the strengths of our differences, we can be a role model to the world. This is the triumph of teamwork.

religious beliefs. Fortunately, that tumour proved benign, but nevertheless, it spread into Laurie's mind.

"It was particularly hard because I didn't know why, and I didn't understand what the rejection was all about. I found that to be an internal struggle. It was far harder than physical rejection. I was rejected as a person."

Very few of the Soviets spoke any English and none of the Canadians spoke Russian. With the Canadians in the minority, rifts quickly developed over all kinds of issues. Disagreements over everything from food and equipment to personnel and personal ideologies were frequent. Considering the physical and psychological stresses they were under, however, it is a testament to everyone that differences of opinion did not become more serious than heated discussions. Their interpersonal conflicts were usually the direct result of overwhelming environmental factors, not only the cold, but the physical and psychological isolation of being unable to communicate.

Day after day, the Arctic put up obstacles. Eyelashes froze together, noses and faces turned black from frostbite and red icicles hung from nasal passages which dried, cracked and bled in the arid air. Faces swelled and blistered in the intense reflection of the sun's rays off the snow. The ice itself was rarely flat, and instead consisted of a never-ending series of frozen ramparts, fissures and open areas. It was like a continuous obstacle course. If you got over a ridge, there was always the possibility that the ice might give way on the other side and you would have to swim. In water this cold, that could be life threatening. Fortunately, because everyone stayed close together, that never happened. Usually, there was at least one pair of hands outstretched to save you.

Every day started at 4:30 a.m., when the man on duty rose in the team's cramped 13-man tent to prepare breakfast. He woke the others at 6:00 and by 8:00 or so, everyone was moving. It sometimes took up to four hours for Laurie to feel his toes again after a long night of shivering in his sleeping bag.

Most of the down sleeping bags lost their loft – their ability to insulate against the cold – early in the expedition. As soon as the moisture in the sleeping skiers' breath hit the minus 40° C air, it would liquefy and soak everything inside the tent. Once the sleeping bags became wet, they lost their loft and all their warmth. Then the condensation would freeze inside the bags, producing hard lumps the size of golf balls. Laurie and the others spent the entire night fully clothed, endlessly shifting and shivering.

"I remember one time when I went into the tent and found Laurie half into his sleeping bag with his parka on," recalls expedition member, Richard Weber. "There was frost and snow all over the place. It reminded me of the movie 'The Race to the South Pole' about the last days of Scott. I asked Laurie if he was okay. I felt really bad for him then. That was rock-bottom."

Skis, poles and bindings snapped in the cold and cracked under the weight of trying to bear burdens of 115 to 135 kg, the men's own weight plus their packs. It was impossible to travel in a straight line because either pressure ridges or open areas of water blocked their progress. Often, they would have to back-track for many kilometres before finding a way around. Or they'd throw clumps of snow and ice into the breach, lay skis over the top and build their own polar bridge to the other side.

Each day was divided into eight to ten marches of 40 to 50 minutes each. When the lead skiers had been moving for the alotted time, a 10 to 20 minute rest break began – but only for the leaders. Those members who pulled up the rear sometimes got little break at all. During those first excruciating weeks, if Laurie was lucky enough to hobble in with time remaining, he would be asleep on his pack within 30 seconds.

The expedition's mental challenges were as great as its physical ones. To survive the daily drudgery, members disappeared into their own little worlds. Some would dream of warm peaches freshly plucked from the trees of summer. Others would think of family and friends thousands of kilometres away. Much of Laurie's thinking was dominated by the time to the next rest stop, the number of marches completed and the number of marches remaining. Aside from the perpetual pressure ridges, cracks and open stretches of water, there was nothing – absolutely nothing. They were the only things alive for hundreds of kilometres, at least above the ice.

269

Sometimes Laurie took advantage of the monotony to pray. Before leaving home, his congregation had given him a small sheet of paper on which a different person had signed to pray for him. Each day Laurie would check to see who was praying for him, and as he skied along, he would pray for them.

The day usually ended around 11:00 p.m. That meant that the most sleep anyone got each night was about six hours. Considering the huge energy output and sheer exertion of surviving day after day in the frigid temperatures and high winds, it was never enough.

Nothing was enough. There was never enough food, drink, warmth, sleep, clothing, space in the tent, time or even letters from home. Any way you looked at it, it was dull, painful and exhausting work, an exercise in prolonged deprivation. And it was lonely.

"The lowest point in the journey was when I got diarrhea during one of the rest breaks," Laurie recalls. "It was really windy and I couldn't find any shelter. I had

The single biggest key to my success is commitment.
– Laurie Dexter

trousers with buttons on them instead of a zipper. I got them undone okay, but by the time I'd done my business, my fingers were so numb, I couldn't do them up. I had to ask Max to do up my fly. It's amusing, looking back on it, but at the time it was the ultimate humiliation."

Long before the team left Siberia, the expedition had dominated Laurie's life. For a year, he had followed a strict training regimen of rising at 5:30 a.m. every day, running 10 km on a treadmill in his basement and cycling on a stationary bike. He had also put on 11 kg of muscle by lifting weights. He further trained by climbing up and down a river bank with 45 kg of sand on his back, and he cross-country skied for hours on end with a heavy backpack.

If all this makes you question why anyone would voluntarily put themselves through such discomfort, you are not alone. Laurie himself questioned the validity of the whole morbid affair on many occasions. His answer was the same as for any project he commits to doing: "Commitment is total. You don't make a commitment unless you're willing to carry it through. Once you've made it, you should already have weighed all the pros and cons. So, that's it."

The Soviets were used to pushing themselves. Dmitri had begun his polar group some 20 years earlier. Since then they had achieved every major polar objective they'd set for themselves. In 1979, they'd skied to the Pole and received the highest accolade bestowed on Soviet citizens, the Order of Lenin. In 1987, they skied over 640 km between two ice stations during the bitter cold and total darkness of the Arctic winter. Some had hallucinations

270

along the way. One member had lost the better part of two toes. In short, they were the most experienced polar travelers in the world. Not only were they used to working together, their philosophy was basic, if not brutal: they would sooner die than be defeated.

The only way to avoid failure is not to take any risk in the first place.
– Laurie Dexter

It was with this knowledge that Laurie faced those gruelling first two weeks of the Polar Bridge Expedition. He was used to life in the Arctic. In 1981, in fact, he'd set out for the North Pole from the Canadian side. Just one week into that trip, however, the journey was aborted when one member came down with pneumonia.

Nothing on that trip, however, could have prepared Laurie for the hardships he was now experiencing. Yet he, too, refused to give up.

271

"When I asked myself what I was doing there, I would think to myself: Okay, Laurie. What if by magic a helicopter could drop in from the sky and say that in two hours you'll be back in your own warm bed? I knew there was no way I would take it. It didn't matter how much I was hurting. I was that committed to our overriding purpose. The only way I would quit was if I got totally incapacitated. I couldn't have lived with it if I knew I still had the ability to go on. As long as I could move, I was going to move."

Things did get better, gradually. His wounds healed and he began to assume his usual spot near the front of the line.

"He pulled himself around," says Richard. "Obviously, he was very mentally tough. I suppose you have to be if you're going to do ultra-marathons. He really hung in there. Even though his body wasn't doing it, his mind was."

Laurie Dexter is not driven by a desire to win, place or show. He is driven by curiosity. He wants to know how far he can go. He admits it's a selfish desire, one which has put his life in danger at times, but he's at peace with his own weakness. "I'd rather die attempting to live up to my potential than have to look back over my life and realize I've failed to do what I could have done."

It was eerie. Someone was following him. He could swear someone was there. Laurie looked beside him – nothing.

Sat. March 19, 1988: They were a quarter of the way to the North Pole. As Laurie chugged along in a light wind, he kept getting the sensation he was not alone. It was uncanny. It was like one of those feelings you get when someone is watching you. When you look up, someone usually is. But this was different. Every time he looked, all he saw was what he always saw: the vast expanse of ice.

"I'm not reading anything into it and I'm not superstitious," Laurie says. "I'm not saying my Dad's spirit was with me. Neither am I denying that I was aware of a presence constantly popping up beside me."

Four days later, Laurie learned that his father had died that Saturday. When he got the news, the wind was howling outside the tent. The men were sitting around looking like a bunch of beleaguered bandits with unshaven faces and scarred cheeks. Laurie was operating the radio.

As he handed one happy message after another to his teammates, the atmosphere in the tent became festive. Then the radio operator paused. "I've also got a message for you, Laurie," the voice said into the earphones. "It's from your wife, Sheena, and it says... I'm sorry to have to tell you, but your dad died last Saturday."

Laurie shut off the radio. He didn't say a thing. He didn't tell anyone. He just lay down and shut his eyes. "The whole atmosphere, the whole scene was such that I just didn't feel I could tell anybody."

Laurie felt like someone had deflated a balloon inside him. All the air went out of him. Pulling one of his sleeping pads on top of him, he forced himself into his frozen sleeping bag. Surprisingly, he was asleep in minutes. For the first time in weeks, he was warm.

"I had been waiting for this for so long," he recalls. "It was as if everything had broken, swept over me, and I just slept."

It's not so much whether you reach the goal. It's the process itself which is the catalyst that opens up the potential. It's the process rather than the gain.

– Laurie Dexter

273

Part way through the next day, Laurie told Max and Dmitri. He knew Dmitri would understand. A few years earlier his Dad had died while he had been on an expedition in northern Siberia. Laurie's relationship with the others was such that he couldn't tell them. He was afraid they might accuse him of weakness if he acknowledged his grief. They were his companions, but they were not his friends.

"Even in something that depends on teamwork, you still have to be willing to accept total responsibility for your own well-being, whether it's mental or physical. You depend on each other for some things, but for your own mental stability, I think it's pretty much up to you. Nobody is free from grief, physical pain or sickness, but the more you experience and the older you get, the more you can accept it."

He accepted it, but it wasn't easy. It took so much energy to simply survive on the ice, there wasn't much left

I measure success in the degree to which I'm able to fulfill what I believe is God's will for my life. Success, ultimately, is an inner thing. It can't be measured in objective ways.
– **Laurie Dexter**

274

for anything else. He thought about quitting, but he knew he couldn't. That's not what his father would have wanted, he knew. Rather than diminish Laurie's forward drive, his father's death only served to harden his resolve. Now, he HAD to make it to Canada.

A few months before the Polar Bridge Expedition began, Laurie had visited his father for the last time. They had discussed his involvement in the expedition at great length. "Dad insisted that I continue the expedition because he saw it as a fulfillment of the life for which he had trained me. We had a complete understanding of each other.

"When the day is done and we look back over our lives, all the plaudits of society, all the medals, the awards and everything else really have very little value. I think that is where this experience with my dad was so important. I looked back over his life and felt that he was successful. He was never well off, or had a lot of material things, but he lived a fulfilled life. I believe he has achieved eternal security."

To understand the influence Laurie's father had on him, you have to go back to Laurie's childhood growing up in the Shetland Islands off northern Scotland. Famous for its ponies and wool sweaters, the Shetlands have a shoreline dotted with spectacular fjords, impressive cliffs and complex caves. Located 640 km south of the Arctic Circle, they are also known for their frequent high winds, especially in winter.

Laurie went to the Shetlands with his parents and older sister, Anne, when he was 4. His father was a minister in the Church of Scotland (Presbyterian). Together they lived in a little house not far from the ocean. There was no electricity, no television and no radio. Oil pressure lamps were the only source of light during the long, dark winters. Time was passed playing games for hours by the peat stove.

Laurie's childhood home was very isolated. It was a kilometre to the nearest cottage and there were less than 100 cottages spread out over a 10-km area.

"My earliest memories are of the sound of the wind howling past the house, the call of the loon and the *aurora borealis* (Northern Lights) dancing across the night sky. Norwegian fishing boats would put in there for shelter during storms, and I used to go down to the pier with my Dad and clamber all over them."

Laurie's father and mother, Nancy, were central to his life of adventure. From as early as age 5, his parents took him and Anne hiking over the Shetland moors. He developed a love of birds and animals. His life was simple, but stimulating. He became fascinated with nature.

As a youngster, Laurie read a lot. In fact, he read everything he could get his hands on. His father had an extensive library. Laurie began with children's books and rapidly progressed to adventure stories. His father had dozens of them: tales of Marco Polo, Magellan, Drake and others. The most fascinating ones for Laurie were about the polar explorers, people like Amundsen, Shackleton, Scott, Byrd, Cook and Peary.

Laurie discovered early that education would teach him more than the three Rs. His primary school teacher had a particular dislike of boys and an even more intense dislike of ministers. So, as a minister's son, Laurie was not the teacher's pet. "I used to go home sometimes with ear aches because of the way he used to grab our ears and pull them."

During class, Laurie was once asked what he wanted to do in life. When he replied that he wanted to be a missionary doctor like David Livingstone, his opinion was met with utter scorn. "There isn't such a thing," his teacher snarled.

"I remember that because it was a dream that had been deliberately shattered. It was one incident out of many where a person was saying, 'You don't amount to any-

---

IGNORE THE DOUBTING THOMASES

Many of our adventure achievers experienced turning points early in their lives. During these moments, their goals and aspirations were specifically and harshly put down by those around them.

While it is important to listen to positive criticism and learn from it, one has to differentiate between what is useful and what is detrimental. If you are doing something for the first time, as is often the case, how are you to know who or what to believe? This is where self-confidence, self-esteem and self-worth – the Three S's – are significant.

You've got to aim for the horizon and never doubt that you'll make it.
– Mike Beedell

The Three S's drive the circular psychology of success. When achievers succeed, their self-confidence, self-esteem and self-worth increase commensurately. Suddenly they are able to undertake even more challenging goals. In other words, success really does build on success.

"The self-confidence you get from accomplishing a difficult goal will make the rest of your worries seem insignificant," says John Hughes. "It's worth millions. It's priceless."

thing.' Perhaps that gives some clue about some of the things I've done since then. That teacher and others like him telling me something was impossible is what has probably pushed me into proving the opposite."

High school wasn't much different from elementary school, at least in terms of how Laurie was viewed by some of his peers. There was a very strong prejudice against the children of ministers.

"It was blatant and open," recalls Laurie. "I was physically beaten, punched and kicked. If any perks were to be given, I was the last to get them. In any team events, I was the last to be chosen. The beatings hurt me more psychologically than physically. The rejection hurt more than the physical pain."

Laurie was relatively small compared to the other boys, so he was an easy target. He tried to defend himself, but it was futile. The experience was so traumatic that he failed his first year of high school. "I remember getting 9 percent in the final Latin exam. The teachers pretty much considered that I wouldn't go on academically. They didn't understand the trauma."

Laurie's saving grace was that his family moved to Glasgow the next year. By then he was almost 13. At school he learned of a place where Christianity was all but banned. He later wrote about this discovery:

"I grew up in Scotland at a time when the word 'Russia' was spoken with fear. The cold war was at its coldest. I remember clearly the national tension as everyone listened to the radio while Kennedy faced off against Kruschev in the waters around Cuba. 'The bomb' had been an ever-present danger for some time, but it seemed that this abstract threat might suddenly become a reality. I also remember classes at school in which Russia loomed large

277

and threatening: physics classes where we learned about nuclear fission; geography classes where we learned of changing borders as Russian troops descended on Hungary and Czechoslovakia, while communist forces took over in China and other Asian countries; history classes where we read of the Russian Revolution and the rise of Marx and Lenin and the communist desire to take over the world. We truly believed the cartoon image of Russia as the rapacious bear with blood dripping from its jowls."

At the same time as he was being introduced to these issues and stereotypes, Laurie also remembers admiring

FOLLOW YOUR INTUITION

Key in our achievers' ability to find their own path was a strong sense of intuition. Sharon Wood naturally gravitated to the mountains; Mike Beedell naturally bought a camera. Intuition is a key component in their strong sense of self.

Trust your instinct to the end, though you can render no reason.
-Ralph Waldo Emerson

"If you really believe that this is what you have to do at this juncture in your life, then do it," insists Laurie Dexter.

In the process of fundraising for the 1982 Canadian Everest Expedition, John Amatt came face-to-face with personal fear many times greater than anything he'd ever faced in his climbing – the fear of rejection. "What kept me going through all the maybes and nos was an intuitive sense that I was doing the right thing. I think intuition is a very important part of achievement. It gets you through the tough times. Just knowing that what you're doing is right and then committing all your resources to it is what makes things happen."

many Russian composers, writers and explorers. He wondered how the image of Russia could be so contradictory.

While in high school, Laurie took his first step toward life in the North. He became interested in whaling. In a bygone era, the fleets of whaling ships used to dock in the Shetlands to pick up their crews. In the process of reading about the industry, Laurie discovered that in a far off place in the Canadian north there existed a breed of people who still relied on whales and other wildlife for their complete survival. They were called Eskimos, or Inuit. "As I read book after book, I came to feel that they must be the toughest people in the world."

The focus of Laurie's reading became the geography, history, exploration and anthropology of the Arctic. It was then that he first felt a preliminary calling to missionary work among the Inuit. In spite of the beatings he had experienced at the hands of his peers, his father's influence prevailed.

279

About this time, Laurie met a girl named Sheena through his father's church. He discovered she was good at Latin, so he asked her if she would tutor him. They became friends.

"He was very shy," she recalls. "My first impression was that he was a bit of a loner and kept pretty much to himself. But even as a youngster, he liked to see how far he could go and push himself. I liked him because he was a little bit different. He was more interesting than the other boys. I never thought it would develop into something."

In the beginning, Laurie and Sheena went for walks in the parks of Glasgow. Gradually, these became hikes in the surrounding countryside, then hill walking and finally serious rock-climbing. "Gradually, it grew into love," she says.

You don't stand around and hope the ball's going to come to you. You get in there and make the ball come to you.
– Laurie Dexter

Years later, they would marry. Before they did, they would face many new challenges together and apart.

One winter's day during his early teens, Laurie was out hiking alone in deep snow. Suddenly, he fell into a cavern. He was able to climb out, but it shook him up a bit. Later that day, as he tried to return home, he had to descend the side of a large gully. It was covered with ice. Step by unnerving step, he slowly lowered himself from tree to tree. The further he descended, the greater his fear became. He knew that if he lost his balance or his grip, the result could be disastrous. "I remember thinking and praying, 'If I can survive this, I'm going to follow through with what I believe is my life's calling.' "

Laurie made it back safely. The trip became one of a series of events which seemed to draw him inexorably toward a pre-determined destiny. It was more than the spiritual influence of his parents. It was something larger.

Then came Sunday, January 5, 1959. Laurie was approaching 14. As he sat in church in Glasgow listening to his father deliver a sermon, the turning point came. Secretly, he had been questioning the reality of his own faith for some time. So, he said a prayer asking Jesus to be part of his life in a real and meaningful way.

"I felt no wave of emotion. In fact, I felt no change at all."

Laurie was wrong. There was a change and it was significant. The very act of asking for some direction created the psychological and spiritual commitment he had been seeking. His life was never the same.

280

"The key to it was the sense of purpose. I still believe we all have a purpose for being here. The sense of call is not some magical thing. It's not a voice in the night. The things I'm talking about are not some sort of big emotional upheaval or high. It's a very logical sequence of events, which are yet supernatural in that sequence. It didn't just happen by chance and so things began to come together and doors began to open which would not have opened through the normal process of events as far as I could see. I knew what I had to do and what I had to be."

For Laurie, that logical sequence of events had started as a minister's son in the Shetlands. It expanded in the wilderness during his early spiritual contacts with nature and progressed during his studies of the Inuit. Finally, it crystallized on that January morning in church.

After high school, Laurie attended college and majored in physical education. All the while, he knew he still wanted to work with the church among the Inuit. He discovered that at the time there were really only two churches working in the Canadian north: Roman Catholic and Anglican. Apart from any theological differences, with Sheena becoming an increasingly important part of his life, the celibacy of Roman Catholicism held little appeal. So, he applied to the Anglicans.

He was rejected.

"They told me not to bother because I didn't know a single Anglican priest for a reference, I had never worshipped in an Anglican church and I certainly hadn't been baptized as an Anglican. Their only suggestion was that I join a local Anglican congregation. Aside from the fact that there wasn't one nearby, my allegiance lay with my father's church."

281

Laurie was undeterred. He wrote back saying that he felt God was calling him to work in the North. Even though it was impossible for him to be admitted as a minister in their church, he asked if they would at least let him go through the selection process. They agreed.

Laurie eventually attended a theological college in England and while there, married Sheena. Before he was ordained, he accepted a position in Coral Harbour, NWT, a tiny settlement on Southampton Island at the north end of Hudson's Bay – an island the size of Scotland. It was the biggest challenge he has ever faced in his life, including the Polar Bridge.

"I left everything I knew – my culture, my family, my country and my language. I was uprooted and, within days, was planted in a foreign country in a totally different geographical environment and among a completely different people who spoke a different language. My task was to be able to relate intimately with those people and have the nerve to be able to say to them, 'I have something of value for you.'"

Laurie and Sheena were in Coral Harbour for eight months. Then, there came an opportunity for Laurie to finish his theological training and be ordained. From Coral Harbour, they moved to Saskatoon, Saskatchewan. After that, it was back to the deep freeze in Pond Inlet, NWT – the most northerly parish in Canada – on the northeastern end of Baffin Island. Laurie and Sheena stayed there for eight and a half years, during which time Andrew and Alison were born. In all, Laurie spent 13 years as a minister in the high Arctic before eventually moving south to Fort Smith.

"In each of his postings, the missions have become self-supporting," says John Sperry, Bishop of the Arctic. "That's absolutely outstanding in the expensive world of the Arctic."

Laurie has always been a bit uncertain about how his church views him, not only as a minister, but as an athlete and adventurer.

"I think the church sees Laurie in two ways," says Bishop Sperry. "Those who know him well recognize his invaluable contribution to the church, but according to one or two letters, some people ask why he isn't in his parish. But Laurie has not lost his zeal for being a missionary. Within the church itself, he has tremendous respect high up."

"The church looks on his activities very positively," says Archbishop Michael Peers, Primate of the Anglican Church of Canada. "For people who work in the church to have another area of excellence is positive. I don't think anyone would view his activities as a waste of time. He has the talent and the discipline. Laurie's an interesting combination of amiability and determination. He has a great capacity to stay with things. People without that kind of determination don't last in the Arctic."

Somewhere near the horizon, Laurie made out the shape of something floating in the air. That must be it, he thought to himself. That must be the North Pole.

As they inched their way closer, burdened as they always were with their heavy loads, things came into clearer focus. Yes, there was something there. There were huge balloons, and flags and even two inflatable tents. They had reached the ceremony site.

At 9:00 p.m. on April 25, 1988, after 55 gruelling days and over 960 km of travel through some of the most inhospitable terrain on the surface of the earth, 13 weary

You reach the top by taking that first step.
— **Laurie Dexter**

men slowly approached the North Pole. They were met enthusiastically by a few Soviet reporters, some supporters and friends. They were the first human beings, in fact, the first signs of life Laurie had seen besides his companions in almost two months. The rest of their welcoming team had been delayed due to bad weather and was not expected until morning.

The dream of reaching the North Pole has been the goal of adventurers for decades. Although the jury remains divided on exactly who was the first person to stand there, many believe it was U.S. Navy Admiral Robert Peary. On April 6, 1909, along with five other men and 38 sled dogs, Peary is reported to have said, "The Pole at last! The prize of three centuries, my dream and ambition for 23 years. Mine at last."

In reality, the North Pole belongs to no one. Those who seek to stand there are perpetually disappointed. The ice around it is no different than the ice hundreds of kilometres away. It is as nondescript and unimpressive as any patch of snow on the planet. What is more, the moment you stand there is even more fleeting than the fame it may bring you. Within minutes, the drift of the ice pack causes the Pole to slip away beneath your feet. In reality, it is more a point in time than it is a point on the earth. It is as evasive – and as elusive – as the end of a rainbow.

Although Laurie was excited to be at the Pole, he was not euphoric. One of his primary character traits is his even temperament. "I don't go through wide swings of mood. Most of the time, I am on an even keel. When things go wrong, I don't get too excited. When things go well, I enjoy it, but I don't really whoop it up.

"I think it's a positive trait, but it may not be viewed so by everybody. While it's wonderful not to experience the depressions that I see some people going through, neither do I get to experience the incredible highs that some people feel."

Success, or the things we call success, are so fleeting. They are so temporal.
– Laurie Dexter

Laurie's rest was, as always, too short. Within hours, the outside world descended on the Pole. It came in the form of noisy helicopters which roused them with abruptness. Within minutes, they were surrounded by a horde of over 180 dignitaries, reporters, sponsors, investors and supporters. The assortment included an eight-year-old boy, a dozen runners calling themselves "The Polar Pacers" and one cold and confused dog.

There was also one surprise guest. As Laurie emerged bleary-eyed from one of the tents, he came face to face with the last person on Earth he expected to see there – Sheena.

"You're here as well!" he exclaimed, as his jaw dropped and his eyes widened in speechless disbelief. "I can't believe it."

Sheena's appearance had been the doing of one of his closest friends, "Arctic" Joe Womersley. Although the wives of expedition members had been strictly prohibited from journeying to the Pole, Joe and his friends had dug deep into their pockets. They had secretly flown her all the way from Fort Smith to Ottawa and on to the Pole – almost twice the length of the country. Not even the expedition's management company had known she was coming. In disguise and travelling under a false name, she had been personally smuggled by Joe and his running friends "The Polar Pacers," through several airports, numerous secu-

285

rity checks and thousands of kilometres of frozen wilderness.

"I just couldn't believe how well Laurie looked," says Sheena. "It was wonderful. It was just like he was home. I felt incredibly guilty, but seeing Laurie's face was just great."

There was, however, one problem. In the midst of the hundreds of questions from the assembled reporters, Laurie and Sheena had no time whatsoever to themselves. About all they had time for was a heart-felt hug and the exchange of a few letters from home. Then Laurie was whisked away to make a speech.

Everyone huddled around a metre-high cylinder of ice that was supposed to be the pole. Radiating out from it were blue lines which had been spray-painted to represent the lines of longitude which came together at that point. Beneath a banner that proclaimed "Welcome to the North Pole" in English, French, Russian and Inuktitut, Laurie spoke:

"We are at the North Pole! All of Earth's meridians meet here. And it seems to us that we are able to see all the mountains and seas, the countries and the people from this vantage point. Let peace be on Earth forever."

When the speeches were done, everyone joined hands and, to a backdrop of coloured flares and balloons, circled around the pole, moving through all of the world's time zones in the process. Somewhere in the middle of this, Joe Womersley and his "Polar Pacers" went for a run. They called it "Around the World in 80 Minutes" even though it only took about half that.

For four hours that sunny morning in the Arctic, there was the biggest party ever held at the Pole. Joe and "The Pacers" had brought piles of exotic food, everything from fresh strawberries, bananas, maple cookies and cakes to bacon, sausages and stew. This was supplemented with government-supplied lobster, coq au vin, pate and, of course, Russian vodka. Helicopters and planes buzzed continually overhead ferrying food, supplies and personnel from a nearby Soviet ice station. There was toast after toast and photo after photo. Champagne flowed freely and everyone smiled from ear to ear. There had never been so much life in such a frozen place.

Unfortunately, the skiers never got to sample the banquet. Everything was gobbled up by the hungry "guests." Richard Weber watched in disgust and amazement as one obese journalist devoured the last of the raw bacon by diving face-first into it. To add insult to injury, a few of the departing visitors removed critical wind-proof clothing from the packs of some expedition members as souvenirs.

287

"Our vital space had been violated," recalls expedition member, Max Buxton.

The locusts disappeared as fast as they had come. By 12:30 p.m., all had lifted off by helicopter in a whirlwind of snow and deafening rotors. Three hours later, the tents were deflated around Laurie and the team. Two hours after that, the only evidence that anyone else had been there was a few pieces of windblown litter, a partially obliterated north "pole" and a lot of footprints in the snow.

To Laurie and the others, the whole affair seemed like a bizarre dream. Over and over he found himself asking, "Did that really happen?" Here they were, about as far from civilization as you could get on this world – and all of a sudden people, food, balloons and banners had dropped from the sky. Now, they were gone. He felt like he'd just communed with creatures from outer space. He couldn't differentiate fact from fantasy, reality from imagination.

His head spun for days in dazed bewilderment.

To ground himself, he went for a short walk and took a Russian New Testament with him. Finding a large outcrop of ice, he opened it and gently put it down as a symbolic offering to God. Then he thought about how much he would have given just to have had half an hour alone with Sheena, or with his father now gone, or his mother now alone.

At the North Pole, the representation of the pinnacle of a lifetime of achievement, Laurie Dexter cried. It was too anticlimactic, surreal. As he stood alone looking out over the cold, empty ice, he realized all he wanted to do was to go home. It was 800 km away – 800 km of the most treacherous ice of the trip.

Laurie and his companions reached the other side of the bridge five weeks later. For weeks, they had been hearing horror stories of a huge expanse of open water many kilometres wide separating them from their destination, Ward Hunt Island on Cape Columbia.

The open water never appeared. Like a reverse parting of the Red Sea, the gap closed up before them. Filling it was one last obstacle: a terrifying jumble of massive ice blocks pitched on end. It was the point of contact between the ever-shifting ocean ice and the land ice permanently frozen to the shore.

They were past the point of caring. All Laurie wanted now – all they all wanted – was to be finished. Painstakingly, they picked their way through it. On the other side, they slid down on their backsides like little children on toboggans. Then, they shook hands and cheered. They were still about 8 kilometres from terra firma, but the danger was behind them. For the first time in 90 days, they were safe.

The final day dawned with all the splendour of spring. June 1, 1988 will forever be etched in Laurie Dexter's memory. It was unseasonably warm – just below freezing. There was bright sunshine and not a cloud in the sky. There was no need to hurry. The end was in sight. They stopped frequently to take photographs, savouring their achievement. It was all so fantastic, like a dream.

Then, they came to their first real "land," an ordinary-looking patch of gravel about six metres across. Dmitri called a halt.

"We do this together!" he declared proudly. "Together."

The things for which people strive with life and limb usually turn out to be vessels with holes in them that let through the things which really bring peace and satisfaction.
– Laurie Dexter

289

There was nothing more to it than to take that last step. Lining up around the patch, they put their ski tips on the edge of the earth. Then, at the signal, they all took that last stride in unison. For the first time in 91 days, they heard gravel beneath their feet. They were home.

Laurie took off his skis and climbed a nearby hill. From there, he looked out over the huge expanse of ice, back toward Siberia. For one magnificent moment, he was filled with an overwhelming sense of awe. "There was this tremendously barren yet unique beauty, and a deafening silence. Everything is so enormously beyond normal human perception in the Arctic. Everything fills your mind."

Then the marble pragmatist spoke: "I felt a sense of great thankfulness and satisfaction at having completed something very difficult. My whole focus had been to finish."

The Bridge to Reality – The Marathon of Life

The battle began at the sound of a horn. As a lone bugler bleated out a charge over the barren Arctic landscape, 30 foot soldiers started their advance. Somewhere in the crowd, the inspirational notes of the theme from "Chariots of Fire" rang out from a tape recorder. The still in the land of the midnight sun was broken.

The runners took off over the gravel road and hurried toward the first corner. There, turning crisply to the left, they headed out of town. The 12th annual Midnight Sun Ultra-Marathon was under way.

Sunday, July 1, 1990; Canada Day, the nation's birthday: It was 5:00 a.m. in the tiny mining town of Nanisivik at the northern end of Baffin Island – just over 600 km north of the Arctic Circle. While most people lay snoozing in their beds, 30 of North America's most committed runners had begun their ordeal. Among the runners that morning was ultra-marathoner Laurie Dexter. He had been Nanisivik's first Christian minister. From his base in the tiny Inuit village of Pond Inlet some 240 km east, he had commuted every three months to Nanisivik and to the Inuit hamlet of Arctic Bay, some 32 km distant.

The mining town of Nanisivik stood virtually deserted, the small cluster of trailers, prefabricated houses and dome-shaped enclaves silent in the sun. Above town, on the crest of a large hill, a lone crucifix overlooked the scene. Below it, the massive inlet of Strathcona Sound was equally serene. It was still covered with ice, and would be for several weeks yet. When the ice finally melted, one of the few supply ships of the year would slowly put into port and deposit a load of life-sustaining supplies for the next 12 months. Then, it would vanish before the long Arctic winter.

It was to Arctic Bay that Laurie and the other runners were headed that morning. The day was glorious. As the sun hung over the horizon, as it would all day and all night for the coming weeks, a brilliant blue sky stretched overhead without a single cloud. The temperature was a cool 4° C and there was a light wind. It was the kind of day marathoners dream of – perfect for running. One local pilot remarked that it was the best weather he'd seen in 28 years.

The contest would last all day, for some as long as 14 hours. It would be a brutal 84 km long – double the standard marathon distance. By the time it ended, there would be casualties. Laurie hoped he would not be one of them.

"The Midnight Sun Ultra-Marathon" is widely acknowledged as one of the world's toughest runs. The most northerly race of its kind, it is famous for its hills, its solitude and its foul weather. Staged annually on the only road that stretches between Nanisivik and Arctic Bay, it attracts some of the globe's greatest marathoners. The gruelling out-and-back course covers a series of merciless hills that gradually shatter resolve. After descending 5 km from the start, during the next 10 km of the route, the runners ascend an astounding 480 m. The next 27 km into Arctic Bay are run mostly downhill. Then, the real running begins. From Arctic Bay they must run back over the same terrain – mostly uphill.

"Just looking at the course is scary," says Laurie, who has run the double or single marathon here every year but one since the race began in 1979. "I get a hollow in the pit

No matter how much I hurt or how slow I may be going, I usually finish because finishing is what's important.
– Laurie Dexter

of my stomach. You can almost smell the fear in the bus that takes the runners to the starting line."

It is not only the topography of the course that causes the casualties of the Midnight Sun Marathon. The landscape is so barren that there are no markers by which to judge your progress. In city marathons, there are always side streets or street lights by which to continually monitor your progress, but here there is nothing. It's like running on a continuous treadmill.

In addition to this, there is the overwhelming solitude of the place. There are no crowds lining the route, in fact no people for many kilometres. The field of competitors is so small that often the only sound is your own breathing, the pounding of your stride, and the wind. It takes every ounce of will to prevent your mind from playing horrible games, games in which you can not only lose the race, but lose yourself in the process. The event epitomizes the loneliness of the long distance runner. Here, every man and woman is an island.

This was the challenge facing Laurie Dexter that glorious morning – the toughest, northernmost, steepest, coldest double-marathon in the world.

Although he'd run this race eight times before, Laurie knew it wouldn't be any easier this time. He knew it was going to hurt. He knew there would be moments when he would ask himself why he was there. He also knew that if he made it, he would not be able to walk without discomfort for several days. Descending stairs would be difficult; climbing into a car very uncomfortable.

292

The obvious question is: Why would anyone want to run 84 km? Why would anyone want to put themselves through such pain, especially here, in the middle of nowhere?

"The failure to finish would hurt me more than all the pain I'm going to put up with during the race. The pain of the race will go away in about a week. But if I didn't finish, I would go over and over that in my mind for months and months.

"I really don't know about this business of failure. I don't think anybody else would think less of me if I didn't finish. But I would of myself."

"Ultra-marathoners," as they are known, are an unusual breed inflicted with a madness for motion. They consider 42-km marathons relative child's play. Their objective is to run double, triple, even quadruple the usual distance and to keep running until they can run no longer. For them, running is not measured in hours, but in days, sometimes weeks. They are the super-achievers of the running world and their objective is clear, but not simple: push themselves to the frontiers of personal discovery. It has long ago ceased to be their passion. It is their absolute obsession.

Before this race, the furthest Laurie had run at a stretch was 640 km. It took him six days. His latest goal is to run 1,600 km with stops only to cat nap.

If there is a gospel according to Laurie, it is running. It has almost become his own private religion. With robes exchanged for runners, his church becomes the vast land through which he runs. He not only moves, but moves his congregation, whether it's a bunch of fellow runners sharing the road with him, or hundreds in a church.

Failure is a very important learning process. You have to analyze it. Once you've analyzed it, then you set up your next dream.
– Laurie Dexter

294

"I don't want to be confined to just a parish ministry. I think that one of the things that's kept me going is that I'm constantly widening the focus of what I believe to be my life calling. I'm not called to be a minister to one group of people. Whoever I'm in contact with, that is my congregation."

Sporting a brand new pair of red tartan shorts and a blue and white singlet with the letters NWT on the chest, Laurie began his battle. His face told a tale of early race tension. He was silent; his forehead furrowed. Within half a kilometre of leaving the start, however, he was out in front and began to relax. I followed along behind on a mountain bike.

From town, he turned and led the pack down the "Crunch." As his pre-race jitters wore off, his stride became crisp and sure, the way you wish it could always be, but which in ultra-marathoning is nothing but a temporary calm before the storm.

At the bottom of the "Crunch", Laurie passed by a building that could easily hold two football fields. It was the storage shed for the refined concentrate from the

DEVELOP POSITIVE DISSATISFACTION

"Positive dissatisfaction" is critical to success. Dreamers, by their very nature, are dissatisfied with how things are. That's why they dream. As they imagine what it would be like, an excitement flows over them. "Some men see things as they are and say why," Robert F. Kennedy said while quoting George Bernard Shaw. "I dream of things that never were and say why not."

town's lead and zinc mine and is probably the largest building in the high Arctic.

On the docks beside the storage shed, Laurie rounded a bucket filled with sand and precisely on pace, started up the "Crunch" for the first of two times during the race.

This was no ordinary hill. While the Boston Marathon's series of climbs ending in the dreaded "Heartbreak Hill" have become legendary in marathoning circles, the comparatively unknown "Crunch" makes Boston's equivalent look like a bump on the landscape. More than 10 times higher in elevation gain, it climbs a slow, agonizing 300 m. It snakes its way through a series of winding switchbacks on the dry gravel road. Except for the storage shed and a noisy refining mill three-quarters of the way up, it is like everything else for kilometres around – barren and exposed. It is also deceptively steep. The struggle continues past Nanisivik to rise an additional 180 m for 5 more kilometres; in all, 480 m in 10 km. "The Crunch" is more than vicious. It is vile.

So far it had been an absolute breeze for me to keep up with Laurie. Coasting effortlessly down the hill beside him on my bike, I had shivered in the early morning air as it whisked by me. Now, at the foot of "The Crunch", I geared down to save energy. Meanwhile, with every hurried pedal stroke I watched Laurie pulling further and further away. As my face became redder and redder, not from exertion but from embarrassment, I imagined spending the entire day playing catch the rabbit. That, I decided, would be the ultimate humiliation – to travel thousands of kilometres to one of the most remote places on earth only to lose the one man I had come to see in the first 30 minutes of the race.

295

Nothing rational can explain Nanisivik – except money. In the local Inuit language, Nanisivik means "a place where people find things." Here they found lead and zinc. The race was originally organized as a fitness and morale-booster for the town's people, but has blossomed into a world-class event. Every June, the company that owns the mine, Strathcona Mineral Services of Toronto, charters a jet and flies 100 or so runners from departure points in Toronto and Montreal. This group of largely ne'er-be-fore-northerners steps off the plane wide-eyed and gaping. "Welcome to the Great White North," they are told. Jet-lagged from a six-hour flight equivalent to a trans-Atlantic crossing, they suddenly realize that Canada is almost as big north to south as it is east to west. Most of that distance is nothing but open Arctic space.

To understand Laurie Dexter, you must see him here. Here, the ultra-marathoner is ultra-polite, ultra-conservative and slightly subdued. To many of the locals and to race organizer "Arctic" Joe Womersley, Laurie is a hero.

"If you wanted to choose a person to be your brother, son, father or uncle, Laurie'd be perfect," says Joe, himself a high achiever who has completed the famous "Ironman" triathlon (swimming, biking, running) in Hawaii and sailed across the Atlantic in a catamaran. "He never complains, he works on a mediocre salary, and he's a man of great honour."

Finally, the road leveled off and I caught up, apologizing profusely to Laurie who, in spite of his climb, didn't seem the least bit tired, let alone upset by my absence. He was as he usually was – forgiving.

By the time Laurie reached the top of the huge hill and made the turn to Arctic Bay, he had been running continuously uphill for over an hour. Laurie hadn't missed a stride. He glided smoothly over the road as effortlessly as if he'd just crossed the street. I shuddered at the thought that this double marathon would also end on this same hill.

Minutes after the turn to Arctic Bay, Laurie passed one of the most significant points on the route – the Terry Fox memorial. It is a monument to the ultimate lonely runner. It stands out starkly against the sky: three bare flagpoles with the ensigns of Canada, the Northwest Territories and British Columbia, Terry's home. A single plaque declares: "He never gave up." It is the only man-made feature visible for many kilometres. With the rock and rubble of the Arctic as its backdrop and with the wind whipping through its flags, it stands as a silent tribute to the one-legged marathoner who died of cancer and who has been immortalized as a Canadian hero.

297

An hour or so after passing the memorial, we crossed a bridge and started up another of the dozens of long, seemingly endless hills on the course.

Suddenly, Laurie stirred from his silence. "Shit! I'm starting to get a blister. We'll have to stop just ahead."

For the first three years of the Midnight Sun, Laurie did not run on Sunday. It was not that he was against competing on the Sabbath, it was just that his professional commitments as a minister precluded his involvement on that day.

In many ways, Laurie is not unlike the famous Scottish runner, Eric Liddell, of the film, "Chariots of Fire". He was a minister who would not run on Sunday. Liddell, who became known as "The Flying Scot" is one of Laurie's greatest heroes.

"If ever there was a man who never surrendered an inch in life, it was Eric Liddell," Laurie says. "People tried to pin him down to a Christian stereotype. Reporters would

What is a runner? A runner is somebody who took one step, and then was a little bit off balance so had to take another step, and another, and so on. That's all achievement is – it's a series of steps. But it takes courage to take that very first step. Once you've made it and broken the barrier, then things begin to roll."
– Laurie Dexter

ask him if, when he ran a race and won, if he felt he was inspired by God and if he felt his faith gave him wings. His answer was 'No. I just don't like to be beaten.'

"Eric was a man of incredible tenacity," says Laurie as his eyes light up. "He never surrendered anything and yet, the fact is, he surrendered all his ambitions, he surrendered all his potential wealth and fame to go abroad to live in circumstances that nobody else would live in. He surrendered his will to God. That level of surrender was, paradoxically, his great source of courage and strength in all the other things. That really means something to me. In everything I do, the ultimate test is how much is surrendered to God. While I'll fight to the bitter end in a race or anything else, I'll never give in. The reason is because I believe I'm surrendered to the will of God."

Laurie's philosophy of life, achievement and spirituality are wholly integrated and inseparably linked. They boil down to one formula: If you never yield to fear, discomfort or pain, you will achieve your true potential. When you achieve your true potential, you bring glory not only to yourself, but to your Lord.

As Laurie descended "Pain in the Ass", the majestic, ice-covered mass of Admiralty Inlet gradually came into view. Bordered on one side by 600-m sheer cliffs, which Laurie at one time climbed, it was a panorama of breathtaking beauty – blue sky, brown rock and white ice.

Slowly, we approached Arctic Bay, now just 10 km away. One kilometre later, the hamlet came into view. Laurie had spent five years here as a minister.

Arctic Bay had not been easy for Laurie. The Inuit had never seen running before. In their eyes, it was a complete waste of time and energy. Why, they asked, would anyone run for recreation when they could hunt or fish? Because few people understood his desire to run, Laurie was treated even more as an outsider.

"A couple of folks said I was the first minister they'd ever known who acted like a child. 'Only children run. Adults don't.' they said. Their reaction was much the same when I wore shorts. I was told that a grown man doesn't go around in shorts."

"Every morning around 6:00 he would go for a run, even on very cold days," recalls Arctic Bay resident Sam Willie, an Inuk. "Nobody does that around here. The only reason we run is when we're with a dog team. At first we thought there was no purpose to it. Now we understand."

Although Laurie was not immediately accepted in Arctic Bay, he was respected. He already spoke Inuktitut and proceeded to adapt to the local dialect. Quietly, he stole his way into the people's hearts. The key was his patience, his polite disposition, and especially his unpretentiousness.

"In order for him to learn our language, he had to bring himself to our level," says Sam. "That's what brought about the feeling he was our friend. Sure, he made mistakes. Before I met him, church was just church. I didn't care much for it. But I got close to him. He had a relaxed lifestyle and manner."

Eventually, Sam became a vestry member in Laurie's church. Laurie was successful in converting many others, but surprisingly, few have become his close friends. He

Unfortunately, to do anything worthwhile in life nearly always involves a measure of sacrifice.
– Laurie Dexter

300

works well in a group, but to this day, continues to be a loner. Independence and solitude is an integral part of his character. From his solo hiking expeditions in Scotland as a youth to his ultra-running as an adult, it has always been his nature.

There were no cheering crowds when Laurie came puffing into town. He was unperturbed. The only human contact and encouragement he received was from fellow runners who had set out early from Arctic Bay on their own marathons to Nanisivik. As they passed each other going in opposite directions, the slower runners applauded Laurie warmly. Pushing hard now to reach his turn point in the scheduled three hours and 30 minutes, Laurie had only enough energy to raise a hand in thanks. The sweat poured from his brow.

"I've really got to take a chance here," he said between breaths. "I feel good. I could hold back and try to conserve some energy for the return but if I do that, I won't be able to maintain the lead. I've got to go for it."

In the world of marathon running, winning has its own definition. Except for the elite competitors, placement numbers are largely meaningless. To some degree, so are finishing times. What takes their place is the battle within yourself, the struggle against your own doubts, fears and discomfort. To win is to overcome yourself – and to finish. To finish fast is a bonus.

At the turn point in Arctic Bay, Laurie was still on pace. It was now 8:30 a.m. on that sleepy Sunday. At a time when most of the world, north or south, was still fast asleep, Laurie Dexter had already completed his first marathon of the day. He turned for home – still another marathon away and mostly uphill.

Marathons of one sort or another are nothing new to Laurie Dexter. During his lifetime, he has made 26 first ascents of Arctic peaks, some of them solo and in the pitch-black of the Arctic winter. A glance at his resume leaves you breathless. He has run eight double marathons, six races over 100 km and is the Canadian aged 40 – 44 record-holder for runs between 300-640 km. He is also the record-holder in his age group for runs of three, four, five, six and seven days.

"I believe that ultra-marathons, perhaps more than any other sport, help turn the clock back for your body. It has completely changed many of our concepts of aging. We have a total misconception about the body slowing down as it gets older. It does slow down and we do get weaker, but nowhere near as much as some people allow it to happen."

Laurie admits that although many people run, not many do so for two and three days at a time. He dismisses charges he's a fanatic. "It's very rare to meet anybody who really believes that I'm crazy for doing these things. If that does happen, I have no quarrel with that. Everybody has to find their own way in life and what's fulfilling for them. I know that many of the things I do have no appeal for them. That's fine, but I would hope that they are generous enough in spirit to be able to look at the things I do and see that they are right for me without making a judgment call."

Although Laurie's running requires a huge time commitment and individual focus, he has not lost sight of others. Running is important to him, but it is not his everything. "It has great value to me, but I do not overestimate what it really means. It really doesn't have any value to the world. People, on the other hand, have life, spirit, soul and eternal value in them.

"Everything we do in life impinges upon other people, and it's up to us to make those paths of crossing meaningful. That's what makes our own lives meaningful, as we learn from, associate with and as we love other people."

Laurie is not like other high achievers, whose goals frequently force them to focus so entirely on themselves that they become one-dimensional. He will try just about anything. Besides running, his skills include hiking, backpacking, climbing, skiing, kayaking and table tennis. He has studied Latin and Greek, knows a little French and Russian, and plays the viola, violin, and mandolin. He can also navigate using a sextant.

Whether at home or on the road, Laurie is a marathon man. His face is gaunt – the way the faces of most marathoners are – and there is direction, even in his forehead. Two curious wrinkles point down and in, like an arrow. The top of his head is covered with short, brown hair that dissolves into silver sideburns in stark contrast to his blue eyes. His upper body is tanned and trim, and his muscles are long, lean and sinewy. They almost glow from the endless hours of life-giving blood pushed through them by the powerful pump in his chest. Aside from his lack of body fat, however, he appears average.

"I'm certainly not different physically from anybody else. When people meet me they're surprised at how very ordinary I am. That's one of the reasons I believe people have far greater potential than they are realizing."

Surprisingly, he is not the most fluid runner. His steps are swift and solid, but he reminds you more of a running bear than a graceful gazelle. His footfalls are heavy and distinct, but unrelenting. He is a plodder.

In more than just physical appearance, Laurie is a man of contrasts. In church and in life, he is unendingly polite, even meek – the way you imagine a humble, small-town preacher should be. He is all but invisible in a crowd.

Aim high. Do the goal-setting bit. But be sure you make time for the things that really count – people.
– Laurie Dexter

But looks deceive, especially Laurie's looks. Like most marathoners, Laurie's greatest strength is contained deep inside, in his heart. It is here, invisible to the eye, that Laurie displays his real power. Fiercely determined and doggedly persistent, he rarely lets go of anything once he's got his teeth into it. It may be a finish line eight hours away, or a piece of nondescript ice at the top of the world, but either way, he gets there.

About 16 km out of Arctic Bay, Laurie reached the bottom of "Pain in the Ass" again. "That hill has always been one of my worst points," he says. "But I decided to take a chance, to push it harder than I really felt was wise. I ran it faster than ever before."

Laurie knew he had gone out fast; he just didn't know yet if it was too fast. After the top of "Pain in the Ass," the road began to drop steeply to a bridge at the base of a valley. By now, busloads of marathoners had begun to pass him going in the opposite direction. They were on their way to the start of their marathon from Arctic Bay to Nanisivik, scheduled to begin within hours. As each bus passed, all its passengers gave a rousing cheer and hung out the windows with cameras, offering encouragement. As always, Laurie politely acknowledged them, but did not give pause. His pace, although strained now, continued unabated.

303

Worth should not be judged on what you do or do not achieve. A person is worthy because they are human. A child should be loved because they are a child.
– Laurie Dexter

304

Laurie wondered where his son, Andrew, was. During the months leading up to the race, he had become Andrew's coach. Andrew was entered in the 32-km event – the longest distance he had ever run. "I never pushed Andrew into running," Laurie says. "He just seemed to catch on to it."

In past years, when the bus-bound marathoners and 32-km runners had passed the ultra-runners, they had often told their bus driver to stop so they could cheer at the roadside. That hadn't happened this year. Since Laurie hadn't seen his son, he assumed he had already passed on his way to Arctic Bay. That saddened him.

Then a bright yellow truck pulled over. Half a dozen people piled out. One of them was Andrew. Laurie's spirits soared. Andrew was only 15. His presence here meant that both of them would be running on the same course, but at different times. Together, they had toyed with the idea of Laurie winning the ultra for the first time and Andrew winning the 32-km race the first time he entered.

"We both knew that it was very unlikely we could win. Yet, deep down inside we both secretly hoped we could. I knew that when he saw me in the lead, even though I might not be confident, I knew he'd think, 'Boy, Dad's going to do it this year.' I knew it would give him a real boost for his own race."

To a rousing cheer, father and son slapped each other's hands in an emotion-charged "high five." Then, without missing a stride, Laurie continued down the hill.

"When I was younger, I looked up to my Dad a lot," says Andrew. "Everything I want to do, he'll try to help me do. Whether he likes the sport or not, he'll put out the money. But he doesn't force me to do what I don't want to do."

Andrew and Laurie enjoy a special relationship. They share far more than an interest in running. They share a mutual fascination with each other's differences. While Laurie is conservative, pragmatic and frugal, Andrew is liberal, idealistic and materialistic. He loves bright-coloured clothing, loud music, and flashy cars. Their banter is an entertaining exchange of open-ended respect for two very different lifestyles.

"I can say things or do things that I would never be able to do in front of other people because I know he won't get mad at me," says Andrew. "Like rap music. It has swearing in it all the time. Sometimes when we run side-by-side I put it on. All he says is, 'I don't really like that Andrew.' But sometimes he listens to my music with me and analyses the words and the tunes and tries to explain why he doesn't like it. And he's not your typical minister. I like that about him. I know every side of him. He doesn't put on an act in public. At home, you wouldn't think he's a minister. He's only 'churchy' on Sunday. After that, he's just a regular guy. He tells dirty jokes, for example."

If there is an interpersonal quality to Laurie as a man and as a minister, it is that he is non-judgmental. His values are his values and he does not impose them on others. You can feel completely at ease around him; you can be yourself.

"He's just fun to be around," says Laurie's daughter, Alison. "He doesn't look down on people. He looks for the best in them."

While he aspires to a higher calling, Laurie knows that he is a fallible human being. One of his greatest fears, in fact, is that as a man of the cloth, he will be put on a pedestal and from there, fall from grace. "Anybody can fall. I have the same temptations as everybody else – emotional, immoral, whatever. If it happened, I would be devastated. It is one of my nightmares.

"If you can gradually show people that there is no pedestal while still maintaining your leadership, then those dangers become less because people now view you on a more equal basis and, therefore, there's less danger of falling."

Adventuring and running are two ways Laurie reveals his humanity. While his strength and endurance are the source of considerable admiration, his struggles do more than just break down his own physical barriers. They break down the psychological barriers imposed on him as a middle-aged man.

"You appreciate your health and your own mortality when you do something like an ultra race, when you hurt and wonder if it's worth going on. You do go on, but you realize that one day this is going to come to an end – not today's race, but the race of life."

"One of the early Christian writers said that the glory of God is a human being truly human," says Archbishop Peers. "That's what Laurie's doing."

Within minutes of meeting Andrew, Laurie was grinding up yet another huge hill, pouring sweat, bent by the challenge. This was "Marathoner's Madness" – another 10-km-long, 300-m-high discomfort.

Laurie was forced to walk. Again, he looked behind him, straining to see any tiny specks that may be hunting him. To his dismay, he could just make out a pair of red shorts blasting swiftly down the hill on the far side of the valley. The competition was closing.

"I'm in trouble," Laurie said as he crested the first of dozens of false summits on his way up "The Madness," "I've really come apart in the last 10 minutes."

Laurie had not urinated in well over two hours. I began to notice he was sweating less and looking understandably pale. I knew these could be the preliminary signs of dehydration.

"That was probably the worst part of the race," he recalls. "Everything felt pretty bad. I had the first feelings of nausea and I had to fight just to keep my legs moving. I felt the temptation to walk that whole hill."

Immediately, he began to ply water into himself, first half a quart, then as much as he could handle every five minutes. He kept running.

We soon learned it was not dehydration. After more than five hours of running, with 58 km covered and 26 yet to go, Laurie had hit "the wall."

"The wall" is perhaps the most feared of all obstacles faced by long-distance runners. When the body exhausts the stores of energy lodged in the muscles, it must switch to burning fat instead. This transition does not happen instantaneously. It takes time. As a result, for a short period, the runner literally runs out of gas. What's left, and what keeps marathoners moving, is something which cannot be described. It is the unseen element that produces all feats of human endurance.

"Running a race like this is probably well over 50 percent mental. Most people would say 70 percent mental-30 percent physical. There comes a point when your body just doesn't have it anymore. From every conceivable assessment, the only thing your body can do is stop. Yet somehow it keeps moving. It's simply because your mind wills it to move. In a race like this, if you are really good from the shoulders up, you can keep plodding on. The key is not to lose it in the head."

"Guaranteed, the only thing that will stop my Dad from finishing is if he is threatened with losing a limb," says Andrew. "No matter how much it hurts, he will keep going until he finishes. Mentally, there's nobody stronger that I know."

Laurie had faced "the wall" dozens of times in his life. He knew how to break through it – with his head. Pinned against "the wall" on one side with his competitors closing in on the other, he had only two options: to quit or to keep climbing. He knew this could be the end, but he was sick of being a bridesmaid. He had finished second four times before. He'd been third once and fourth twice. This time, he wanted to be first.

"Marathoner's Madness" seemed to go on and on forever. The pain became etched in Laurie's face, then slowly became deeply engraved. I started to feel nauseous just watching.

When the Terry Fox Memorial came into view again, it was little comfort. Although Laurie knew now that only one hill remained, there was no respite. The spectre of the "Crunch" hung over him.

"He never gave up," came the words. "He never gave up." After turning toward Nanisivik, Laurie began his last, long, downhill stretch to the docks on Strathcona Sound. At 12:15 p.m., after seven and a quarter hours of running, Laurie rounded that bucket of sand on the docks. His energy ran out.

"I'm dead on my feet," he said, his voice lifeless. "I'm dead on my feet."

Then, the inevitable happened. That had been hunting him suddenly appeared on its way down. It was 32-year-old Jack Butler, a veteran marathoner with a reputation for finishing first. His best previous time for 84 km was almost a full half hour faster than Laurie's goal that day. And, with 15 years between them, he was a serious threat.

"When I saw Jack, I thought, 'Where did he come from?' He seemed to appear from nowhere. That really startled me."

What happened next startled me. When Jack reached Laurie, rather than keep blasting down the slope en route to ultimately passing him on the way up, he stopped suddenly. Extending his hand to Laurie, he said smiling, "Great effort, Laurie. Great effort." Then, he applauded Laurie.

This is the real magic of the Midnight Sun Marathon. While competitors in most southern races are often little more than numbers on a runners' list, here they are human beings with faces, names and personalities. The course is so terribly lonely, so incredibly demanding and so ultimately extracting that a mutual respect and bond develops between the competitors. It is unique. In the process, this frozen, seemingly heartless land somehow brings them together in the warmest possible way. Gone are the egos and selfish desires to eliminate the opposition. The human spirit is revealed. The only thing that matters is finishing. It is sport as sport should be, where winning is not measured in medals, but in mettle, and where the last man's achievement is as significant as the first's. Here, if you survive, you win.

"It was one of the finest gestures I've ever seen," Laurie said. "That is what this race is all about. In past years, it's usually been me in that position."

Physical strength and endurance and the ability to endure does not decrease with age. In fact, it may very well increase with age.

– Laurie Dexter

310

Laurie stopped running suddenly. "I'm going to have to walk this next section," he said as his voice evaporated.

My eyes darted to my watch, then back to Jack, now disappearing from sight on his way down to the docks. I lost all objectivity. I forgot my journalism training. I couldn't bear to see Laurie lose, not after all he'd been through, not after he'd so tenaciously hung on for so far and so long. His goal had become mine. I entered into the experience.

"C'mon Laurie," I screamed. "This race is yours! Go get it! It's yours!"

He looked back over his shoulder again. My heart sank. I was sure he had given up.

The next 30 minutes of that run will remain with me for the rest of my life. As I pedalled slowly alongside him barking continuous encouragement, I was witness to the most moving display of grit I have ever seen.

With an exhaustion approaching collapse, Laurie Dexter somehow continued to move up the "Crunch," crawling at a snail's pace. He squeezed every step out of himself like it was being willed through a tiny hole in his soul.

The inner man emerged then, not the straight-laced preacher or the quiet sensitive listener, but the scrapper, the warrior. Long depleted of all his physical reserves, he attacked the slope with his will. As the sun beat down, he went to a place I have never seen anyone go before.

He was wheezing again – wheezing and groaning. You could almost hear his legs screaming. With head bent forward and shoulders rounded, the steps came out in slow-motion – one after the other after the other.

The torture went on for what seemed like hours. I almost cried. I shared his pain.

Then, it ended. He turned the final corner into town.

"If I was forced to stop through external injury, fair enough, I'd accept that. But if I failed to finish just because I was hurting, then I wouldn't be able to live with myself afterwards because I wouldn't have lived up to my potential, to my aim. I would have allowed myself to be defeated."

A lot of people fail to achieve their objectives in life because they don't push through the pain.
– Laurie Dexter

Laurie was not defeated. He conquered the "Crunch" that day, as they all did. Jack Butler never took the lead. He reached the docks and had nothing left.

"I'm not sure I would have passed Laurie even if I'd been able to," he said later. "I have too much respect for him. This was his year. He beat me fair and square."

"I run 83 kilometres so I can enjoy the 84th," Laurie says. "I don't enjoy the first 83, but I'm willing to run them because the 84th is the important one. The reward is in finishing. Finishing is what's important."

Laurie strode triumphantly across the finish line just three minutes under eight hours. My heart went into my mouth. I felt a tingle go up and down my spine. It was not the finish that moved me. It was all that had gone before.

At last, he stopped and looked at his watch. For the longest time, he just stood there staring at it, silent and swaying. For the first time in hours, he was alone not in pain, but in victory. He had won. He had overcome himself.

Moments later, he was helped into a waiting truck and whisked away for a relaxing shower, massage, food and

311

Success is measured in a person's level of achievement in relation to their potential.
– Laurie Dexter

drink. As I watched him go, the magnitude of what he had done hit me. His achievement went beyond spiritual strength or dogged determination. It hit you in the heart. It was the strength in his face. It was power amidst pain. It was courage.

About an hour later, Andrew also pounded across the finish to win the 32-km race. Laurie was there to cheer him in. Years earlier, at the finish of Laurie's second ultra, Andrew, then 7, had been there to cheer Laurie. The two had been photographed as Laurie crossed the line, father in front, exhausted, and son running along behind, jumping for joy. Now, the roles were reversed. Well, almost. Laurie was too sore to jump.

When the two hugged each other in the most visibly emotional embrace of the day, a cheer went through the small crowd of onlookers. Laurie seemed as happy about his son's achievement as he was about his own.

"I was just absolutely thrilled. I was bubbling up inside with joy for him."

"Half of it was for him," Andrew said. "Half was for me."

"We must not allow ourselves to become overly impressed with performance, or with the level of performance – the coming first," Laurie says. "When it's all said and done, the things that we achieve are of passing value. So we climb a mountain, or we run a distance that we have designated in a time system we have made up. So what? Really, these things have no objective value in themselves. It's only insofar as they change what we are within that they have value."

Laurie Dexter, Anglican minister, Christian, a man of peace, is a warrior in a war of one. He loves to do battle with his fears, his pain and even, at times, his boredom and loneliness. Yet he can never really appreciate the fight until it's over. Dead on his feet, but never more alive, he will crawl across the finish line if he has to, but he will never surrender. His excellence is enduring.

I have done my best in the race.
I have run the full distance and
I have kept the faith.
– 2 Timothy 4:7

314

Conclusion

Rediscovering the Adventure Attitude

Attitude is the key to success – not skill, not knowledge, not education – ATTITUDE.
– John Amatt

My university gymnastics coach, Ken Allen, used to say that your attitude at the beginning of a task largely determines your attitude at the end of a task. At the time, I thought it was a ploy to get me to believe that the four-hour workout I was about to endure was only going to hurt in my head.

When Sharon Wood said: "Adventure isn't an experience. It's an attitude that goes with an experience" a light went on. If what they're saying is true, the only difference between the ordinary individual and the extraordinary one is what goes on in their minds.

This book has attempted to explain what's in the minds of five high achievers. It has shown how what these people think – their attitudes – have formed their lives and enabled them to reach their pinnacles of success.

In the process of examining their achievements, we have pinpointed five "elements of excellence" that comprise the "adventure attitude." These primary elements are: courage, persistence, curiosity, teamwork and endurance.

Four more elements of the "adventure attitude," while sometimes less apparent, are no less critical to high achievement. When added to the five listed above, they form the basis for an expanded "adventure attitude."

The Nine Keys to Personal and Professional Success

The following nine elements are common to all our achievers. They are considered to be the hallmarks of success. Separately, they seem to be just a collection of ideas. Together, they give us a powerful acronym that describes the adventure attitude which enables us to take that one step beyond and into a successful life.

317

A   Achievement internally; success is self-satisfaction.

D   Dream big and dream often; imagine the ultimate.

V   Value your values; be true to yourself.

E   Excel under pressure; cultivate courage.

N   Never say die; endure endlessly.

T   Trust others; be great in a group.

U   Understand your commitment; give it your all.

R   Risk-take carefully; plan meticulously.

E   Exude energy; triumph relentlessly.

Adventure Attitude Element #1

Achieve Internally

We do not conquer mountains nor tame the elements. The true conquest lies in penetrating the self-imposed barriers, those limitations within our own minds.
– Sharon Wood

Society has established visible indicators of success. These include material security and wealth, fame and power. None of our adventure achievers use these scales. They value personal contentment, satisfaction in themselves, integrity, happiness and independence more than anything. More important for them is the satisfaction and deep sense of self-worth they acquire from their achievements. They have little need to prove anything to anybody because they have proved it to themselves. They are, as psychologists say, "self-actualized."

318

KNOW YOURSELF

A strong sense of self and a stubborn adherence to personal values is one of the most powerful "elements of excellence" displayed by people with the "adventure attitude." They intuitively know what's important to them and they stick to it. It may be that the severity of soul-searching they had to go through to find themselves creates such clarity and resolution. Whatever it is, once adventure achievers discover who they are, they are as rigid in their loyalty to values as they are in pursuit of their goals. That's because their goals and their values are integrated and inseparably linked. They pursue what's important to them, not to anyone else.

Examples:
• By monetary standards, Mike Beedell is poor. By experiential measurements, he is a billionaire.
• John Hughes says: "As a whole, society has moved away from testing one's mettle to measuring everything by certain standards: the size of your house, the number of cars you have, your income, etc. I'm not saying those aren't nice to have, but I don't think they should be what we as individuals measure ourselves by."

The "adventure attitude" challenges us to re-think our conventional standards of success. It isn't, at least to the people you've just read about in this book, an external, objective condition. It's an internal, subjective reality. But it is still measurable: by how we feel inside ourselves. Sharon Wood says: "Success is contentment."

Laurie Dexter says, "Success, ultimately, is an inner thing. It's not something that can be measured in objective ways." Laurie Skreslet comments that, "Success, to me, is the sense of deep satisfaction you get when you're doing what you love. Money is a side issue."

If personal contentment and satisfaction are really the true measures of happiness and success, it would appear that somebody has hoodwinked the western world. While our consumer economy depends to a large degree on a "buy-your-dream" mentality to ensure the demand for goods, it may be steering some people in the wrong direction – to the cash register instead of to the jackpot within themselves. Is your personal Utopia a custom-built home in the suburbs with two cars, a motorhome and a boat? Or is it a sense of inner peace, a feeling that you've done the very best you can do?

319

There is no question that if we hope to survive in the twenty-first century, we will have to severely curtail our consumption, not only of goods, but of the resources required to produce those goods. A shift from consumerism and planned obsolescence to "sustainable individualism" based on the renewable and positive energy within ourselves may be part of the solution. Our locus of control and reward must shift from outside to inside.

Adventure Attitude Element #2

Dream Big and Dream Often

Achievement is the constant process of going one step beyond your previous experience.
– John Amatt

Those with the "adventure attitude" not only dream big, they think big – very BIG. First they make gigantic mental leaps of faith. Then they make equally quantum leaps in reality. This capacity to think far beyond the realm of "reasonable," separates great achievers from aspiring achievers.

Examples:
• Mike Beedell's daily daydreaming.
• John Hughes' constant setting of new goals once old ones have been achieved.

When John Hughes first seriously considered sailing solo around the world he had no boat, no sponsor and almost no solo sailing experience. At the time John Amatt attempted the mile-high Troll Wall in Norway, the tallest thing he'd climbed was a mere 90 metres high.

The Dream Process: Five Steps

If you take it one step at a time, even the impossible becomes possible.
– John Amatt

Step 1: Be Positively Dissatisfied

"Positive dissatisfaction" is critical to success. Dreamers, by their very nature, are dissatisfied with how things are. That's why they dream. As they imagine what it would be like, an excitement flows over them. "Some men see things as they are and say why," Robert F. Kennedy said while quoting George Bernard Shaw. "I dream of things that never were and say why not."

Step 2: Take Action and Adapt

Dreams are not enough. Positive dissatisfaction must be channelled into action. The dream, or vision, must be internalized as a motivating desire. Then a plan must be prepared, executed and constantly modified in the face of a changing world. In this way, the dream goes from the head to the heart and out through the hands and feet. In short, it goes from an internal idea to an external action.

Central to this process is the ability to take that first step. Without exception, all of the adventurers in this book have had the faith and the courage to do that. Once taken, it leads to successive steps which eventually lead to the realization of their dream.

"If I'm different," says Hughes, "it's maybe that I'm just a thread less cautious than most at the start."

"Everyone has the ability to achieve great things," says Mike Beedell, "if they're willing to take the risk and take that one step beyond."

Step 3: Accumulate Experience and Learn the Lessons

Before "the big dream" is attempted, complete the groundwork. The DREAM BIG philosophy is always preceded by years of digested experience. Although Mike Beedell had almost no sailing experience before attempting the Northwest Passage with Jeff MacInnis, he nonetheless had a lot of expedition and Arctic experience. Before attempting Everest, Sharon Wood had spent years acquiring experience on other mountains.

"Experience that is unconsidered remains merely experience," John Amatt says, quoting psychologist Dr. Layne Longfellow. "But experience that is considered becomes learning."

322

Step 4: Focus

"Disciplined focus," as one achiever said, "is what distinguishes those who make things happen from those who watch things happen."

All of our achievers have the ability to focus intensely. They know exactly what they want to do and they go after it.

"Your moment of strength is when you have the greatest amount of singleness of purpose," Laurie Skreslet says.

We saw the force of focus in Hughes' unwavering drive to finish. For him, as for Laurie Dexter, the goal is to finish. "No matter how much I hurt, and how slow I may be going," Dexter says, "I usually finish because finishing is what's important."

Adventure achievers focus on their goals, but they also keep a watchful eye on the world around them. This peripheral vision is what keeps them alive. They have the direction of a thoroughbred, but they do not wear blinders.

Focus must not be achieved at the expense of awareness.

Once the dream is conceived through positive dissatisfaction and followed up with action and experience, it must be kept alive through constant focus. It is easy to lose sight of your goal.

In future years, maintaining focus will become pivotal to success. As the speed and complexity of our world continue to increase, there will be many distractions. With a vision of the future, the forward action of our ambition, the accumulated weight of our experience behind us and our focus on our goals, we can achieve success.

Step 5: Enjoy the Journey

Adventure achievers don't adventure just to reach a summit, cross a finish line, or make it to a goal. They are there because they have a genuine love for the unknown, whether it takes the form of the sea, the mountains, the Arctic, or simply a long and winding country road. That is why they get involved in adventure and that is why they stay involved. Their primary motivation is not to arrive, but to travel. Success to them is not a destination, but a journey.

"It is the process of getting to a goal that really turns me on, rather than reaching the goal itself," Sharon Wood says.

This dichotomy of travelling and arriving is critical to success – and happiness.

"Reaching the summit is not the significant thing, because you learn nothing on the top," says John Amatt. "It is during the journey that the learning takes place. The important thing is to digest the experience, to learn what it was that got you there. Then you can apply this new knowledge to the future."

323

Visualize Your Dream

All of us have dreams – big ones, little ones, seemingly impossible ones. The next time you're lying in bed at night, close your eyes and concentrate on visualizing every facet of your dream. Start with the basic concept and embellish it from there. See if you can put yourself into your dream – actually feeling, tasting and smelling it. Then let yourself drift off to sleep. The next night, repeat the process. After a week, watch what happens. If your desire – and your dream – is strong enough, imagination will become action. Some terms for this process are "creative visualization," "mental imagery," or "visioneering." Whatever you call it, it works.

324

You can accomplish a lot in 10 years. From now to the turn of the century, imagination will be as important as intellect. In fact, it may be more important. The dreamers of yesterday who act today will be the achievers of tomorrow.

Adventure Attitude Element #3

Value Your Values

The only way to be happy is to do fully what you are destined for.
– Sir Francis Chichester

A strong sense of self and a stubborn adherence to personal values is one of the most powerful "elements of excellence" displayed by people with the "adventure attitude." They intuitively know what's important to them and they stick to it. It may be that the severity of soul-searching they had to go through to find themselves creates such clarity and resolution. Whatever it is, once they discover who they are, they are as rigid in their loyalty to their values as they are in their pursuit of their goals. That's because their goals and their values are integrated and inseparably linked. They pursue what's important to them, not to anyone else.

Examples:
• Laurie Skreslet's first ascent of Louise Falls: "As I was climbing it, there was such a strong sense that 'this is right.' It was a feeling that permeated my whole body. There didn't have to be a reason. I just knew it."
• Laurie Dexter's call to do missionary work among the Inuit, which he achieved in spite of the criticism of his teacher and the initial refusal from the Anglican church.

325

With the possible exception of John Hughes, all of our adventurers went through long periods of soul-searching struggle before they finally discovered what it was they wanted to do with their lives. After being apprehensive, confused and frustrated for a time, they just seemed to stumble on the answer. Once they found it, they never wavered from their paths. As they progressed, a set of underlying principles or values became increasingly important. It was Laurie Skreslet's unwavering belief in the teamwork principle, "If you go up the mountain together, you come down together" that he maintains put him on the top of Everest. It was John Hughes' dogged determination to be true to himself which compelled him to sail around the Horn with a makeshift mast. And it was Mike Beedell's love of nature and his desire to share it with others that have enabled him to become one of North America's finest outdoor photographers.

The Importance of Intuition

Key in our achievers' ability to find their own path was a strong sense of intuition. Sharon Wood naturally gravitated to the mountains; Mike Beedell naturally bought a camera. Intuition is a key component in their strong sense of self.

Trust your instinct to the end, though you can render no reason.
– Ralph Waldo Emerson

Our achievers did not stop using their intuition once they'd found their paths; they used it even more. High in Everest's rarefied air, Sharon Wood and Dwayne Congdon decided to go to the right through the Yellow Band, in spite of the fact that most past parties had gone left. Mike Beedell intuitively sensed that he could survive the break-up of the ice pan on which he and Jeff MacInnis had been sleeping.

"If you really believe that this is what you have to do at this juncture in your life, then do it," insists Laurie Dexter.

In the process of fundraising for the 1982 Canadian Everest Expedition, John Amatt came face-to-face with a personal fear many times greater than anything he'd ever faced in his climbing – the fear of rejection. "What kept me going through all the maybes and nos was an intuitive sense that I was doing the right thing. I think intuition is a very important part of achievement. It gets you through the tough times. Just knowing that what you're doing is right and then committing all your resources to it is what makes things happen."

The next time you are faced with a major life decision, go with your gut feeling. Toss aside your rational mind.

Forget about listing or evaluating all the pros and cons. React instinctively. You may be surprised with the results.

The Value in Your Values

Increased Clarity of Purpose

The more you trust your intuition, the more aware you will become of who you are and what's important to you as a person. Once you know who you are and where you're going, your vision will become clear – and exciting. Suddenly, you will see your own personal path.

Empowering Independence

If we can endure the discomfort of being different, we will garner a new-found sense of strength and self-worth. Independence is empowering. It unlocks many doors to greater achievement because it gives us the confidence to know that we can depend on ourselves. No longer are we burdened with the weight of self-doubt and the goals of others.

327

I took the [road] less traveled by, and that has made all the difference.
– Robert Frost

If you know who you are, you can dare to be different. However, it is sometimes very difficult to be different. Anyone who has tried to step out from the flock understands that to do so involves a measure of personal sacrifice that may cause criticism from others, self-doubt and isolation.

All of our adventure achievers experienced some degree of difficulty before they saw their ultimate objective and stepped out from the crowd. For Sharon Wood, there was the frustration of not fitting in at school. For Mike Beedell, there was the realization that he would never be a great mathematician. But they overcame their frustrations and grew to achieve an independence that empowered them.

Success, The Three "S"s and The Circular Psychology of Success

All of us could take a lesson from the weather. It pays no attention to criticism.
– North Dekalb Kiwanis Club *Beacon*

Many of our adventure achievers experienced turning points early in their lives. During these moments, their goals and aspirations were specifically and harshly put down by those around them.

When Laurie Skreslet overheard the words "I hope he falls and kills himself," he became hardened to ignore the "doubting Thomases." Laurie Dexter refused to listen to the childhood school teacher who insisted there was no such thing as a missionary doctor.

In John Hughes' case, the dean of his marine navigation college insisted he wouldn't last two weeks.

Despite these personal attacks on them at a relatively young age, these achievers all responded by using the incidents as motivators, rather than deterrents. Laurie Skreslet climbed all the way to the top of the bridge at the zoo. John Hughes not only survived the marine navigation program, but graduated at the top of his class. And Laurie Dexter succeeded in proving his teacher wrong.

While it is important to listen to positive criticism and learn from it, one has to differentiate between what is useful and what is detrimental. If you are doing something for the first time, as is often the case, how are you to know who or what to believe? This is where self-confidence, self-esteem and self-worth – the Three "S"s – are significant.

You've got to aim for the horizon and never doubt that you'll make it.
– Mike Beedell

The Three "S"s drive the circular psychology of success. When achievers succeed, their self-confidence, self-esteem and self-worth increase commensurately. Suddenly they are able to undertake even more challenging goals. In other words, success really does build on success.

"The self-confidence you get from accomplishing a difficult goal will make the rest of your worries seem insignificant," says John Hughes. "It's worth millions. It's priceless."

The Circular Psychology of Success, like a wheel, can roll forward and backward. If we don't succeed, our three "S"s suffer and the circular psychology begins to work in reverse. Instead of our circle of success increasing in diameter and rolling forward to bigger and bigger projects, it shrinks and begins to move backward. Or, as John Hughes says, "When you come to a wall, you either climb over it or you go back. But once you've given up, you can't always return for another try. If you quit before you've given it your all, I think that takes a toll on your self-respect." Success for adventure achievers is not measured in the attainment, but in the effort.

To create happiness in our lives, we need to succeed at something – no matter what it is. It might be success at work, in a relationship, or just in feeling good about ourselves. Along the way, we will encounter many who will doubt us. With the three "S"s firmly in place, we can prevent the external doubts of others from becoming internal ones within ourselves. "Success boils down to not being mentally encumbered by other people's ideas of what you should or shouldn't do," says John Hughes.

Latent Leadership, Individuality, Grounding

Most powerful is he who has himself in his power.
– Seneca

Leaders are people who have enough self-confidence to be different. Other people immediately sense high self-confidence and gravitate towards it. It is part of the unspoken language of leadership. Without saying a word, you make a statement.

Of course, we cannot all be free spirits. Society as we know it would collapse. But there are those among us who are latent leaders. You may have already made the decision to be different. But in what way?

In our busy, crowded world, it is easy to lose touch with ourselves and our values. With so many possible roads to follow, it is sometimes impossible to decide in which direction to go. The choices can be overwhelming. This is when it is critical to know yourself and what is important to you, your values. What if you're unsure?

The method I recommend is to answer this question by asking yourself another question: If you had a whole day to do anything you wanted, what would it be?

Once you have an answer, figure out a way to do it. Better still, figure out a way to make a living at it every day.

That way you'll be paid for what you love to do. And if you love what you're doing, you'll be successful at it.

Studies show that a large percentage of the work force is unhappy in their jobs. For some, it is the nature of the work, the workload or the stress. For others, it is simply that they have fallen into the trap of earning an income at the expense of happiness. They have a job, a home, a car, a VCR and all the other comforts the western world can offer, but they have become possessed by their possessions and addicted to the security of a steady pay cheque. If they could somehow get up the courage to leave their jobs and go to work doing something they love, they might easily find greater happiness, even though they may be earning less money. The critical value question is: At what price happiness?

The issue of how much money you can make in your chosen activity should not enter into your decision. Money may or may not be a healthy by-product of doing what you love. Even if you don't become a millionaire, you will be infinitely wealthier in terms of personal happiness. That's because you'll be in touch with what's important to you.

What we get from this adventure is just sheer joy and joy is, after all, the end in life. We do not live to eat and make money, we eat and make money to be able to enjoy life. That is what life means, and what life is for.
– George Leigh Mallory

Adventure Attitude Element #4

Excel Under Pressure

Without adversity, without change, life is boring. The paradox of comfort is that we stop trying.
– John Amatt

Fight, not Flight

When the chips are down and the gauntlet thrown, those with the "adventure attitude" don't just rally, they attack. For many of them, it is the times of testing that are as much the adventure as the exploration. The mountaineers have a chance to challenge not only the mountain, but the mountain environment. More importantly, however, is that it gives them a chance to challenge themselves. "We do not conquer mountains, nor tame the elements," says Sharon Wood. "The true conquest lies in penetrating those barriers of self-imposed limitations within our minds."

Examples:
• Mike Beedell's tenacious effort to escape the ice pack.
• "When the situation starts saying, 'Pack it in! Call it quits now! Better go home because now it's going to get really difficult!' That's when something comes up inside me and says, 'Ah, now it's getting interesting.'" – Laurie Skreslet

It is an achiever's ability to perform under pressure that is the acid test of their attitudes and abilities.

The five figures in this book switch to a fight, rather than flight, mode when the going gets tough. For some, like Laurie Skreslet, the courageous warrior is an integral and obvious part of his character. For others, such as mild-mannered Sharon Wood or Laurie Dexter, the courage is less visible. Nonetheless, when the heat is on, that aspect of their personality moves into the foreground. Coupled with instantaneous, pragmatic action, they become formidable.

Overcoming Fear

Fear in all its forms – physical, emotional, spiritual, financial – is one of the biggest barriers that stands between us and our dreams. Fear is a four-letter word. It simultaneously terrifies and immobilizes. Yet to confront fear is to flourish.

Every one of our achievers feels fear – lots of it. It can be physical fear, such as the kind Laurie Skreslet felt when he was temporarily trapped high on Mount Yamnuska. It can be the fear of rejection that Mike Beedell battles with in relationships. Or it can be the kind Laurie Dexter battles with in being a minister. For John Hughes, it was as much his fear of failure and the resulting sense of self-deprecation that motivated him to continue sailing in spite of overwhelming odds.

"When you run away from fear, it gets bigger," Laurie Skreslet says, "but when you advance towards it, it shrinks." Someone once said that there are three barriers to success:

1. Fear of failure.
2. Fear of being ridiculed.
3. Fear of the unknown.

John Amatt agrees: "The only limiting factor to our achievements in life is our fear of the unknown."

Adventure achievers have a unique way of dealing with fear. First, they acknowledge that it is there. John Hughes is not some fearless fighter. He is an intelligent strategist – and self-analyst. Rather than letting his fear control him,

333

he channels his energy into achieving success. Rather than focus on fear, he focuses on what he must do to overcome it.

"Fear must be dealt with," he says. "There is no option. If you don't stay in control, then you can be in serious trouble. You have to suppress fear and cope."

Over the years, I have met many people who look at me as a self-employed person and say: "Boy, it must be great to be your own boss. I've always wanted to open up my own business, but I'm afraid to. I've got a wife and children to support. What if it doesn't work out?"

While it is true that dependents can significantly alter your perspective, there may still be a way to realize your dreams. It might be possible to set aside some money each month, say, some of the money you might be reserving for your retirement. You could invest that in your dream. In this way, you would not compromise your commitment to your family at the expense of compromising your commitment to yourself. With the fear of financial insolvency at bay, you would be free to focus on how you might open your business, prepare a marketing plan, decide on possible office space, etc. As Mike Beedell says, "The only fear you should have is the fear of mediocrity."

By continuing to be unhappy with where we are now, are we not in essence guaranteeing that we will be unhappy five, ten or twenty years from now if we don't act on our dream? Today is our chance for tomorrow.

If you want to master your situation, control your fear. Life is such a waste when you're confused, when you're filled with self-doubt. To hell with that! Cross the bridge and get moving.
– Laurie Skreslet

Resolute Decisiveness

It is said that he who hesitates is lost. No one knows this better than an adventure achiever. The ability to make big decisions quickly, even life-threatening ones, is one of the hallmarks of those with the "adventure attitude." From Laurie Skreslet's decision to try to climb higher on Yamnuska instead of waiting to fall, to Sharon Wood's decision to leave Dwayne Congdon behind in the dark high on Everest, all adventure achievers display a resolute decisiveness.

John Hughes did not think about the future when he cut away his broken mast. He knew that to leave it unattended could be self-destruction. So, he cut it away knowing full well that the short term danger of inaction was more life-threatening than the long term implications of having no means of self-propulsion. Considering he was 2,880 kilometres from land, it was an astounding decision. And he made it in a matter of minutes.

335

Turning Negatives (Obstacles, Adversity, Uncertainty and the Unknown) into Positives

A key factor in excelling under pressure is the ability to see opportunities where everyone else sees only obstacles. Adversity, uncertainty and the unknown can be motivators, not deterrents, when attacked with sufficient resolve, creativity and adaptability.

Obstacles are like nutshells that, once cracked, reveal meat inside that nourishes you.
– Laurie Skreslet

Four deaths and the ensuing team rift could have scuttled the 1982 Everest expedition. But the team saw the opportunity for a renewed attempt and made a miraculous comeback. Likewise, the higher Sharon Wood climbed on Everest and the more conditions worsened, the more her attitude became central to her success. "I looked at the wind as just another test and if I could pass the test, I'd be better able to deal with the hardships ahead of me."

The Success in Failure

Failures can also be viewed in much the same way that obstacles can be seen as opportunities. "Failure is delay, not defeat," said William Arthur Ward.

Sharon Wood used her unsuccessful attempt on Mt. Makalu as a springboard to the top of the world. Over and over again, those with the "adventure attitude" return to places of previous failures. They do so not only out of sheer persistence, but because they are slowly gathering knowledge that they know will eventually lead to success. For them, failure is used as a foundation for future success.

"The only failure in life is when we fail to learn the lessons from our experiences," John Amatt maintains. It is this ability to turn negatives into positives, obstacles into opportunities and failures into successes, that, more than anything, will help us to succeed in the twenty-first century.

Experience is not what happens to you. Experience is what you do with what happens to you.
– Aldous Huxley

When the "fight or flight" response is activated in business or in life, it is not appropriate to start swinging, nor is running away an effective action. But we can react positively. First, we must not recoil from our challenge. We must move directly toward it. If a critical business decision must be made, we must make it, usually quickly. The economic livelihood of many employees and years of time, effort and money may be at stake. A key opportunity may be lost.

It is unclear whether the ability to perform under pressure can be developed or whether it is innate. In some, it may lie dormant. In others, it's definitely overt. One thing is certain: the twenty-first century will call for leaders who can face their fear of the unknown and learn quickly from their mistakes. That leadership must begin with each individual. To expect a handful of others to lead the way will not be enough. We do not have to manage others, but we do have to manage ourselves.

Adventure Attitude Element #5

Never Say Die Through Endurance, Persistence and Toughness

You've got to hang on to your dreams. Great dreams don't happen overnight.
   – John Amatt

The Excellence in Endurance

People with the "adventure attitude" can endure physical discomforts that border on unimaginable. Throughout intense effort and extreme pain, they are able to hold fast to their dreams. While they are actually struggling, there is tremendous malaise. But if they are able to overcome that discomfort, they meet with invaluable rewards. The greater their struggle, the greater their reward.

Examples:
• Laurie Dexter's ability to endure tremendous physical and psychological discomfort during the Polar Bridge Expedition.
• Sharon Wood's successful Mt. Everest summit attempt.

"In order to make a difference, we have to be willing to leave our comfort zones," says Sharon Wood. "In doing so, we start to struggle and it's in the struggle that we're given the opportunity to tap our unutilized reserves. This is when we see our personal best – in the struggle. The conquest lies in penetrating those barriers of self-imposed limitations and getting through to that good stuff – the stuff called potential, 90 percent of which we rarely use."

Struggle is central to success. The trouble with struggle, of course, is that it often hurts. It can hurt physically, psychologically, spiritually, emotionally or financially. It's easier and a lot more comfortable just to avoid it. But no goal of significance is ever achieved without struggle. Those who endure will excel. Those who avoid it survive, but they fail. Struggle is the separator between the winners and the also-rans.

A lot of people fail to achieve their objectives in life because they don't push through the pain.
– Laurie Dexter

The Power of Persistence

Closely linked to physical endurance, persistence is mental endurance.

B.C. Forbes said, "Nobody can fight their way to the top and stay at the top without exercising the fullest measure of grit, courage, determination and resolution. Anyone who gets anywhere does so because they are first firmly resolved to progress in this world, and then have enough "stick-to-it-iveness" to transform their resolution into reality. Without [persistence], nobody can win any worthwhile place among their fellow men."

For Laurie Skreslet to get himself back into the game on Everest, he had to do more than decide he wanted back up through the Khumbu Icefall. He had to figure out a way through it – alone.

In a similar way, John Hughes had to creatively and systematically think his way out of the loss of his mast. At a time when most might have lost their heads, his persistence to stay in the BOC was unbending. His response to the danger was as emphatic and pragmatic as he is: no mast – no problem. He created a structure that was, like his persistence, "bulletproof."

As Laurie Dexter so accurately points out: "There comes a point when your body just doesn't have it anymore. From every conceivable assessment, the only thing your body can do is stop. Yet somehow it keeps moving. It's simply because your mind wills it to move. In a race like this, if you are really good from the shoulders up, you can keep plodding. The key is not to lose it in the head."

Most of today's challenges are cerebral. Now more than ever, the one who wins the game is the one who wins the

339

mind game. Politics, outside economic factors and natural disasters aside, "Life's battles don't always go to the stronger and faster. Sooner or later, the one who wins is the one who thinks they can."

Although the economic or corporate climate for your big dream may not yet be right, hang on to it. Chances are that the situation will eventually change. Or, you may want to change it yourself. Either way, dig in and be prepared psychologically for a long fight.

Bear in mind, if you are going to amount to anything, that your success does not depend upon the brilliancy and the impetuosity with which you take hold, but upon the ever-lasting and sanctified bull-doggedness with which you hang on after you have taken hold.
– Dr. A.B. Meldrum

The Temper of Toughness

Toughness is more than physical endurance or mental persistence. It is an overall capacity to bear life's storms – physically, mentally, financially, emotionally and spiritually. Endurance and persistence are components of toughness in the same way as the serve and volley are parts of tennis. Endurance and persistence are both a part of the larger game of life.

If there is one characteristic which is common to adventure achievers, it is toughness. Their personal ideologies may be closely attacked, as were Laurie Dexter's religious beliefs, or they may have to survive extended separation from loved ones, as John Hughes did. Because they have the "adventure attitude," they are able to go on.

This strength emanates from somewhere deep within them – a place invisible from the outside. They have it not so much in their bodies as in their hearts and minds.

I discovered it wasn't a matter of physical strength, but a matter of psychological strength.
– Sharon Wood

When a person or a company goes through difficult financial times, or there is a death or serious illness in a family, it is easy to become disheartened and disillusioned. During these times of adversity, it is those who are able to dig deep and find the hidden reserves to continue who will achieve ultimate success. This does not mean they should deny their pain. It means they should acknowledge it, but work to overcome it.

341

Life is a series of struggles. We can meet them as our adventurers did, if we have the fortitude. Or, as one achiever with the "adventure attitude" said: "Expect trouble as an inevitable part of life and when it comes, hold your head high, look it squarely in the eye and say, 'I will be bigger than you. You cannot defeat me.'"

To reach the twenty-first century successfully, we'll all have to be just as enduring, persistent and, ultimately, as tough as our toughest challenge. The next two decades will test us as never before. But having met the challenge, we will come out of it stronger than when we went in.

Adventure Attitude Element #6

Trust Others, Retain Your Independence, But Work Productively As a Member of a Team

The essence of teamwork is to use the strengths of others to offset our own limitations so that the strength of the team becomes greater than the sum of the individual parts.
– John Amatt

The Triumph of Teamwork

342

Far from being self-serving individuals determined only to reach self-appointed goals, the adventure achievers in this book are individuals and team players at the same time. Each maintains their own independence while working collectively toward a common goal.

Examples:
• During his voyage, John Hughes was in constant contact with his "home team." Ultimately, they played a critical role in his success by providing him with a replacement for his lost mast.
• The Everest '86 team effort which helped put Sharon Wood on top.
• "Working as a team, you can overcome unbelievable odds and achieve things that others believe to be impossible," said Mike Beedell in reference to the Qitdlarssuaq Expedition.

Teamwork is not restricted to corporations, associations or athletic teams. It has been a part of Canada's history since the days of the fur trade. Then, French-Canadian voyageurs worked with indigenous guides to open up a continent.

The 1990s will be a decade of struggle for Canadians. As our efforts to redefine our national identity and political structure continue, the need to work together will become even more important. While differences between West and East, English and French, the haves and the have-nots may threaten to pull us apart, they can actually be used to hold us together, because it is precisely these differences that make up our national identity.

Canada is a country of diversity – not just linguistic and economic, but geographic, cultural, climatic and social. Unlike some nations whose essential character can be described with less difficulty because of their size, geography or cultural makeup, there is no stereotypical Canadian. While we have been wrestling for decades with our national identity, it's been staring us in the face. Our face is many faces – and places, customs, climates. The one thing we have in common is the potential to become a team.

Differences can be seen as positives or negatives. Since adventure achievers have the ability to turn negatives into positives, the differences which have threatened to divide us can easily be used to unite us – if they are approached with the right attitude. If we work together and build on the strengths of our differences, we can be a role model to the world. This is the triumph of teamwork.

343

Adventure Attitude Element #7

Understand Totally Why You've Committed To A Mission Before You Commit To It and Be Ultimately Accountable For Your Actions

W.H. "Bill" Murray, a Scottish mountaineer, wrote in his book on his expedition to Mount Everest:

Until you are committed there is hesitancy, the chance to draw back, ineffectiveness. There is one elementary truth about all acts of initiative (and creativity), the ignorance of which kills countless ideas and splendid plans: the moment one definitely commits oneself, then Providence moves. All sorts of things begin to happen to help you that would never otherwise have occurred. A whole stream of events issues from that decision, raising in your favour all manner of unforeseen incidents, meetings and material assistance, which you couldn't have dreamt would come your way.

I have learned a deep respect for one of Goethe's couplets, which bears repeating:

Are you in earnest? Seize this very minute. What you can do, or dream you can, begin it. Boldness has genius, power and magic in it. Only engage and then the mind grows heated.

– Goethe (Faustus)

Examples:
• Sharon Wood's commitment becoming greater the higher she climbed on Everest.
• "The single biggest key to my success is commitment," says Laurie Dexter.

The Command of Commitment

Our adventure achievers don't commit themselves in a casual way. They commit with their heart and soul. But before they do, they thoroughly think through what it is they are proposing to do, what sacrifices it will entail, what heartaches and what pain. Most importantly, they know why they want to do it. Then, if and when things get difficult, they don't waste time and energy in the paralysis of self-doubt. They know why they're there and they want to be there – regardless of how difficult the challenge becomes. Of course, since they are human, they will occasionally feel hesitant, but that hesitation is never long enough to significantly stop their forward movement.

Those with the "adventure attitude" seem to be of one type of mindset: circular. They set out from the start and when they encounter a major obstacle, their minds return automatically to "go." Here, they re-affirm their reasons for starting, draw again from their original motivational well and continue.

"Somewhere along the line you ask yourself, What am I doing here?" says John Hughes, as he clearly articulates another example of The Circular Psychology of Success. "It is then that you must think back and remember that it was the right thing to do at the start. Therefore, it's right to carry on and finish whatever it is you've committed to."

The minds of great adventure achievers function with this type of "broken record" mentality. When the needle of their mind hits an obstacle and skips, it automatically jumps back to the start. It does this until the ultimate objective is reached. It is, as Laurie Skreslet described Sharon Wood's summit assault, "...like watching a cybernetic torpedo lock onto a target. She just kept re-correcting herself and going for it."

Level of commitment equals level of performance.
– Sharon Wood

True commitment goes beyond determination and tenacity, however. It is rooted in your values. Values are the foundation of commitment. Without them, no house of any strength can be built.

Commitment will be critical to our future. As the number and significance of obstacles and challenges increase, it will be necessary for us to possess a commensurate level of commitment. Without it, we will be overcome. With it, we will triumph.

346

Ultimate Accountability is Ultimately Empowering

O.J. Simpson said: "The day you take responsibility for yourself, the day you stop making excuses, that's the day you start to the top." Once an adventure achiever makes a decision, they totally accept the consequences of it. If Sharon's partner, Dwayne Congdon, had not come back, she would have had to live with that. John Hughes was willing to risk his life to go for the Horn. Laurie Skreslet knew he might fall to his death if he didn't cross that crevasse in the Khumbu Icefall.

"Don't pretend that other things are stopping you from reaching your goals," says John Hughes. "They only stop you if you let them."

While few of our everyday actions have life-threatening consequences, our achievers show us the great potential of the human spirit. Theirs is a simple but prepotent rule: ultimate accountability can produce ultimate success.

This adage seems distant from life as some know it today. We live in a sue-happy society in which millions of hours and dollars are spent trying to prove the other guy was at fault. In the end, the only winners are usually the lawyers.

"It seems to me more and more that nobody wants to take responsibility for what they do," says John Hughes. "If you lose your job, you got fired because management was at fault. If you have a car accident, there's insurance. Almost everything we do is insurable. And it's always somebody else's fault if bad luck comes our way. I'm not saying that isn't true in some cases, but it never tests you."

"Ultimate" accountability is just that – ultimate. To put your life on the line for what you believe in is not only the ultimate sacrifice, but ultimately empowering. As Laurie Skreslet discovered when he crossed the crevasse in the Khumbu Icefall, "I looked around and it was like a blanket had been taken off me. It was clear what I was here to do. For the very first time in my life, as I moved away from that bridge, I realized that if you're lucky, once in your life, you come to a place where you realize you must make manifest what you profess to believe."

If we profess to believe that we can succeed in the future, we will need to commit completely and be ultimately accountable. If we do everything else right, we should be ultimately successful.

Adventure Attitude Element #8

Risk-Take Carefully

When forced to confront fear, a lot of people step back. Those who step forward, move forward.
– John Amatt

None of the people featured in this book are daredevils. All have spent a lifetime acquiring skills, knowledge and experience which enables them to move smoothly and in relative safety through some of the most demanding and dangerous environments on earth. For them, there is a very clear distinction between reckless foolishness and cool, calculated risk-taking. One can be fatal; the other fantastic.

Examples:
• John Hughes' decision to sail around Cape Horn was well thought out.
• Mike Beedell: "I don't see what I do on the level of risk the same way that people on the outside see it. All my risks are seriously calculated."

All of us are faced with risks on a daily basis. Every time we get into an automobile or step out onto the street to catch a bus, we assume risk. Life IS risk. Getting out of bed in the morning is a risk. Riding the subway is a risk. Taking out a loan is a risk.

To laugh is to risk appearing the fool.
To weep is to risk appearing sentimental.
To reach out for another is to risk involvement.
To expose feelings is to risk exposing our true selves.
To place your ideas, your dreams before the crowd is to
*   risk loss.*
To love is to risk not being loved in return.
To live is to risk dying.
To hope is to risk despair.
To try is to risk failure.
But risk we must, for the greatest hazard in life is to risk
*   nothing.*
The man, the woman, who risks nothing does nothing,
*   has nothing, is nothing.*
-Unknown

Our society discourages risk. It starts with parents cautioning their children from venturing too close to the top of the stairs. It is, on one hand, an instinctive parental reaction. But it forms the basis for North American society's "security syndrome." In kindergarten, students are taught not to play with matches. In elementary school, they are told not to venture too far from home and in high school, they are disciplined for staying out too late. All of these controls can be healthy, and often are. Yet they can also produce generations of adults who, as Mike Beedell says, are "strangling in their security blankets."

Security is mostly a superstition. It does not exist in nature,
nor do the children of men as a whole experience it.
Avoiding danger is not safer in the long run than outright
exposure.
– Helen Keller

The Calibre of Courage

Risk assessment is nothing without the courage to take the risk, if the risk is acceptable. Laurie Skreslet faced the ultimate risk when he leaped across the crevasse. He knew that if he fell and his rope system didn't hold, he would likely die. Likewise, John Hughes knew that if he failed to make it around Cape Horn, he would likely perish.

Courage is not only the ability to risk your life, it is the ability to stand fast when everything else around you is falling apart, to remain calm when everyone else around you is losing their heads. In the simplest sense, it is getting up every day to make a better life for yourself, or starting a new job, or re-marrying, or moving to a new city.

If you are faced with a decision, no matter how small, ask yourself if you are acting out of courage or out of fear. If you are acting out of fear, the result will be predictable. If you are acting out of courage, success could be within your grasp.

Successful individuals in the 1990s and in the twenty-first century will be those who learn to take courageous, calculated risks. They will move with courage but care from the known world of the present into the unknown world of the future.

Success for the next generation will mean cool-headedness. We'll need to have more entrepreneurs and gutsy business and political leaders to make it happen. All of us can prepare now by doing our homework: acquiring the skills, knowledge and experience needed to enable us to assess our risks and make those critical decisions.

Having done that, like Laurie Skreslet, we must then have the courage to leap into the void if we are to reap the rewards. To do so may be contrary to our basic natures and nurturing, but our very survival may depend on it. Those who prepare their wings now will fly later.

Adventure Attitude Element #9

Exude Energy, Enthusiasm and Curiosity

Enthusiasm is the propellor of progress.
– B.C. Forbes

The Energy in Enthusiasm

All adventure achievers exude boundless enthusiasm. They seem like children in how they pursue their passion with fervour. Listening to Laurie Skreslet describe a challenging ice climb is as riveting as hearing Mike Beedell talk about an exciting photographic experience. You are immediately captivated.

351

Youth is not a time of life...it is a state of mind. Nobody grows old by merely living a number of years; people grow old only by deserting their ideals. You are as young as your faith, as old as your doubt; as young as your self-confidence, as old as your fear; as young as your hope, as old as your despair.
– Unknown

Examples:
• John Hughes' abiding love for the sea.
• Mike Beedell: "The thing that is special to me is the actual exploration, of going around the next bend, of just seeing what's beyond. That for me is the greatest joy."

It is sometimes hard to be youthfully enthusiastic in our everyday life. Traffic jams, foul weather and irritable co-workers can make it extremely difficult. Yet those who are enthusiastic stand out immediately. And, as with great leaders, there is a gravitation to their enthusiastic energy.

Enthusiasm is energy. And it can be tapped. If everyone else is dragging themselves through the day, an injection of enthusiasm can work wonders. If at first it is rebuffed, persevere. Those who are genuinely enthusiastic are genuinely valued in any organization, in any situation. If you want to be valued, be of value.

The Capacity of Curiosity

Mike Beedell's enthusiasm is coupled with a curiosity that enables him to achieve. In fact, enthusiasm and curiosity, more than physical or photographic ability, have been two of the keys to his success. He's like a kid in a candy store. Everywhere he looks there's something new to taste, touch, feel or experience.

Although all our achievers are adults, they have not lost their childlike curiosity. They are far older than their years in many other ways, yet this part of them seems to be forever locked in the past.

Skilled managers know that to maximize the productivity of an organization they must selectively delegate jobs to specific individuals. An employee who is enthusiastic and curious in their work can outstrip the productivity of a nonmotivated employee within hours.

If you are a manager, consider ways to stimulate the curiosity of your staff. It might be a simple thing like asking them some thought-provoking questions about their work. Or ask them to give you a list of projects or ideas which would most interest them. Then see if you can match your organization's goals to their interests. If you can, you will have hit on a potent formula: Curiosity Plus Opportunity Equals Productivity.

With energy, enthusiasm and curiosity, the next millennium can be tackled with the same kind of success with which Beedell and MacInnis attacked their dream of windsailing the ice-choked Northwest Passage for the first time in history. In fact, for people like Mike Beedell, the newness and novelty of it all will make every new year not only exciting, but enticing.

Given the degree and rate of change in the last two decades, by extrapolation we can expect thrilling advances in the future. For some, that will be unsettling. For others, it will be exciting. The choice is ours.

353

One Step Beyond

This purpose of this book is to show that the way in which achievers look at our world and its challenges is central to their success. As John Amatt says:

Adventure isn't hanging on a rope on the side of a mountain. Adventure is an attitude that we must apply to the day-to-day challenges of life – facing new challenges, seizing new opportunities, testing our resources against the unknown and, in the process, discovering our own unique potential.

In the process of researching this book, I got to know the achievers in it very well. They have shared their doubts and dreams with me, their failures and successes. The thing that struck me most about all of them wasn't what they were on the outside. None of them were super athletes or brilliant intellects. In fact, they appeared ordinary in every way. They had fears and weaknesses just like all of us. They were human. The only differences I could find were in how they perceived the world.

Sharon Wood: "The way I perceive my environment is the only thing that makes me different – nothing else."

Laurie Skreslet: "It's not what you go through in life that makes you what you are, it's how you react to the world you're going through."

John Hughes: "It's not what you have. It's what you do with what you have."

All of this inspires us to a very clear, but propelling conclusion: that personal success and happiness is largely a matter of what we do in our minds. The mind, and what we choose to put in it, determines greatness. Our grey matter is what matters.

We CAN be happier and more successful. We CAN achieve our dreams. The power IS within our control. It's not some arbitrary set of circumstances, fluke or chance that molds great people. Great people are the product of what's in their heads and hearts. Provided we have been raised in an environment which gives us the basic tools to choose, we can excel. In fact, we can dream, and realize our dreams. Perspective is power.

Wings are not only for birds; they are also for minds.
– Toller Cranston

For yourself, and for others, may this end now become a new beginning. All that remains is for you to take that first step – and then that one step beyond.

If you start something, you might just succeed. But you'll never know until you start.
– John Amatt

About the Author

Alan Hobson can write and speak about achievement because he has experienced achievement first-hand. A nine-time All-American gymnast (although he is Canadian), he was a member of six US national championship gymnastics teams. While at university, he won the William Randolph Hearst Award for excellence in newswriting and began his career as a newspaper reporter with *The Citizen* in Ottawa, Canada.

Since 1983, he has been a full-time freelance writer, journalist, broadcaster and public speaker, specializing in adventure and achievement. His travels have taken him all over Europe, from which he has reported to Canada's national media. In 1988, he was author of the official retrospective book on the Olympic Torch Relay, *Share the Flame*. In 1991, he made Canadian communications history by sending the first live Canadian radio reports off Mount Everest via satellite.

His interests include hang-gliding and ice-climbing, and he has at one time or another participated in parachuting, bobsleigh, luge, rock-climbing, whitewater kayaking and marathon running.

He lives in Calgary, Alberta, just east of his favourite playground, the Canadian Rockies.

Alan can be reached through the One Step Beyond office in Canmore, Alberta.

John Amatt

One Step ▲ Beyond

MEETING THE CHALLENGE OF CHANGE

One Step Beyond is a unique educational and motivational company, dedicated to the development of effective teamwork and personal peak performance in corporate and professional life. Through the primary vehicles of inspiring keynote presentations, wilderness-based seminar experiences, and creative business meetings, One Step Beyond assists its clients throughout the world in developing innovative strategies to meet the challenges of change represented by the 1990's and the 21st century.

One Step Beyond was organized in 1983 by the principal members of Canada's first successful expedition to climb Mount Everest. The corporate name evolved from the desire of this group to go "one step beyond" their Everest experience and to apply the lessons of Everest to the challenges of personal and professional life. Today, One Step Beyond associates specialize in applying the "adventure metaphor" as a learning tool in the uncertain and unpredictable times of this decade. Every year, John Amatt, Sharon Wood and the other adventurers profile in the pages of this book inspire hundreds of thousands of people to become more adventurous in their own lives and to climb their own pinnacle to success.

Since 1983, One Step Beyond associates have addressed thousands of audiences, sharing their adventure experiences as a powerful metaphor for "reaching the top" in the challenging global environments in which we must now operate. Renowned for their emotional impact, these presentations and seminars offer a strong analogy for the vision, courage, commitment, resourcefulness, endurance and teamwork that must be brought to bear in any field of endeavour. Illustrated by magnificent photography and first person experience, these highly innovative sessions are particularly valuable for addressing the issues of teamwork and change in corporate structures.

For further information on One Step Beyond, or to request a presentation on the "adventure attitude" articulated in this book, contact:

John Amatt, President & Founder

One Step ▲ Beyond World Wide

Suite 200, 838-10th St.
Canmore, Alberta, Canada T1W 2A7
Phone: (403) 678-5255 / Fax: (403) 678-4534
Toll-free: 1-800-661-9400

- Keynote Presentations & Seminars
- Team-building Seminars
- Audio-Visual Modules
- Creative Mountain Meetings
- Peak Performance Audio & Video Tapes